PENGUIN BOOKS

THE ART OF WARFARE ON LAND

D1240334

Dr David G. Chandler was educated at Marlborough College and Keble College, Oxford. He served four years in the army, two spent in Nigeria as a captain in the Royal Army Educational Corps. He taught at the Royal Military Academy Sandhurst for over 33 years and became Head of the Department of War Studies. He retired in 1994. He has been a Visiting Professor at Ohio State University, the Virginia Military Institute and the US Marine Corps University, Quantico, and has lectured all over the world. He is Honorary President of the British Commission for Military History, Fellow of the Royal Historical Society, Honorary Founding President of the European Union Re-Enactments Society and Special Historical Consultant to the International Napoleonic Society. For six years he was a Trustee of the Royal Armouries at HM Tower of London and Leeds. He was awarded a D.Litt. at Oxford University in 1991, one of only four military historians to have received this distinction since the end of the First World War.

David Chandler is well known for his writing on Napoleon and Marlborough, and has brought this period of history alive through his many books. His books include *Marlborough as Military Commander*, *The Campaigns of Napoleon* and *Waterloo: The Hundred Days*. He has been a military consultant and adviser on a number of television programmes, notably to the BBC during the production of the twenty-part serialization of Tolstoy's *War and Peace* (1971–3) and for the Channel Four series *Great Commanders* (1992–3).

DAVID G. CHANDLER

THE ART OF WARFARE ON LAND

PENGUIN BOOKS

This book is dedicated to the many officer-cadets and young officers I
have been privileged to instruct at the Royal Military Academy, Sandhurst

PENGUIN BOOKS

Published by the Penguin Group
Penguin Books Ltd, 27 Wrights Lane, London W8 5TZ, England
Penguin Putnam Inc., 375 Hudson Street, New York, New York 10014, USA
Penguin Books Australia Ltd, Ringwood, Victoria, Australia
Penguin Books Canada Ltd, 10 Alcorn Avenue, Toronto, Ontario, Canada M4V 3B2
Penguin Books (NZ) Ltd, Private Bag 102902, NSMC, Auckland, New Zealand

Penguin Books Ltd, Registered Offices: Harmondsworth, Middlesex, England

First published by Hamlyn 1974
Published as a Classic Penguin 2000
1 3 5 7 9 10 8 6 4 2

Printed in Great Britain by Martins the Printers Ltd, Berwick-upon-Tweed
Cover repro and printing by Concise Cover Printers

CONTENTS

PREFACE

This book is intended as an introduction to the study of the art of war on land from the earliest times until the near present. It sets out to describe the salient developments in the types of wars as the centuries and millennia have unrolled. Man has probably always faced the challenge of armed struggle, but war's face has taken many different forms. Closely linked to such considerations have been the evolution of weaponry, of the administrative systems and organizations needed to supply men at war, and of the strategies and tactics required to make effective use of the constantly changing kaleidoscope of conflict, which has become steadily more complex over the generations–and never more so than over the past quarter century.

For reasons of space it has been decided to concentrate on land warfare at the expense of naval or air developments, and to conclude the historical part of this study at 1945. This is not to aver that the past thirty years have been markedly peaceful, or that technological progress has ceased. The very opposite is true. In the case of Great Britain there has only been a single year since 1945 which has seen no military casualties attributable to hostile action. The postwar period has witnessed successive conflicts, many of them linked with the emergence of former colonies to independent status, and many more caused by international friction over ideological, political or economic rivalries, as the bitter struggles in Korea, Indo-China, Vietnam and the Middle East bear witness. But most of these wars have not been total (although the recurrent crises in the Middle East, the Korean War and the prolonged Vietnamese struggle have approached conventional totality at varying times) owing to the unique circumstances that have existed since the late 1940s and early 1950s. We have thus witnessed an unparalleled revolution in the art of warfare.

The advent of new weapons has periodically shaken the prevailing strategic balance, but no development, not even the introduction of gunpowder, has rivalled the impact on diplomacy and warfare of missile-borne thermonuclear warheads. Formerly, the dictum that 'peace was diplomacy without fighting, and war diplomacy with fighting' had a certain validity. Since 1945, however, the distinction between war and peace has almost disappeared. The major powers no longer *dare* to go to war in pursuit of total objectives for fear of the retaliatory nuclear destruction they would almost certainly court. Consequently, military men have no freedom of action–every decision has now to be taken at the top political level. Furthermore, sea, air and land warfare have become increasingly interdependent, involving helicopters, commando-carriers and missiles, another justification perhaps for concluding at 1945, when the distinctions between land and other forms of warfare were already becoming blurred.

Nevertheless, warfare continues on a restricted scale, employing more subtle but no less important means. The age of nuclear stalemate has spawned the age of the revolutionary guerrilla. Guerrilla warfare is by no means a new phenomenon, but the present international climate, dominated by fear of nuclear war, is unique. Consequently, the military implications of even the smallest confrontation may prove immense. 1945 saw the passing of what General Beaufre has called the Classical Age of Warfare, and this study is restricted to the years of recorded history leading up to the end of the Second World War. However, as this would leave a vital period uncovered, the principal implications of the new age are described in the Introduction.

Nevertheless, in certain respects the past has never been more relevant to the present than in our own troubled times. Certain features of war have, moreover, remained immutable. Foremost amongst these have been the basic requirements of leadership and generalship. The qualities that go to make a successful commander are many; a number are of great importance. The control of armies may have become less personal since the days of Napoleon or Marlborough, but the responsibilities have become greater. A general then needs the moral courage to accept the responsibility of having to risk the lives of a great many men. Science has depersonalized some of the control and communication processes, but the hard decisions have still to be taken. The late Lord Wavell, himself no mean judge (although an 'unlucky' general in the Second World War), placed this robustness and ability to withstand the shocks of war as the first requirement in a general. None would deny the need for a commander to be at the peak of personal fitness, both mental and physical, if the situations he faces are to be assessed quickly and the necessary decisions firmly taken. A general must similarly know his men–their characteristics, strengths and weaknesses, and he must know how to make the most of the former and how to minimize the dangers inherent in the latter. This is where the skills of man management come into play: he must know how to win both their respect and their affection. A good general must also know how to select reliable subordinates, be willing to place the maximum trust in them, and back them to the hilt. He must be firm but fair, clear yet flexible, bold yet cautious. He must have a thorough grasp of his profession and of the capabilities of the weapons and instruments available to him, and be prepared to adjust his preconceived notions to suit unforeseen circumstances, for von Clausewitz was correct when he claimed that war was pre-eminently the sphere of the unexpected. One last quality demands notice. Napoleon, before appointing a general, would ask, 'Is he lucky?' By this he really meant, 'Is he competent at taking calculated risks?'– for much of a general's professional skill is tested under difficult conditions and on the basis of incomplete knowledge, and a commander's ability to inspire confidence in his political superiors and his military inferiors is always at stake. Another recurrent theme of every chapter that follows, therefore, will be an attempt to assess the principal qualities and characteristics of the great soldiers of history.

Precept without example is of little value. A fourth purpose of this survey, therefore, will be to give brief descriptions of selected actions and battles which illustrate the main points mentioned in this preface. Here special emphasis will be placed upon well-chosen and properly annotated illustrations–for a good picture can save many thousands of words. And lastly, in the Select Reading List, I have attempted to suggest a number of reliable sources for fuller information than it has been possible to include in a volume of this length and type. The shortcomings of this work will be all too evident to the skilled student in military affairs–but any author must exercise the right to choose themes and illustrations that he deems to be of importance. And if a number of readers, after sampling these pages, are tempted to delve deeper, then this book will not have been conceived and written in vain. Thomas Hardy was never more accurate than when he wrote, in *The Dynasts* . . . 'War makes rattling good history; but Peace is poor reading'.

The author is grateful to Major-General H Essame CBE, DSO (retd) for permission to base part of the introductory chapter on an article he published a number of years ago.

INTRODUCTION

Man has always displayed the aggressive side of his nature. Over the 3,650 years of recorded history, it has been estimated that the human race has known only 292 years entirely free from the horrors of organized warfare, and one suspects that in those supposedly peaceful years much overt hostility was detectable, even if only on a small scale. The study of the art and science of warfare provides an important, if bloodstained, insight into both the constructive and the destructive sides of human nature, and at the same time reveals much about the development of civilized societies, technology and government. This book sets out to examine the development of warfare in its more obvious professional and technological aspects, while for reasons of space the equally important political and sociological factors will be treated only in passing.

Warfare is without doubt the most complex form of activity evolved by man in the 2 million years of his evolutionary existence. As an introduction, therefore, this chapter sets out to achieve three objectives: to describe the salient features of the subject, with definitions; to trace the evolution in the broadest terms of military strategy so as to set the scene for chapters to follow; and to outline the seven basic tactical manoeuvres of war which have reappeared time and again and in one form or another regardless of technical developments in weaponry, means of communication and methods of supply. Although every war and campaign must be regarded as a unique occasion with special features, there are nevertheless certain aspects that bear marked resemblances and similarities, struggle after struggle, generation after generation.

The Strata of War
The phenomenon of warfare can be studied at five levels. Each is closely connected with the one before and the one that follows, except in the case of the fifth, which forms part of all the previous four. It should be noted that the demarcation zones are not clear-cut—one level merges almost indistinguishably into the next.

Grand Strategy is the highest level. It is primarily concerned with the formulation of policy, the selection of realistic war aims, whether offensive or defensive, and the building and main-tenance of alliances. Decisions of grand strategy, therefore, are taken at governmental level and are the responsibility of cabinets and ministries (or, in an earlier age, monarchs), acting on the advice of their professional heads of services. At this level objectives and priorities are defined.

Strategy has been well defined by the late Sir Basil Liddell Hart as 'the art of distributing and applying military means to fulfil the ends of policy'. Thus if grand strategy lays down the aims of a war and the broad form it is to take, strategy determines the methods by which the aims are to be achieved, and those of the enemy confounded. In other words it decides the 'how', the 'when' and the 'where' of military operations. This is the province of a country's chief of staff and senior advisers, acting in consultation with their allies to ensure coordination of efforts at both national and arms-of-the-service levels.

Grand Tactics is concerned with the actual planning of major operations in all their complexity. The frontier with strategy is often very blurred, for more than any others these two strata merge into one another at their limits. General Nathan Forrest's classic dictum that strategy meant 'gitting thar fustest with the mostest' applies equally to grand tactics in two of its most important aspects: the achievement of speed and the concentration of force. Others include the selection of intermediate objectives, the allocation of the correct number and types of forces, the achievement of proper coordination, and the maintenance of a reserve to exploit success or to remedy unforeseen difficulties. Generally speaking, grand tactical decisions are taken at all levels from army to brigade or regimental group, and sometimes even at battalion level, or lower, in the case of special operations involving only minor forces.

Minor Tactics govern the actual methods of fighting and manoeuvre, and involve every combatant from battalion commander to senior soldier or pfc. The actual application of force to achieve the immediate objective, be it only a single house or copse, is the province of tactics. Of course, the success of tactical operations is as vital to the success—or failure—of a battle, campaign or war, as the selection of a correct aim and plan. A chain is as strong as its weakest link, and if minor operations go awry the effects can be far-reaching, for the smallest detail can be the dominant factor between overall success and failure.

Logistics comprises the provision, movement and supply of armed forces. Its range is, therefore, all-embracing, covering the mobilization of whole national economies and populations, the design, testing and manufacture of weapons and ammunition, the provision of communications–radar, satellites, computers and other electronic devices–the organization of transport, and the provision and distribution of the myriad stores modern forces require in the field. Logistical considerations must be taken into account at all levels of warfare; it is as useless for a prime minister to demand an immediate strategic bombing offensive if the aircraft, escorts and bombs are not available, as it is for a second lieutenant to order an attack on an enemy-held ditch without having the necessary ammunition and grenades at his disposal. Nevertheless, such decisions are often unavoidable even if the material means are not available; in war, so confused and subject to friction, shortages and delay, great risks have often to be accepted. The ideal situation rarely occurs, particularly as regards supplies, fuel and munitions, and a general who is unduly concerned with quartermaster problems is unlikely to be a very effective leader. Rommel demonstrated his greatness as a general by maintaining an effective campaign in the Western Desert from 1941 to 1943 in an exceedingly difficult logistical situation. On the other hand, nothing is surer to lead to ultimate failure than a rash disregard for the requirements of logistics at every level, and one secret of Montgomery's success at Alamein was his refusal to attack before all was ready. Today, one of the greatest problems stems from the fact that to sustain a single combat soldier in contact with the enemy requires between a dozen and eighteen men in various support and logistical roles. The contrast with the self-sufficient guerrilla of Malaya or Vietnam, who requires only simple weaponry and ammunition, and a single bag of rice a week, together with a strong sense of purpose, does not need to be laboured here.

To illustrate the last few pages, let us examine briefly the decision to mount D-Day on 6 June 1944. At grand strategical level, Churchill, Roosevelt and Stalin were committed to gaining the unconditional surrender of Nazi Germany and Imperial Japan; they had to decide whether Europe or the Pacific should take priority, and decided, upon Stalin's insistence, to go for Germany first; they had to choose between an invasion of north-west Europe and launching the major onslaught in the Mediterranean–through Italy and the Balkans or southern France. They settled for north-west Europe. Lastly they had to select the Supreme Commander–Dwight D Eisenhower. All these grand strategical decisions were progressively considered and resolved by the Allied leaders at a series of conferences, with the aid of their respective chiefs of staff and key advisers.

The implementation of the decision to attack north-west Europe in 1944 was then passed down to the joint planners, the strategists. They had to decide between the merits of three possible landing areas–Normandy, western France or the Pas de Calais–and settle the problems of dates, tides and time. They had to agree what was the minimum force in terms of aircraft, ships, tanks, guns and men required to make a successful assault landing and *then* win the following build-up race to achieve a local victory and a breakthrough to the Rhine, and thence to the industrial heartland of the Third Reich, the Ruhr. To fool the enemy, the strategists also

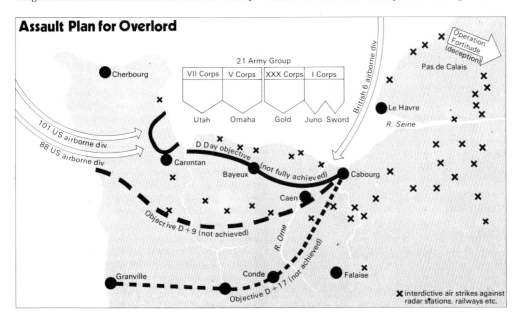

Assault Plan for Overlord

21 Army Group

VII Corps	V Corps	XXX Corps	I Corps

Utah · Omaha · Gold · Juno Sword

Cherbourg

101 US airborne div
88 US airborne div

D Day objective (not fully achieved)

Carentan

Bayeux

Objective D+9 (not achieved)

Caen

R. Orne

Cabourg

Conde

Objective D+17 (not achieved)

Granville

Falaise

British 6 airborne div

Le Havre

R. Seine

Pas de Calais

Operation Fortitude (deception)

X interdictive air strikes against radar stations, railways etc.

devised Operation Fortitude, an elaborate cover plan which in the event proved a great success in deluding the enemy for several critical weeks into believing that the Calais area would be the prime target of the invasion.

The choice eventually fell on the Normandy area. The problem then became one of grand tactics: the formulation of an assault plan, based on intelligence of the enemy's preparations, on the number and siting of beaches, the sweeping of minefields, the collection of shipping, the loading of men, material and munitions, the mounting of air operations to isolate the bridge-head area and secure the flanks from enemy counterattacks by the use of bombing, strafing and paratroopers, the provision of a floating reserve in case of emergencies, and the coordination of all these activities with those of the French *maquis*. The generals, air marshals and admirals worked on these problems under General Morgan and produced the COSSAC Plan by mid-1943; this was subsequently massively amended in early 1944 by General Sir Bernard Montgomery, who doubled the invasion area, called for five assault divisions instead of three, increased the airborne attack force from two brigades to three whole divisions, and generously recommended the postponement of the attack from May to June 1944 to allow time for these changes to be implemented!

Ultimately the planning was passed down to the tactical level to the regimental assault team commanders, the paratroop leaders, the air and naval squadron commanders. They decided how many aircraft or supporting ships should attack which sea wall or beach obstacle on a designated beach at exactly what time, which bridges the paratroopers would destroy, and which they were to leave intact.

At every level there were key considerations of logistics to be taken into account. The heads of state had to decide how many landing-ships-tank (LSTs) could be spared from the Pacific and Mediterranean theatres of war, facing remonstrations from Admiral King and General Alexander respectively. At strategic level there was the building of the secret Mulberry harbours' components, and the finding of the great mass of extra aircraft and shipping made necessary by Montgomery's radical amendments to the original plan. The problems of beach obstacles and local defences were countered by ordering the design of the 'funnies' – swimming DD tanks and other specialist armour. At the lowest level there was the need to provide every soldier, sailor and airman with a small guidebook to France describing the country and its inhabitants, whilst every American paratrooper was given a clicker to aid mutual identification in the confusion of a night landing on a hostile countryside. Last, but not least, was the provision of anti-seasickness pills for all personnel moving by sea. Every last detail had to be anticipated and everything kept secret until the last moment.

The result was the most famous and most successful amphibious assault in the annals of military history. It is hoped that something of the complexity of the planning and mounting side of Operation Overlord has emerged from the preceding paragraphs: every single item listed had to be settled *before* the first ship left. Such is the complexity of modern war. Nevertheless, William the Conqueror faced similar problems in 1066, albeit on a much smaller scale. On both occasions the weather played a determinant role. In 1066, adverse winds delayed the sailing of the Normans, and this helped them to surprise Harold's Saxons, redeployed to Yorkshire to meet a Norse attack. Just under 900 years later the sudden blowing of an unseasonable gale almost caused the decision to postpone D-Day for at least a month, and Eisenhower's supremely difficult decision to proceed, taken on the advice of a single meteorologist who believed that there was a *chance* of a temporary lull, substantially contributed to the surprise of the German commanders, and thus to the initial success of the operation.

The Evolution of Military Strategy through the Ages

Although it is always dangerous to generalize and attempt to impose artificial patterns on or apply external criteria to warfare as a whole, it is nevertheless useful to trace the development of major trends from age to age with a view to obtaining an over-view into which the more detailed study of historical periods can be fitted.

Earliest man indulged in primitive warfare. This was closely associated with hunting, and appears to have consisted of surprise or flee

Operation Overlord posed special logistical problems, especially for the critical post-landing build-up phase. Two prefabricated Mulberry harbours, towed across the Channel and reassembled, were one answer. In fact, however, gales put one out of action and crippled the other.

tactics–a gambit that has been reapplied in certain aspects of modern guerrilla warfare. Primitive man gathered in tribes for mutual protection against beasts and other men, and most conflicts were little more than brawls over women, herds, grazing land and, later, cultivated areas. Eventually, to help overcome the state of constant insecurity that must have surrounded early peoples, man sought refuges–often caves with barriers of rocks thrown up to protect the entrances–and thus began the art and science of fortification. This in turn posed a challenge to would-be aggressors; ill-coordinated horde tactics would no longer suffice, so they came to appreciate the need for a chief, a strong man skilled in the arts of primitive warfare, who could devise crude means of overcoming these fortifications. In this way the concept of military leadership was probably born.

About 4000 BC primitive conflicts began to give way to what may be termed classical warfare. The need to overcome more sophisticated protected places postulated the creation of real armies; the men belonging to them were looked upon as representatives of the race, and although all men capable of bearing arms might be called upon to serve in a crisis, in principle they delegated their defence to a select number. Wars came to centre upon the major confrontation– the battle, sometimes referred to as the judicial combat, when large masses of men met to settle outstanding issues between their peoples by recourse to arms. Tactics remained simple; most early battles resolved themselves into a mass of personal combats, warrior against warrior. Attempts to outflank or turn the foe's battle line led to the extension of the battle lines, but this

process could weaken the centre, so the basic principles of turning a flank or penetrating the centre evolved. Chariots conferred mobility, early bows and javelins added missile power, and wars and armies became more elaborate. Psychological warfare also came to be deliberately applied, the early warcry being supplemented by imposing helmets and armour, or by weapons designed to unsettle the enemy, such as the Chinese use of firecrackers.

Battles were now more complex, but they still followed broadly predictable patterns based on a number of variations. Such actions were hardly ever spontaneous and it took time for the elaborate arrays to be drawn up. One result of this was that large battles only took place by the mutual consent of the commanders concerned, for unless he was inextricably trapped with his back to an unfordable river or other obstacle, one antagonist would very often refuse combat and retire to a strong position where he was virtually unassailable. The art of war, and therefore the test of a commander, remained, until the late eighteenth century, the ability to force action by surprise or other means on an unwilling foe at a place and time of the aggressor's choosing. Means of inducing a foe to fight included ravaging his territory or direct attack upon his refuges. This second variant led to ever more complex siege warfare, in which part of the attacking army conducted the investment whilst the bulk formed a covering force and waited at some distance for the foe's field army to arrive in an attempt to interfere with the siege. Manoeuvres against supply lines and more refined battle tactics also developed.

The French Revolution, and above all Napoleon, shook up this pattern, which may be said to

Four diagrams illustrating the changing face of war from earliest times to 1918.

Classical Warfare

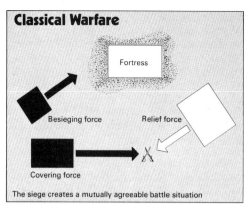

Fortress

Besieging force

Relief force

Covering force

The siege creates a mutually agreeable battle situation

The Napoleonic Variant 1796–1813

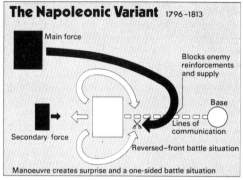

Main force

Blocks enemy reinforcements and supply

Base

Secondary force

Lines of communication

Reversed–front battle situation

Manoeuvre creates surprise and a one-sided battle situation

The Extending Front

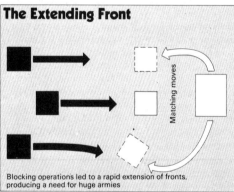

Matching moves

Blocking operations led to a rapid extension of fronts, producing a need for huge armies

The Continuous Front 1915–18

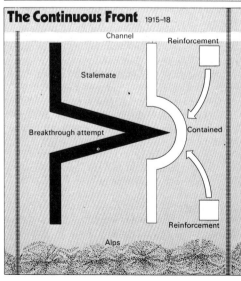

Channel

Reinforcement

Stalemate

Breakthrough attempt

Contained

Reinforcement

Alps

have dominated much of classical warfare in Europe from the days of Caesar to those of Marlborough and Frederick the Great. Napoleon's great contribution to the art of war was his fusion of manoeuvre, battle and pursuit into one continuous sequence; his predecessors had always rigidly distinguished between marching and fighting, adopting different formations for each, which took much time to adapt. Thus Napoleon exploited the superior fire power available by the end of the eighteenth century to move his army in self-contained detachments spread in a wide net across the countryside, which assisted logistical support or 'living off the countryside', and made for far faster strategic movement. He specialized in using part of his force to attract, and pin, his adversary, whilst the rest swept round a flank to attack the enemy's communications, and thus compel him to choose between fighting on ground of the French choosing in a reversed-front battle (see p. 155), and early surrender. The French marched dispersed in a highly flexible network of corps, and concentrated in order to fight. One after another, the old-fashioned armies of the Continent succumbed.

However, by 1813, France's opponents had learnt enough of Napoleon's methods to discover an antidote. The counterploy was to match French detachments with similar Allied detachments, and to ignore any attack towards their rear. Thus was set the scene for the nineteenth century, which saw the rapid extension of fronts from mere local affairs to whole theatres of war of 100 miles or more in length; the string of detachments being thickened up to produce, by 1915, the continuous Western and the Eastern fronts of the First World War. The terrible deadlock continued until 1918.

These continuous fronts, associated with still further increases in artillery firepower, greatly favoured the defence rather than the offence; barbed wire, machine guns and shell-pitted terrain made frontal assaults inordinately expensive in terms of casualties, and yet there seemed to be no alternative to direct attacks, as there was no flank to turn. Successive technical expedients such as gas and the tank failed to solve the impasse, and only in 1917 (in the East, where the front was always more fluid) and 1918 (in the West) did the Germans develop a partial answer: infiltration tactics by shock-troops. By 1918, however, it was too late for Germany to exploit this discovery. The reason was another major development in warfare: the increasing effect of the political and psychological aspects of the struggle on the civilian population. To find the huge armies needed to hold the vast fronts, nations were for the first time mobilized for industrial war; with the armies in a state of deadlock at the front, the side that would win the war would be the one that could stand the economic and social strains of total war the longest. In 1917 it was the Russian national morale that cracked, rather than that of its armies, and in

1918 Germany shared the same fate, *internal* cohesion snapping on each occasion; this was the signal for total defeat and ultimate capitulation. Thus the Napoleonic system had been reversed; the enemy's army *per se* was no longer the ultimate repository of the will to resist; this lay with the peoples themselves.

The inter-war years saw British, French and German strategists seeking a solution to the front-line deadlock. The Germans were the first to appreciate and adapt the infiltration shock-tactics of 1917–18 by making use of fast-moving armour supported by mechanized infantry and dive bombers (in place of heavy artillery). The aim was to make a penetration through the enemy front on a limited scale, avoiding strong points, and then thrust rapidly towards the rear to engulf the enemy's headquarters and logistical resources. This was the *Blitzkrieg* war, based upon a handful of Panzer divisions, which so nearly brought Hitler total victory in 1940 and 1941–42. Right through to 1945, however, the test of successful generalship remained the ability to foresee new weapons and appreciate their possible effect. The ultimate aim remained military victory and psychological persuasion – linked to compel a foe to capitulate by destroying his physical and moral cohesion.

In the meantime, on a separate plane, a different form of war had been developing since the nineteenth century – that of colonial warfare. The early colonial conquests had largely proved to be a matter of sending an expeditionary force to crush or overawe a primitive opponent with superior arms and organization. Where resistance was protracted, the colonial power learnt to persuade part of the local population to share in the liberation of the stubborn areas, engendering a state of civil war, and ultimately benefiting from this to spread, mile by mile, so as to engulf the dissident zone. This system worked well enough until the end of the century, when improvements in education and in methods of mass communication enabled the dissidents to adopt and disseminate an ideology, not only to bolster their own resistance, but also to undermine the colonial power's morale by means of direct propaganda appeals to liberal elements within the power's homeland and, most significantly of all, to friendly third parties. The Boer War thus saw highly emotive Boer propaganda aimed with some success at both the English Liberals and Kaiser Wilhelm's Germany. The former caused great political friction within Great Britain but ultimately failed to undermine the resolve to win the war, as the 'Khaki election' of 1900 demonstrated; the latter exerted international pressure in favour of the Boers (albeit unsuccessfully) and sent them some material aid. Here we see the beginning of colonial revolutionary war, in which a small but determined group, often employing guerrilla means, mobilizes liberal and neutral opinion to undermine its opponent and acquire material

help. The colonial powers tended, after 1945, to place too much importance on achieving military victory through operations and hardware, whereas the political and psychological/ideological aspects were now, for perhaps the first time in history, the most vital.

The result was the collapse of the old empires as colony after colony achieved independence, often after *losing* a struggle in purely military terms. The aim of revolutionary movements was to hold out (employing guerrilla tactics if necessary) until the combined effect of international liberal pressures and sheer exhaustion induced the colonial power to give way. Thus battles were no longer the *sine qua non* of successful warfare – a lesson the colonial powers were slow to learn.

There were, of course, more complex variations of classical wars. For instance, there were *indirect* wars, in which one belligerent attacked its foe through a third party, by paying subsidies, applying moral pressure and some degree of direct aid. In the nuclear age this form of war has become common; historical examples include Britain's use of continental coalitions against both Louis XIV and Napoleon. A modern example is provided by the Korean conflict, in which Russia indirectly challenged the United Nations and the United States by supporting the North Korean aggression in every way short of actual intervention, using the new Communist state of China as a pawn to provide about a million 'volunteers' to prevent a complete United Nations victory.

Nuclear warfare – or rather the threat of it – has again revolutionized military strategy. However, the capacity of both of the super powers to destroy each other has produced a nuclear stalemate. This took some time to achieve, but by the late 1960s a state of impasse had been reached, which has been accepted by Russia and America in the 1972 SALT talks. However, the proliferation of nuclear weapons over the years to include Britain, France and China complicates the situation, introducing a possible third-power situation of basically the same sort that complicated classical war. Nevertheless, future struggles for power and prestige are more likely to follow the pattern of such indirect super-power confrontations as the Six-Day War in the Middle East in 1967, when both Russia and the United States backed rival parties in a regional dispute, or the Vietnam conflict where, once again, Russia inspired and supplied the North Vietnamese and Viet Cong in their protracted struggle against the United States. As in the French Indo-China struggle, the prime target was not the fighting forces but international opinion and the resolve of the populations and governments involved.

Thus the future is likely to hold a number of indirect clashes by the big powers, who are mutually aware of the impossibility of all-out direct confrontation with the havoc that this would probably cause. The Middle East is likely

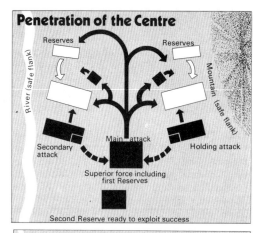

Penetration of the Centre

Reserves

Reserves

River (safe flank)

Mountain (safe flank)

Secondary attack

Main attack

Holding attack

Superior force including first Reserves

Second Reserve ready to exploit success

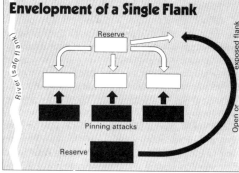

Envelopment of a Single Flank

River (safe flank)

Reserve

exposed flank

Pinning attacks

Open or

Reserve

below
The battle of Gazala, 1942, in which Rommel's Afrika Korps overran the southern flank of the British Eighth Army holding the Gazala line: an example of the envelopment of a single flank.

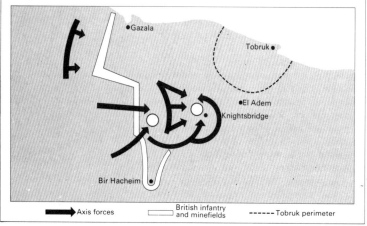

Battle of Gazala

21st Italian Corps

Gazala

Tobruk

XIII Corps

XXX Corps

El Adem

Knightsbridge

150 Brigade

Bir Hacheim

Gazala

Tobruk

El Adem

Knightsbridge

Bir Hacheim

→ Axis forces   British infantry and minefields   ------ Tobruk perimeter

to remain a tension point, and it is not beyond the realms of possibility that other situations will arise in both Africa and South America, as the Communist super powers encourage revolutionary ideologies, and provide moral and material aid–even volunteers and advisers–to the dissident elements. It is also probable that the emergent countries will indulge in nationalist-type struggles amongst themselves, again backed by third parties. Until she mobilizes her military potential China remains an enigma. Of great significance in this respect is the current deployment of over one-third of Russia's land forces along her borders with China.

The Seven Classical Manoeuvres of Warfare

From time immemorial commanders have striven to apply one or more of the seven basic movements. The advent of new weapons and other technological miracles has not radically altered this pattern's validity–only affected the method of application. However, as will be seen, the modern age has spawned an adaptation of the seventh manoeuvre which may, in the fullness of time, become recognized as the eighth gambit.

1 **Penetration of the Centre** This is probably the oldest tactical manoeuvre, dating almost from the creation of effective armies. The very earliest battles seem to have taken the form of an advance to contact, covered by a shower of missiles, whereafter they developed into a mass of individual combats until one side or the other gave up. At some specified moment in time, a commander realized the importance of a reserve and employed it to punch a hole through his opponent's tiring battle line, thus destroying its cohesion and battle power.

Many of these early engagements were fought wholly on foot. As late as 1066 both the Anglo-Saxons and the Danes chose to fight dismounted at Stamford Bridge. However, cavalry had played a vital role in other parts of the world for well over a millennium, chariots or horsemen being used to make the vital breakthrough in the enemy's centre. The central thrust had many later exponents: the Duke of Marlborough won three of his four great battles by using a carefully reserved cavalry force to pierce the centre of his enemy's line when this had been properly prepared by preliminary moves and distractions. In the Second World War, the German breakthrough around Sedan on 14–15 May 1940, or Montgomery's great success in the third stage of Alamein in late October 1942, provide further telling examples.

This method is often applied when continuous or extensive fronts exist. Its advantages include the possibility, once penetration has been achieved, of encircling large parts of the sundered army, or of exploitation towards his rear bases (see 7 below). Potential disadvantages include the excessive weakening of the flanks to produce sufficient striking power in the centre (thus inviting a telling counterstroke by a cool opponent), and the possibility that a break-*in* will not lead to a break-*through* if the foe makes use of exterior lines to rush aid to the threatened sector: the battles of Cambrai (see pp 211–213) and the Somme provide good examples.

2 **Envelopment of a Single Flank** As early armies adopted chariots, elephants or cavalry, their powers of manoeuvre developed according-ly. A skilful general, whilst pinning his foe's attention by frontal attacks with his infantry, would suddenly unleash his mounted forces in a wild dash intended to turn one or other extremity of the enemy line. If successful, this manoeuvre might enable its originator to roll up the hostile battle line, and again crack its cohesion. An alert opponent was obviously watchful for this possibility, and could counter it by reversing his own mounted forces ready to meet the threat.

The method has enjoyed much popularity in both ancient and modern times. At Gaugamela (331 BC) Alexander employed it to smash the Persian army. Two thousand years later, in late May 1942, Erwin Rommel unleashed the Desert Afrika Korps to envelop the southern flank of the British Eighth Army holding the Gazala line. His ultimate success led to the capture of Tobruk, and a German advance to the threshold of Alex-andria and the Suez Canal.

This manoeuvre, therefore, offers the prospect of totally disrupting an enemy by threatening his line of retreat and by enveloping part of his army. The balancing danger in employing this method lies in the excessive weakening of one's centre to build up sufficient force on the flank – thus inviting a telling riposte. This is what hap-pened to the Russians and Austrians at Austerlitz in December 1805 (see pp 165–166).

3 **Envelopment of Both Flanks** If successful, this manoeuvre can lead to the total annihilation of the trapped opponent. To be feasible, it requires either great superiority of strength, or quite exceptional skill in a general. The method connotes the complete encirclement of the enemy, leaving him with no alternatives but to surrender or face extinction. The great classical example was at Cannae (216 BC), where Hannibal with only 50,000 troops so out-generalled the Consul Varro and his 80,000 Romans that only 10,000 fugitives lived to tell the tale of Rome's greatest defeat (see pp 38–40). In 1914, the double envelop-ment carried out by Hindenburg (aided by von François) destroyed two Russian armies at Tannenberg in East Prussia (see pp 209–211). Thirty-seven years later, an even greater tac-tical triumph was achieved at Kiev, when Generals Kleist and Guderian trapped Marshal Budenny's Red Army Group with their fast-moving Panzers, capturing half a million Rus-sians in the process. Hitler claimed that this was the greatest battle in the history of the world, but strategically it proved counterproductive. Two years later a similar fate was meted out to some 200,000 Germans of the Seventh Army in the battle of the Falaise Gap in Normandy.

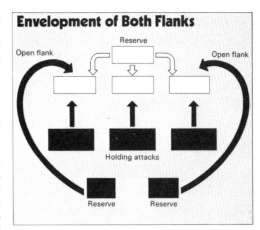

Envelopment of Both Flanks

This method holds the alluring prospect of eliminating the enemy. On the other hand, it can easily lead to over-extension of resources in order to achieve a complete ring, and unless this ring is extremely strong and resilient, the foe may be able to smash a way out and even turn the tables, as at Kohima-Imphal in Burma in 1944.

4 **Attack in Oblique Order** In this manoeuvre, a commander masses steadily increasing strength against one wing of his enemy's battle line until it buckles, while using smaller forces on other sectors to hold the foe's attention and hinder his transfer of reserves to the threatened flank.

The battle of Kiev, 1942, in which the Russians under Budenny allowed themselves to be trapped in a salient by an infantry army, and then enveloped by tank groups in a wider encirclement.

Battle of Kiev

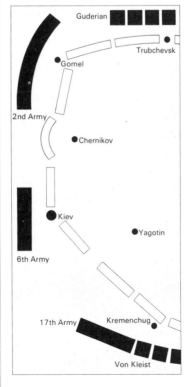
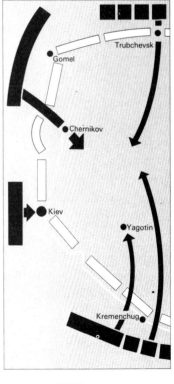

☐ Budenny's Army Group ■ German Armies ■■■ German armoured Groups

Attack in Oblique Order

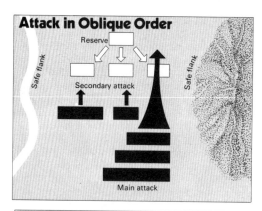

Reserve

Safe flank

Safe flank

Secondary attack

Main attack

Battle of Leuctra

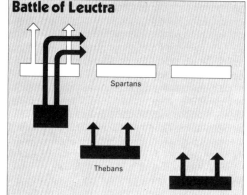

Spartans

Thebans

below
The battle of Salamanca,
1812. Wellington caught
Marmont's army
dangerously strung out
and seized the opportunity
to gain a decisive victory.

Battle of Salamanca

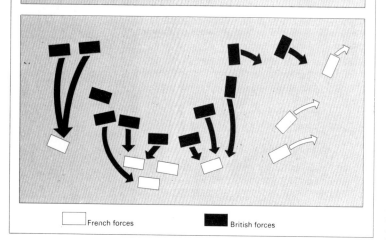

Aldea Tejada
3rd Div
D'Urban's
Cavalry
6th Div
Portuguese
7th Div
Le Marchant
5th Div
4th Div
Clausel
Thomières
Ferrey
Sarrault

French forces | British forces

Used probably for the first time against a Spartan army in 371 BC at the battle of Leuctra by Epaminondas of Thebes, this manoeuvre was associated in later times with Frederick the Great, who employed a similar tactic to great effect at Leuthen in 1757 (see pp 147–148), where he smashed the Austrian left wing by remorselessly applied pressure. In a considerably adapted form, it also provided a major feature of Napoleon's battle techniques as employed at Castiglione (1796) and Bautzen (1813). In essence, it involved the concealed build-up of a *masse de rupture* opposite the selected sector, and in this respect has some similarity with the first manoeuvre described in this section.

Properly employed, this gambit can destroy an enemy's cohesion and shatter his line. If matters go awry, however, the attacker runs the risk of unbalancing his own forces and thus inviting a strong counter against one of his own weaker areas.

5 **The Feigned Withdrawal** This manoeuvre has often been associated with the double envelopment. Its aim is to induce a foe to abandon a strong position, or to blunder forward into an ambush, by tempting him with an apparent flight and the prospect of an easy victory.

At Cannae, Hannibal ordered his weak centre to give ground before Varro, who obligingly reduced his legions into an inchoate mass by packing them forward against a narrow front. On reaching the River Aufidus to their rear, however, the allies of Carthage, who included Egyptian infantry, turned on their pursuers, enabling Hannibal to use his superior cavalry, much of it from Spain, Gaul and Numidia, to surround the Romans, with the result already described. At Hastings in 1066 William the Conqueror similarly tempted the ill-disciplined Saxon fyrd to abandon Senlac Hill; their subsequent massacre in the open ground laid Harold's steady shield wall of thegns open to envelopment and destruction.

A similar gambit was employed by Wellington before Salamanca in 1812. The apparent full-scale Allied withdrawal towards Portugal induced Marshal Marmont to over-extend his French forces in an attempt to get ahead of Wellington's army, whereupon the Duke turned at bay, took the French in flank in disjointed segments, and shattered all but the rearguard. In previous centuries this had also been a favourite gambit of the huge but loosely organized Turkish armies. Their feigned flights several times induced the Austrians to move prematurely out of their barricaded battle positions in the hope of securing loot; well might Prince Eugène declare, 'I fear the Turkish army less than their camp.' In modern times, General O'Connor deliberately traded space for time in falling back from the Libyan frontier in 1940 before striking back against the lumbering and ill-coordinated Italian Tenth Army, which ultimately disintegrated. Rommel, too, was adept at this method, as he proved in January 1942 when he turned in his tracks near Agheila, after a long retreat from the Tobruk area, and inflicted a series of blows to the over-extended Eighth Army, which was consequently forced to relinquish Benghazi and much of Cyrenaica. The dangers associated with this method are, however, considerable. Once troops begin to retreat, even if this is planned, it does not need much to convert feigned withdrawal into headlong and genuine flight. The morale of troops called upon to attempt this manoeuvre must be very high, or, as at Cannae, they must be brought up short by an impassable obstacle which offers them no recourse but to fight or die. If employed by a cool general with a great sense of timing, this manoeuvre is better designed than most to surprise an enemy and throw him off balance, for its psychological impact is powerful.

6 **Attack from a Defensive Position** Napoleon once wrote: 'The whole art of war consists in a well-reasoned and extremely circumspect defensive, followed by a rapid and audacious attack.' In adopting this method, an army prepares a strong sanctuary or defensive position, on to which it proceeds to lure the enemy. When the enemy has exhausted his energy in useless attacks against the perimeter, the garrison sallies forth to accomplish his defeat. Clearly, this manoeuvre is often associated with the one described previously, but it is open to many variations. In the simplest form, the foe is induced to attack troops holding a strong natural or man-made position; this is the story behind Bannockburn, Crécy, Poitiers and Agincourt (see pp 74–76), where pot-holes or hedges of sharpened stakes proved impenetrable to charging knights, and gave cover for the Scottish pikemen or the English archers to reap their grim harvest. In another form, the general forces battle on a foe by besieging an important town, and then deliberately allows his own army to be besieged in turn before switching to the attack. Such was the bold risk courted deliberately by Julius Caesar at Alesia (52 BC), and again by Prince Eugène at Belgrade (1717), on both occasions successfully.

A refined example of a third variation was Wellington's use of the secretly prepared Lines of Torres Vedras in Portugal to confound Marshal Masséna. After luring Masséna on to the Lines by a lengthy retreat, Wellington turned at bay within a triple line of impregnable positions, and used scorched-earth and guerrilla tactics to starve and harass his foe before issuing forth against a retreating opponent. In modern times, no better example can be cited than the battle of Kohima-Imphal fought by Slim's Fourteenth Army in Burma. His IV Corps lured Mutaguchi's reinforced Fifteenth Japanese Army into attacking the carefully prepared 'boxes' athwart the vital all-weather road leading through the Assam Hills towards India. Then, supported by air supply, General Scoones withstood all attacks until exhaustion set in among the Japanese, and

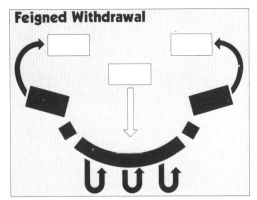

Feigned Withdrawal

then attacked in turn in June, driving the shattered enemy back to the River Chindwin in the famous monsoon advance.

Such attempts can, however, go awry. At Stalingrad (1942) Hitler listened to Goering's blandishments that the *Luftwaffe* could maintain von Paulus' beleaguered Sixth Army indefinitely, but the collapse of air supply was the most important single factor in the disaster that ensued. Again, in 1954, the French in Indo-China deliberately set up a defensive position at Dien Bien Phu far behind the Vietminh's lines and athwart a vital supply route into Red China, inviting Giap to accept battle. Thus far the plan worked, but the struggle ended with a humiliating

The battle of Kohima-Imphal, 1944, in which Slim's Fourteenth Army launched a devastating offensive against the Japanese after the latter had spent their force against carefully prepared defensive 'boxes'.

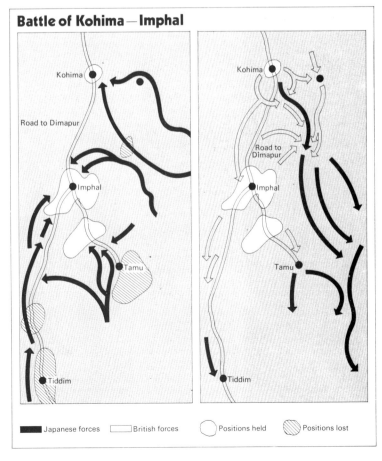

Battle of Kohima — Imphal

Kohima

Road to Dimapur

Imphal

Tamu

Tiddim

Kohima

Road to Dimapur

Imphal

Tamu

Tiddim

■ Japanese forces   □ British forces   ◯ Positions held   ▨ Positions lost

French defeat which cost them Indo-China—largely due, once again, to the breakdown of air supply and support, together with a fatal underestimation of the enemy's capacity, particularly as regards medium artillery. It is interesting to note that Giap did not wish to try his luck twice in this respect, and when the Americans set up a similar situation at Khe-Sanh in 1969, the wily warrior did not press his attack beyond the point of no return, but drew back when he sensed trouble.

Properly employed, this manoeuvre can, therefore, lead to decisive results. It can also, however, lead to dangerous defensive thinking—exemplified by the French belief in the Maginot Line in 1940. To work, the method requires that the foe accept the challenge; the danger is that the defence may wait indefinitely for an attack that never comes, or that it may come from a disconcerting direction, as was the case in early 1942 when the Japanese advanced on the seaward-orientated fortress of Singapore from the landward side.

7 **The Indirect Approach** This concept is based on absorbing the foe's attention by means of secondary operations whilst a major force marches to envelop his flank and rear *strategically*. The effect of such a manoeuvre, if successfully completed, is to interrupt the enemy's supplies, shake his composure and force him to turn in his tracks and accept a reversed-front battle (i.e. each side facing *towards* its base) which, if lost, can only result in disaster, as the foe has no line of retreat. The criteria of speed and surprise are vital to success.

This method, applied with many variations, was perhaps the supreme manifestation of offensive warfare down to 1945. It was attempted many times in Classical Antiquity by such great commanders as Alexander, Hannibal and Caesar, but was rarely completely successful due to the relative lack of mobility of armies at that time. It came nearest to perfection in the hands of Napoleon, underlying no less than thirty of his major manoeuvres between 1796 and 1812, of which the magnificent sweep across Germany in October 1805 to trap General Mack in Ulm must suffice as an example. It proved equally important during the American Civil War, being used with telling effect by Robert E. Lee against Pope in the Second Bull Run campaign of 1862.

The gambit can be associated with others. In 1940, for example, the Germans converted an initial breakthrough against the Allied centre near Sedan into a telling manoeuvre of strategic envelopment as the Panzers raced for the Channel coast far to the rear of the front line, and bottled up the 330,000 troops of the British Expeditionary Force in a hopeless position. The miracle of Dunkirk saved the troops, but not their equipment. An even more successful application in modern times was in central Burma in 1945, when Slim pinned Kimura's attention at Mandalay whilst the major blow was being prepared, over the Irrawaddy, far to the south, against the key Japanese supply centre of Meiktila. Once this key position had fallen to the Fourteenth Army, the Japanese defence of Burma was on the verge of collapse.

This system's advantage is the promise of decisive results, and its endowment of the ability to force action on an unwilling opponent, who cannot ignore the manoeuvre's implications. It requires, however, considerable superiority of force and a well-developed sense of timing to be successful. If indulged in too rashly, moreover, it may lead to catastrophic results, as an alert opponent can counter the implied threat, as happened to Napoleon in 1813 and 1814, by taking steps to meet and thwart each outflanking attempt in turn.

8 **The Modern Application of the Indirect Approach—Offensive Revolutionary and Guerrilla Warfare** The greatest and most lasting lessons to be derived from all the preceding seven manoeuvres, taken together, are the importance of gaining and keeping the initiative, and the significance of throwing the enemy off balance whilst maintaining one's own. These principles remain true of the latest manifestation of warfare, although in certain vital applications the forms of war have changed dramatically since 1945.

Since that date, many struggles have centred around winning independence from colonial powers, and thereafter the succession to power within the new state. Furthermore, owing to the threat of nuclear war, the use of guerrilla warfare as the major means of enforcing a revolutionary concept and overthrowing a society has become increasingly prevalent. By its very definition guerrilla war is based upon indirect means—terror, raids, sabotage, propaganda—

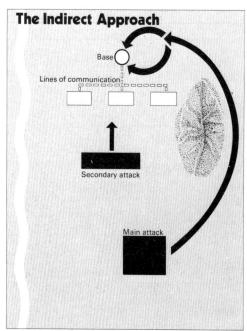

The Indirect Approach

Base

Lines of communication

Secondary attack

Main attack

French paratroops drop into Dien Bien Phu, November 1953, to set up a large fortified area deep in Vietminh controlled territory. They lived to regret it, for next year this was the scene of the French army's most humiliating defeat, at the hands of General Giap and his guerrilla divisions.

but its *offensive* use as a means to gain political dominance and psychological superiority is a new development. Guerrilla war was defined by Napoleon as 'A war without a front', an aspect stressed by Che Guevara when he claimed that the revolutionary aimed to create the impression of being 'everywhere but nowhere'. Until 1945, however, guerrilla tactics were employed only as a last resort, the intention being to stave off total defeat by forming a nucleus for continued resistance to an aggressor, as in Spain (1808–14), South Africa (1900–01) or Yugoslavia (1941–44). Since 1945, however, guerrilla warfare has gained a new significance as a principal means of conducting offensive but low-key operations.

Part of its originality lies in the relative unimportance of conventional military success. The revolutionary cause, indeed, may even be able to absorb conventional military defeat and still emerge as the ultimate political winner. The political aim is now twofold: to persuade the uninvolved part of the population to support the guerrilla programme; and to convince the third-world nations, and the liberal elements within the power whose influence is under attack, that right and justice, as well as convenience, lie in recognition of the new regime and in persuading the former territorial power to acquiesce in this as soon as possible. The Third World War, therefore, is being fought now on the political and psychological planes, rather than upon the conventional military level. The value accorded to winning battles *per se* has almost been reversed; the French army won the war in Algeria, but French power collapsed soon afterwards. The British defeated the Mau Mau in Kenya, but victory served only to hasten the granting of independence.

Armies in the traditional sense are no longer deemed to be the main repositories of power in a conflict situation. Undoubtedly, insurgent forces on occasion adopt conventional methods, as in Indo-China, while they prepare the *coup de grâce*, but essentially their target is the morale and staying power of the enemy's home population and government. Once they reach the stage at which they are sustaining an acceptable degree of damage *and* at the same time are inflicting an unacceptable amount upon their opponent, victory is in sight.

This system has proved highly successful against the French in Indo-China and Algeria, the Dutch in Indonesia and the Americans in Vietnam. The only long-term solution is the divination of genuine social and economic and political grievances, and prompt action to reform these before the stage of confrontation is reached. All other methods are at best palliatives; when military action is resorted to, however, the objective should be to separate the guerrilla from the population on which he depends for intelligence, food and recruits. Only when the infrastructure has been penetrated and neutralized will any purpose be served by giving full priority to hunting down guerrilla groups themselves. This was the secret of the temporary and localized British success in Malaya (1948–60).

Thus warfare has probably reached a period of major change. Conventional wars, such as the Korean, Arab-Israeli or Indo-Pakistan struggles, will indubitably occur from time to time, but it would seem likely that they will concede primacy in the spectrum of warfare to guerrilla and revolutionary struggles in which the political and psychological factors predominate over the military. An eighth manoeuvre of war–one that apparently favours the physically weak (but strongly motivated) group over the physically stronger but less inspired conventional power–may therefore be justly recognized.

A South Vietnamese tank in action outside Quang Tri, South Vietnam. The overwhelming logistical superiority of the Americans and the South Vietnamese was frequently of little use against their guerrilla opponents.

CLASSICAL WARFARE

The Middle East was the cradle of civilization: it was also the birthplace of organized armies and viable weaponry. It would seem, from the scanty evidence available, that the empire of Sumer (c. 3000 BC) was one of the earliest to rise above a purely tribal approach to warfare. Sumer developed heavy infantry, armed with smelted copper spears and simple bows and arrows, and also cumbersome two- and four-wheeled chariots drawn by mules. The former were trained to fight in dense, close-order formations with linked shields–the earliest form of the phalanx. Their engineers are also credited with building the first elaborate fortifications–the city refuge of Ur was their strongly defended capital–and with developing the concomitant skills of siege warfare. Improvements in weapons inspired better protective clothing, and the earliest shields of wicker or wood were replaced by helmets and simple body armour, this often taking the form of metal scales sewn upon a leather undercoat.

At much the same time, the Nile Valley saw the development of an independent military power in Ancient Egypt of the Old Kingdom. The earliest Egyptian armies were largely based on unwieldy militias or citizen levies, but through the period of the Middle Kingdom (2150–1800 BC) and into the New Kingdom, these forces became professional, full-time and better armed. By 2000 BC, swords and axes of bronze were making an appearance, supplementing the simple bows and javelins of earlier generations, but the advent of the light chariot (carrying a driver, archer and shield bearer) provided the first true mobility on campaign and shock action in battle, and forged a viable instrument of distant conquest. Led by such notable leaders as Pharaoh Thutmosis III, Egypt first repelled predatory tribes and rebellious vassals and then proceeded to conquer the area of the Sudan and modern Libya, and lands as far as the Euphrates. By 1800 BC, the Egyptian armies were some 20,000 men strong, divided into five major units and sub-divided into formations 1,000 and ultimately 100 men strong, led by the hereditary aristocracy. Little tactical subtlety was attempted for many generations, but eventually the chariots found their way to the flanks, whilst lightly armed archers and slingers skirmished ahead of the main body of foot soldiers. Such battles were attritional in character, the penalties of defeat being massacre, enslavement, and, on occasion, genocide. Vast fortresses of mud and stone sprang up by 1980 BC along the extending frontiers. However, periods of decline and obscurity lay ahead, and the end came at the hands of Alexander the Great in 332 BC.

Meanwhile the fertile crescent between the rivers Tigris and Euphrates had become the scene of many transient civilizations. Sumer gave place to Akkad (2350–2150 BC), which specialized in light infantry armed with javelins and more powerful composite bows of wood, sinew and horn. The great ruler Sargon is known to have defeated up to 15,000 foes in battle with only 5,400 men, c. 2200 BC. Then came Babylon (1850–1650 BC), but the emergence of Assyria, c. 1380 BC, was the next milestone in the development of warfare.

The Assyrians formed a state organized wholly for war. Their main aim was booty, and their reputation for ferocity became legendary. Armed with weapons of forged iron (the process may have originated c. 1400 BC amongst the Hittites, who were also noted for their light chariots and their discipline and training) and protected by conical helmets, breastplates and shields, they became feared throughout the Middle East. Under Shalmaneser III, they built up an army of 20,000 infantry, 1,200 chariots and–uniquely–some 12,000 light cavalry armed with spears or bows. These represented both the first organized cavalry and the first horse archers.

The Assyrians also perfected the Sumerian skills of siegecraft. Under Tiglathpileser III, master of siege war, they reached their peak. They triumphed by the use of treachery, blockade and assault, specializing in the use of huge mobile siege towers, battering rams and mine galleries to storm over ramparts or through breaches in the foe's walls. Assyria developed the first corps of military engineers, and few cities or peoples could withstand the Assyrian attack. Their victories led to wholesale plundering and the deportation of entire populations into slavery, but at length in 612 BC they succumbed to the

From the very earliest times, hilltops afforded sanctuary and security. One of the largest sanctuaries in Western Europe was Mai Dun (or Maiden) Castle in Dorset. Occupied since at least 2000 BC, it was fortified in the Iron Age c. 300 BC. Its perimeter measures over two miles, and its four main lines of ramparts rise eighty feet.

Medes and Babylonians acting in concert, and Nineveh, their capital, was destroyed.

The Medes were soon assimilated by the more numerous Persians, and another great empire emerged, c. 559 BC. Inspired by the great Cyrus (reigned 559–530 BC) and his son Darius, the Persian realm expanded to include, by 333 BC, most of what is now modern Turkey as well as much of the Levant and Arabia. Persian conquests were organized into twenty efficiently administered satrapies, linked to Persepolis by a network of roads and mounted messengers who were expected to cover 200 miles a day. Uniquely, the Persians earned the acquiescence and even the goodwill of their conquered peoples by respecting local customs and faiths.

The Persian army was several hundred thousands strong, organized in divisions of 10,000 men mainly provided by levies on the satrapies, and was the first force to be paid in coin. Its training and discipline was impressive. It comprised heavy and light infantry, cavalry, chariots and war elephants, and a camel corps – each beast bearing an archer and a driver. Darius also instituted a *corps d'élite* of 10,000 Immortals. Apart from the great war bows used for sieges, they introduced few new weapons, and their tactics remained relatively crude. Moreover, they permitted their armies to be encumbered by immense baggage trains of women, slaves and comforts, which made their marches slow and laid their lines of communication open to attack. Nevertheless, the Persians developed the most effective military administrative system up to their time.

If the Persians were to a large extent the heirs of the Assyrians, the military traditions of the Ancient Greeks were closely linked to those of Ancient Egypt. These had been passed on by the Hittites and Cretan Minoans to the kingdom of Mycenae, and thence to the Greek city states. The great struggles of the fifth century BC between Greece and Persia thus represented a conflict of cultures, Western and Eastern. After years of mounting tension the huge Persian host, 60,000 strong, attacked Greece itself in 490 BC and was decisively defeated by the 10,000 Athenians and Plataeans at Marathon. Xerxes fared no better ten years later, but was forced back into Asia after the great naval battle of Salamis, and the action at Plataea (479 BC).

The origins of Greek warfare antedate the siege of Troy in 1200 BC, but Homer reveals little of its features, save the importance of infantry combat by heavily armed soldiers. From the start, the basic Greek strategical weakness was lack of unity; only the direst peril could inspire a degree of inter-city cooperation. The later writers,

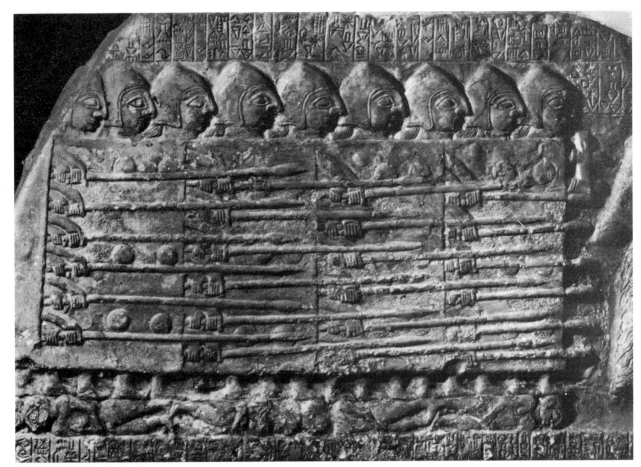

Herodotus and Thucydides, provide much incidental information. Cavalry was slow in appearing in any numbers owing to the terrain, and to the democratic distrust of a social élite; when it did come on the scene the lancers were usually hired mercenaries. The typical Greek soldier remained the hoplite, heavily armoured with helmet, back and breastplate, circular shield and greaves, and for the most part armed with the twenty-one-foot *sarissa*, or pike. These warriors formed up in close order, eight ranks deep, to form a phalanx, the standard Greek battle formation, which was supported by numbers of *psiloi* and *peltasts*, lightly armed troops employing slings, javelins or bows. All male citizens were liable to the call to arms when need arose.

Tactics were for many years little more than crude trials of strength, although Miltiades convincingly outmanoeuvred the Persians at Marathon, and it was only in 371 BC that Epaminondas of Thebes defeated a Spartan army near Leuctra after forming up his three phalanxes in the oblique order, thus bringing superior force to bear at the critical place and time. Grand tactics had been born. Athens meanwhile had become a naval power, whilst Sparta preponderated on land, but in 405 BC a Persian-Spartan coalition destroyed the Athenian fleet, and in the

following year Athens surrendered. The scene was now almost set for the appearance of one of the greatest commanders of all time.

Philip II of Macedon (reigned 359–336 BC), a small kingdom to the north of Greece, set about exploiting Greek divisiveness by reorganizing his state for war and creating an effective army. The peasant-based phalanx remained the core, but it was armed with fourteen-foot pikes and trained to be more flexible and manoeuvrable. Philip also created the Royal Army, a force of élite cavalry some 2,000 horsemen strong, of whom the Companions, the aristocratic royal

Even earlier, warfare had become organized in the Middle East. This bas-relief shows Sumerian foot soldiers formed in an early version of the phalanx, with spears presented, *c.* 2500 BC. Note their helmets and studded shields – also their foes being trampled underfoot. From the 'stele of the vultures' at Ur. *Louvre, Paris.*

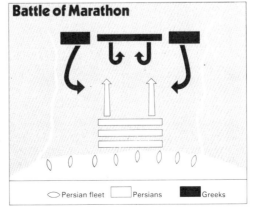

Battle of Marathon

Persian fleet | Persians | Greeks

23

Ancient Egypt evolved a sophisticated military system by 2000 BC. This funerary model from a tomb near the city of Meir shows Egyptian spearmen of the Middle Kingdom, possibly Nubian allies. Note the devices upon their shields, which are being held upside down, the left hands being raised; this may have been a ceremonial posture, the equivalent of 'reversing arms' as a token of mourning, as in later armies. *Museum of Egyptian Antiquities, Cairo.*

The ancient kingdoms of the Fertile Crescent produced fast-moving chariots by 1000 BC. Here we see Assyrian chariots in action, each bearing a driver and archer, and drawn by a pair of horses, *c.* 850 BC. *British Museum, London.*

bodyguard, were the most important part; they were armed with ten-foot lances and short swords, and were supported by 3,000 highly trained light infantry called *hypaspists*. This force was highly professional, and had no peer at this period. The cavalry were still not equipped with stirrups, using the knee grip to remain mounted, but they would clinch almost every major battle.

Philip also added a sophisticated artillery train to his army as well as a bridging train. Orders were transmitted by trumpet, smoke and beacon signals, and a rudimentary staff also came into existence. His army, totalling some 35,000 men, was centred around the Royal Army and four phalanxes, which formed up on a frontage of 256 men and were sixteen ranks deep. In terms of tactical training great stress was laid on combined action and cooperation between horse and

The Assyrians met Arab camel archers during their frequent campaigns. This detail comes from the palace of King Ashurbanipal (668–627 BC) at Nineveh. *British Museum, London.*

foot, and a truly balanced force appeared covering a battle-front of some 1,400 yards. Following his victory at Chaeronaea (338 BC), Philip was virtual master of all Greece save Sparta, and the power-base was thus formed for his brilliant son and successor, Alexander the Great, to exploit in some of the most dramatic conquests of history.

For ten years (333–323 BC) Alexander led his army in a continuous series of challenges and achievements. The motives behind this expansionist adventure were a combination of economic necessity (the newly emergent naval power of the Phoenicians had successfully taken over much of the Greek trade), personal ambition, and a belief in a theory of racial superiority. This heady combination, allied to Alexander's specific gifts of leadership–which will be analysed later in this chapter–took the Macedonian army and its allies, rarely over 35,000 men in all, from Greece through Egypt, Syria and the vast expanses of Persia, to India. A mounting list of great battle and siege successes were a testimony to Alexander's greatness and the value of the forces he led: the battle of the River Granicus in 334 BC;

the great success at Issus over Darius III in November the next year; the seven-month siege and capture of the naval base of Tyre in 332 BC, where Diades employed *telamons* and 'crows' to batter walls and storm strongpoints; the clinching victory of Gaugamela the following October, where the Macedonian attack in the oblique order shattered the Persian army yet again, and effectively completed the overthrow of Persia–these were the achievements of no common mortal. More was to follow, as Alexander pressed eastwards through modern Uzbekistan and Afghanistan into modern Pakistan, winning the battle of the River Hydaspes (see below), before reaching the Indus.

At last even the devotion of his men could not still the clamour for a return home, and Alexander concurred. After crossing the Indian Ocean, he marched his men through hostile Arabia towards Babylon, adapting his methods to meet the guerrilla tactics of local tribes, who exploited every type of natural obstacle and terrain to check his progress. Babylon was safely reached, but there Alexander suddenly died from illness

right
The Hittites also specialized in chariot warfare. Relief from Carchemish, possibly 850 BC, now in Ankara.

opposite, top
The battle of Gaugamela, 331 BC, in which Alexander the Great enveloped the left flank of the Persian army, winning a decisive victory at little personal cost.

opposite, bottom
The Assyrians were early masters of siege warfare. Here they use scaling ladders as they storm the city of Kharmanu. A bas-relief from the North Palace of King Ashurbanipal (668–627 BC) at Nineveh. *British Museum, London.*

at the age of thirty-three. Following his death, his three successors proved incapable of preserving his achievements, and within 150 years almost all his conquests had been assimilated by the next great martial power to emerge–the Roman Republic. Alexander's empire had rested too much on the personality and abilities of a single man, who, for all his undoubted genius, was unable to institutionalize his work. However, none could have foreseen Alexander's premature death. As it turned out, the resultant power vacuum proved fatal, but this in no way detracts from the greatness of this military saga, in which both leader and led were tested in almost every conceivable combination of circumstances.

Meanwhile a new state, Carthage, had established a maritime empire based on sea power. Led by generals such as Hamilcar, Hanno and Hamilcar Barca, its armies marched far from their North African homeland into Spain, Gaul, Sicily and other Mediterranean islands. It was inevitable that this expansion would lead to a clash with another power in the making, Rome.

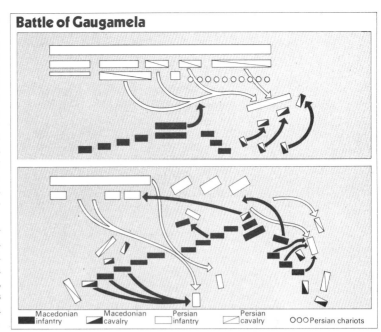

Battle of Gaugamela

| Macedonian infantry | Macedonian cavalry | Persian infantry | Persian cavalry | OOO Persian chariots |

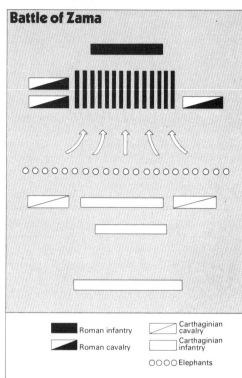

Battle of Zama

Roman infantry
Roman cavalry
Carthaginian cavalry
Carthaginian infantry
○○○○ Elephants

An Assyrian battering ram, covered by archery fire. Note the impaled enemies in the background. *British Museum, London.*

above, centre
The battle of Zama, 202 BC: the successful application of the principle of attack from a defensive position.

By 265 BC, the efficient and disciplined people living on the seven hills near the Tiber had fought their way to paramountcy on the mainland of Italy, and, unlike the Greeks or Macedonians, had transformed their local conquests into a lasting political organization. They then directed their energies beyond the confines of the peninsula; building a fleet, they defeated the Carthaginians at sea and seized Sicily in the First Punic War (265–241 BC). Her appetite whetted, Rome moved on to take Sardinia and Corsica. In 218 BC the young Carthaginian general, Hannibal, moved his army over the Alps from Spain and proceeded to demonstrate his great military gifts. For fifteen years Rome was forced back on the defensive; between 218 and 216 BC Hannibal inflicted three massive defeats on the forces of the Republic: Trebbia, Lake Trasimene and then Cannae (see below).

Fortunately for Rome, Hannibal proved unable to exploit his success to the full, and the peoples of Italy remained loyal to the Republic. The Romans could also learn from their mistakes. Even before Cannae they had appointed a dictator, and after the culminating defeat Fabius Maximus adopted methods of guerrilla war to contain the menace, avoiding direct confrontations. By 207 BC this Fabian strategy had induced Hannibal to return to Carthage, and Rome prepared to switch to the offensive. The result was the invasion of North Africa, where the Roman commander, Scipio Africanus, finally confronted Hannibal at Zama (202 BC) close to Carthage. First the Carthaginian elephants were beaten back by the Roman countermeasures

–including areas strewn with iron spikes (the Classical World's version of the modern minefield), fire arrows and flexible tactics, which channelled the maddened beasts' harmlessly through the Roman lines. Then the Roman and mercenary cavalry swept the Numidian horsemen from the field, the triple line of legions advanced, and Carthage was doomed to defeat. Hannibal was exiled, and killed himself in 183 BC. This sad end notwithstanding, his achievements in the years of his prime had earned him the accolade of being second only to Alexander amongst the generals of the Ancient World.

Scipio's triumph inaugurated the period of Rome's greatness. During the Punic Wars the instrument of empire–namely the Roman legion –had been considerably altered in organization. In the earliest years of Rome the legion had been barely distinguishable from the phalanx, but the tactical limitations this imposed had led to the creation of the maniple legion, *c.* 300 BC. Each numbered about 5,000 men, organized into thirty maniples of 120 legionaries apiece, with a reserve of a further five maniples. Flexible attack tactics replaced the brute shock of the phalanx charge. Almost half the troops were lightly armed *velites*. These skirmished ahead of the maniples, which advanced in three lines of units arranged in chequerboard fashion. The front line comprised *hastati*, armed with javelins. After flinging their missiles, the troops closed with shields and swords, supported by the *principes* of the second line, who were armed with heavier spears. Behind them waited the veteran *triarii*, experienced soldiers one and all, and the

Battle of Zama

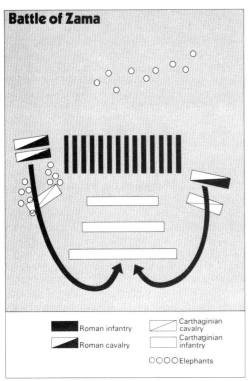

Roman infantry
Roman cavalry
Carthaginian cavalry
Carthaginian infantry
○○○○ Elephants

velites (who had re-formed after completing their skirmishing function). These were essentially citizen forces, every Roman of military age being liable for service. Early armies comprised two legions under a consul, but later two allied legions were added.

The Punic Wars showed Rome her need to raise a paid professional army. The outcome was the cohort legion of 6,500 men. The cohort replaced the maniple, containing 400 to 500 men, divided into centuries of 80 men, which again were split into 10 parties of 8 men each. By this time a regular chain of command had also evolved, running from the Consul (commander-in-chief) through quaestors (staff officers) to the legionary hierarchy, headed by the legate. He in turn was aided by tribunes, centurions and decurions.

Hannibal also taught Rome the need for better cavalry. At first, mounted service had been restricted to the wealthier citizens, but eventually Spanish mercenary horsemen were added. Soon every legion included 24 *turmae* (troops of 32 men) forming 2 *alae* (or wings). Later, each legion also included a train of *ballistae* and other artillery weapons, and thus became an all-arm force of mixed capacity—the most sophisticated military formation (about 10,000 men in all) until the creation of Napoleon's *corps d'armée* 2,000 years later. The legions were first and foremost an

above
The storming of a fortress by Assyrian troops during the campaigns of Tiglath-pileser, *c.* 750 BC. *British Museum, London.*

below
An Assyrian mobile battering ram with a siege-tower attachment. *British Museum, London.*

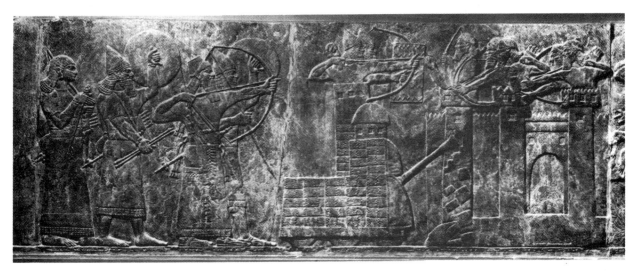

In southern Europe the mounted cavalryman was more popular than the charioteer. This bronze representation of a Greek warrior is full of action. *British Museum, London.*

infantry force throughout the great years, and only with the challenge of the mounted barbarian hordes–first appreciated *c.* 33 BC when Parthian horse archers destroyed the legions of Crassus at Carrhae–was greater emphasis placed on the mounted army. The adoption of the stirrup, *c.* AD 200, encouraged this trend, and eventually a full quarter of Rome's forces was mounted.

Superior tactical training and high-class equipment underlay the legions' long tale of success. Each legionary was armed with two seven-foot javelins (with soft metal shanks behind the point to preclude their re-use by the enemy), a broad short sword with a two-foot blade and a dagger. Many also carried a tougher spear, and light troops carried slings or bows. All wore a metal helmet with ear flaps, carried an oblong shield and wore body armour comprising shoulder guards, a breastplate, a leather apron reinforced with metal studs and greaves or shin-guards. On the march each soldier carried two stakes (for the stockaded camps built each night), fifteen days' rations and personal kit including a cooking pot. The load, weighing some eighty pounds, was partly carried on a large forked

stick, nicknamed 'Marius' Mule' after Marius, who systematized the cohort system and introduced many other reforms, *c.* 108 BC. The long-service native soldier, serving for pay and an award of land upon retirement, soon became the normal type for the main infantry, although mercenaries were still hired in large numbers for service in the *velites* and the cavalry *alae*.

The Roman army also produced first-class engineers and artillerists. They built roads and fortresses that have survived the passage of millennia, and acquired great skill at siege warfare. First isolating the target with lines of circumvallation and contravallation (facing outwards and inwards respectively), they would proceed to blast the defences with engines of war –catapults and *ballistae*–thirty of which were attached to every legion by the time of Julius Caesar. Caesar himself was a master of siege-craft, as his celebrated success at Alesia in 52 BC demonstrated. Having laid siege to the town, he routed a relieving Gallic army of some 250,000 as well as compelling Vercingetorix's garrison of 80,000 men to surrender–all with a bare 70,000 Roman troops. The legionaries were also trained to form the *testudo* to protect mining parties by interlocking their shields over their heads and backs. As in all Roman activities, success was the product of discipline, training and sweat; at some sieges the troops would raise vast ramps of earth to the height of the ramparts–as at Masada in Palestine.

The Romans were nothing if not thorough, and in essentials their legion-based armies changed but little over the 500 years which saw the burgeoning of their empire to take in the whole of the Mediterranean world, Gaul, half of Germany and the British Isles, besides vast provinces in Asia Minor and North Africa. For centuries the legions, patrolling key strategical roads and barriers such as Hadrian's Wall (built AD 122) imposed the *pax Romana* on the civilized world. Eventually, however, the over-extension of frontiers, the spread of corrupt practices and civil strife in latter-day Rome, and a growing reliance on hired mercenary tribes for the defence of the Empire from the mounting barbarian attacks from the East, led to decline and fall. In AD 378, the armoured horsemen of the Goths crushingly defeated the legions at Adrianople. In AD 409, Rome itself was sacked by Alaric, and the Empire in the West soon foundered.

It remains to assess the three truly great captains produced by the Ancient World, namely Alexander, Hannibal and Julius Caesar. These three exerted a pre-eminent influence both on their own times and, whether directly or indirectly, on posterity.

Alexander has been termed the 'father of strategy', and certainly warfare became a sophisticated art in his hands. In many ways a superb opportunist, Alexander nevertheless grasped the principles of strategy; for example, to remove the threat to his communications posed by the

The layout of a Roman camp

	Allied troops	Rear gate Roman troops				Allied troops	
	Foot	11	13	14	12	Foot	
	Horse	12	14	13	11	Horse	
	Foot	11	13	14	12	Foot	
	Horse	12	14	13	11	Horse	

Trench and ramparts

Gate — 9 — 10 Via Principalis 10 — 9 — Gate

5	4	2	1	3	4	5
8		6 7		6 7		8

Front gate

1 Commander's hq	6 Special cavalry units	11 Hastati
2 Quaestor's area	7 Special infantry units	12 Principes
3 Forum	8 Reserves	13 Triarii
4 Special guards	9 Officers' tents	14 Cavalry
5 Special guards	10 Tribunes' tents	

The Roman *testudo*, or tortoise, a formation used for getting a body of troops close under enemy defences to undermine or storm them. Reputedly, a well-formed testudo could carry the weight of a chariot drawn by two horses on the interlocked shields. Detail from the Antonine Column, Rome.

Persian Mediterranean fleet, he did not waste time building a navy, as he was advised, but instead marched his army to seize the foe's naval bases, including Tyre, one by one. He was also inspired by a strong desire to fight. Whatever the weather, climate or terrain, Alexander sought the great battle as the surest road to success, and—equally important—he pursued his defeated foes ruthlessly. Underlying all his achievements were great qualities of personal leadership. In the first place he had an unprecedented ability to inspire confidence in his troops. He showed solicitude for his men's welfare, provided for his sick and wounded to the limits of his ability, and was careful to praise and reward, as well as to punish. Secondly, his great desire to excel in all aspects of the military profession led him to accept every challenge. Thirdly, he could make decisions both rapidly and correctly (the benefit, probably, of his education as a youth by Aristotle). Of course, he had the advantage of owing responsibility to no higher authority, and although this could lead to distortions of judgement and headstrong decisions it was the true mark of his greatness that he proved capable of controlling his weaknesses and making the most of his qualities. Throughout his short but lustrous career, he remained essentially humane and considerate—even towards the defeated—and above all he possessed a comprehensive knowledge of himself. In an age when the calibre of one man—the leader—was so important, Alexander set a standard that few have emulated and none have surpassed.

Hannibal, the greatest soldier produced by Carthage, was also a commander of the first rank. Like Alexander, he was both bold and capable of inspiring his troops. His feat in passing an army, complete with elephants, over the Alps had never been attempted before, and on several occasions only his personal drive and example prevented his men from turning back. The invasion of Italy was a brilliant strategic concept, with its purpose of carrying war deep into the enemy's camp—but what ensued was less strategically sound, although a good illustration of Hannibal's calibre. The first three years of the invasion saw three great battle successes based on Hannibal's skill at laying ambushes, achieving surprise, and controlling his men in action. Thereafter, he was unable to consolidate his success. Yet for ten long years, and despite all the resources of Rome, he managed to keep together his army of some 18,000 men in conditions of considerable adversity, rarely reinforced, in the prosecution of what almost amounts to a guerrilla war, cut off from Carthage by the Roman superiority at sea and their conquest of Spain. Adversity is perhaps the truest test of a leader's mettle, and Hannibal emerges triumphantly as a master exponent of personal leadership.

Thirdly, we must consider Julius Caesar. His military career is all the more remarkable in that, like Oliver Cromwell, he was a politician by inclination, and, again like Cromwell, only took up his first military command at the relatively advanced age of forty. Highly ambitious,

The archetypal soldier of the Greek city states was the *hoplite*, or heavily armoured infantryman, equipped with cuirass, round shield, crested helmet, leg greaves, spear and sword. This amphora dates from *c.* 500 BC. *British Museum, London.*

he saw that the most likely avenue to political supremacy lay through military mastery, and moulded the post-Marian army into a personal weapon. As a general, he could be erratic, and one of the special aspects of his genius was his ability to escape triumphantly from tight corners of his own making. He was not an original tactician, neglecting cavalry and employing the traditional three-line legion throughout his career. Nevertheless, he was the greatest of all Roman infantry commanders, and it is a tribute to the staunchness and dependability of the Roman army that it could rise above the problems he set it. Caesar was at one and the same time a supreme, even rash, opportunist, and an example of Roman method and efficiency. Before his assassination in March 44 BC, he had campaigned in Gaul, Germany, Spain, Egypt, Africa and Asia Minor, and in the process secured a pause in the Roman civil wars and extended the Roman boundaries as far as the Channel and the Rhine–thus spreading Roman concepts to new areas of Europe. His *Commentaries* on the Gallic wars, intended to further his political ambitions, provide a full picture of the post-Marian Roman army and of the man who led it.

The Battle of the Hydaspes, 326 BC
Following his crushing victory over the Persian forces at Gaugamela (331 BC), and its exploitation through Babylonia and Parthia, Alexander the Great marched on with the Macedonian army of possibly 20,000 men as far as the kingdom of Porus in north-west India (328–327 BC). By the spring of 326 BC, Alexander had reached the north bank of the River Hydaspes, a tributary of the Indus. The river appeared to present an impassable obstacle, being a full half-mile wide and swollen with floods. On the further bank was deployed the whole army of King Porus, some 30,000 strong, ready to contest any attempt at a crossing. A particularly imposing part of this array was a force of over 100 elephants and 300 chariots.

Alexander faced a double problem: how to pass over the dangerous river at a disputed crossing; and how to defeat a well-equipped and competent opponent. To achieve his first objective, Alexander set himself to lull Porus into a state of false security. To this end rumours were deliberately spread to the effect that Alexander had no intention whatsoever of crossing until the river level fell, and the Macedonian army set about building an elaborate camp to foster this illusion. Nevertheless, Porus did not relax his vigilance. Next, Alexander mounted a large number of small feint night attacks and probes up- and downstream from his encampment, forcing Porus to take defensive measures practically every night. The King soon wearied of this ceaseless vigilance and relaxed his efforts, thereby helping to create the opportunity that Alexander had been waiting for.

Alexander had already selected a crossing place some sixteen miles from his camp, and at dead of night he moved with 5,000 horse and 6,000 foot to this point, leaving General Craterus with a considerable force to keep Porus' attention

The Ancient Greeks proved themselves time and again in battle against the Persians. Late fourth century BC marble from Sidon. *Archaeological Museums, Istanbul.*

above
A stricken warrior, from
a temple at Aegina,
c. 490 BC. *Staatliche
Antikensammlungen und
Glyptothek, Munich.*

right
A Greek archer in
kneeling firing position.
The sculptured figure
(reputed to be Hercules)
is wearing a cuirass and
short skirt made of metal
strips on a leather
backing. From a temple
at Aegina, *c.* 490 BC.
*Staatliche Antiken-
sammlungen und
Glyptothek, Munich.*

The Etruscans of the Italian peninsula possessed chariots. This is the main shield, seen from the front; it is made of wood with bronze sheathing. Greek influence is clear from the sculptured warriors depicted. The remains of this chariot were found at Monteleone.
Metropolitan Museum of Art, New York, Rogers Fund, 1903.

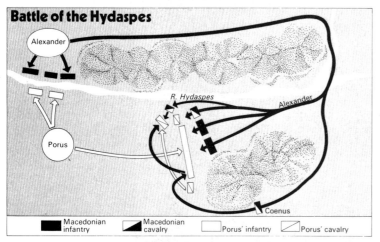

Battle of the Hydaspes

concentrated towards the main camp. By this means, Alexander succeeded in passing his main force over the Hydaspes undetected in the midst of a storm, although at one moment his men faced disaster when they mistook an island in the river for the far bank. Porus gradually became aware that some sort of crossing was in progress, and dispatched his son with 2,000 cavalry and 120 chariots to investigate. This weak force was promptly annihilated by the Macedonians already over the river, and the crossing was duly completed.

Porus, now fully alerted, took up a strong defensive position with flanks protected by the river and a low range of hills. He had at his disposal fully 30,000 infantry and 4,000 cavalry, as well as his elephants and war chariots, which had scythe blades attached to their wheels. The elephants were drawn up before the centre, charged with frightening the Macedonian cavalry (whose horses would not face the beasts) and then trampling the phalanxes; the mass of the Indian infantry filled the centre, and the flanks comprised the chariots and cavalry.

Covered by his cavalry, Alexander advanced rapidly and made a quick reconnaissance. Appreciating that his outnumbered men would never win a frontal battle, he devised a double envelopment. The main army would advance against the Indian left flank in oblique order, half the cavalry leading, whilst General Coenus led off a further mounted force unseen behind the hills so as to be ready to fall on the Indian right. Thus Alexander made the best use of his only advantage, his superior cavalry arm. The plan worked brilliantly. Porus' attention was wholly held by the frontal action, where the Macedonian spearmen caused the elephants to turn about and flee, trampling their own centre.

top
Alexander the Great, supreme soldier of the West, whose military achievements have never been surpassed. Mosaic found at Pompeii. *Museo Archeologico Nazionale, Naples.*

right
Julius Caesar, the pre-eminent Roman statesman and soldier. Coming to high command only in middle life, he proved a dauntingly capable general.

far right
Hannibal, scourge of the Roman Republic and its armies. The rough lessons he administered in the third century BC led to major Roman military reforms.

Two Babylonian archer-spearmen, probably of the royal guard. They are equipped with quivers as well as short composite bows.

Then, at the moment when Porus had ordered his right wing to sweep down and outflank the exposed Macedonian left, Coenus attacked their flank and rear, whilst the Macedonian phalanxes attacked the Indian left. With his foe thrown into considerable disorder by these developments, Alexander charged, at the head of his Companions. After a fierce struggle, the Indians fled and Porus was captured. Thus by skilled use of deception, offensive action and a surprise attack against a flank, Alexander triumphed. These methods were emulated by Napoleon 2,000 years later.

The Battle of Cannae, 216 BC
Following his crossing over the Alps (218 BC), Hannibal set about conquering Italy, winning victories at the Trebbia and Lake Trasimene.

In the spring of 216 BC he moved southwards from Gerunium to seize the important Roman food depot of Cannae, south of the River Aufidus (today the Ofanto), hoping thereby to lure the Romans into risking another major battle. They reacted as he had anticipated and soon 80,000 infantry and 6,000 cavalry, Roman and Allied, were massing at Canosa, several miles west of Cannae, where they built two camps, one on each side of the Aufidus. They were led by the two consuls, Varro and Paulus, who exercised command on alternate days. On his day of command, Varro ignored the cautions of Paulus, and determined to force battle on Hannibal's 40,000 infantry and 10,000 cavalry as soon as possible.

On the morning of the battle Hannibal moved his men over the river and drew them up in battle

The challenge before which the Roman Empire in the West finally succumbed – the barbarian horsemen from the Eurasian heartlands. *Landesmuseum für Vorgeschichte, Halle.*

array across a loop of the Aufidus, thus guarding his flanks. On his left he placed the Spanish horse under his brother Hasdrubal, on the right the 2,000 Numidian cavalry, and in the centre he drew up his infantry – Gauls and Spaniards in a slightly advanced position, with his crack Carthaginian spearmen on their flanks. Varro had already crossed the river before Hannibal moved, and the Roman array, with the cavalry on the wings and the fifteen legions in their usual triple line drawn up in the centre, advanced to the attack.

As soon as the skirmishers of both sides were engaged, Hannibal ordered his superior cavalry forward, and soon routed the Roman horsemen on the flanks, Hasdrubal riding completely round the Roman army to take their left – already engaged by the Numidians – in the rear. Mean-while, Varro's legions pressed forward to attack the exposed Gauls and Spaniards, who recoiled in apparent terror before them. In fact, they were executing Hannibal's orders. The exultant Romans pressed forward into the concave Carthaginian centre, disordering their ranks in their eagerness to clinch the apparent victory. Suddenly Hannibal wheeled his best troops against the flanks of the surprised legions, and the Romans were finally surrounded when Hasdrubal returned to the field after pursuing what was left of the Roman cavalry. Packed into a dense and immobile mass with enemies on all sides, the Romans were butchered like cattle. Varro managed to fight his way out with some 370 cavalry, and perhaps a further 3,000 legionaries made good their escape, but 70,000 were put to the sword and 10,000 taken prisoner. This

The Romans were notable military engineers. Besides many roads, bridges and fortresses, they built such great edifices as Hadrian's Wall in Northumberland, the northernmost frontier of the Roman Empire. Some 90 miles long, it was originally 15 feet high with a 6-foot battlement. Seventeen large forts were scattered along its length, including that at Housesteads, seen rear right; there were also ninety mile-castles and signal stations. This great work was started in AD 120, and abandoned two and a half centuries later.

The legions of Rome set a new standard for military efficiency and all-round effectiveness. Here we see a typical group of Roman legionaries from the Antonine Column in Rome. Note the helmets and varying types of body armour, the short throwing spear or *pilum*, the eagle standards and *bucinae* (trumpets carried by soldiers wearing lion, leopard or wolfskin headdress). The circular shields – often reserved for allied legions – were less typical than those of rectangular shape. Below the frieze is a depiction of the interior of a permanent Roman camp, with houses of stone and huts of wood, all behind a stout wooden palisade and earthen bank reinforced by earth and timber bastions.

total victory cost Hannibal only 6,700 casualties.

'Never, perhaps', wrote the German historian Mommsen, 'was an army of such size annihilated on the field of battle so completely, and with so little cost to its antagonist . . .' The complete success of Hannibal's double envelopment of the Roman centre has deservedly become regarded as a masterpiece of the military art. Imagination, cunning and ability had triumphed over numbers; more than anything else, it was Hannibal's active leadership that had supplied the moral strength so necessary to sustain his hard-pressed centre during the crisis of the battle. As for the Romans, they at least learnt the need to implement military reforms and take extreme measures to meet the Carthaginian threat. The Senate soon appointed a dictator, Fabius Maximus, nicknamed *Cunctator* or the Delayer, who avoided direct confrontation with the foe and led, instead, a guerrilla-type struggle of evasion and small attacks.

Many generals, in later centuries, have attempted similar envelopments, apeing Hannibal's great achievement. None were more successful than the German generals Hindenburg, Ludendorff and von François (who, in this way, won a great victory over the Russians during 1914 at Tannenberg), or von Rundstedt in Soviet Russia during 1941–42. Indeed, ever since Cannae the concept of double envelopment has been a constantly recurring feature of the art of warfare.

Battle of Cannae

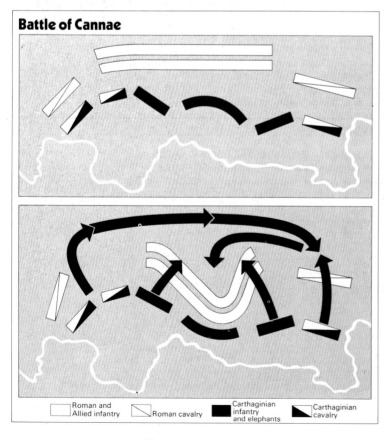

Roman and Allied infantry	Roman cavalry	Carthaginian infantry and elephants	Carthaginian cavalry

ASIA

The Chinese, Indians and Mongols

The development of warfare in the Ancient Mediterranean World was paralleled in time and intensity in the Far East. For many centuries it was an independent process, there being scant contact between East and West until Alexander the Great's fleeting visit to north-west India in 326 BC. However, with the great surge of migrations from Eurasia that began in the second and third centuries AD, both the Western and Eastern Roman empires became increasingly subject to attack by great tides of barbarian horsemen originating from the heartland of the steppes.

By that time, the Chinese had already been combating similar challenges for many generations. The scanty nature of existing records of early Chinese history makes it difficult to describe with any exactitude the events prior to 200 BC, for the emperors of the Ch'in Dynasty ordered the destruction of almost all records prior to their own era, in the hope of placing their dynasty in the forefront of recorded history.

It is, however, possible to distinguish between a number of periods in Ancient Chinese history, and give some idea of the various struggles and issues that affected the development of the military arts. First, between 1500 and 1100 BC, there seems to have been a series of grave contests between the Chinese, desirous of permanent settlement to cultivate land, and various barbaric nomadic peoples. Thanks to their superior organization, the cultivators triumphed over the nomads, but these early struggles seem to have been very primitive indeed. Next, from about 800 to 400 BC, there extended a lengthy period of Chinese feudalism, and wars took on the complexion of power struggles between magnates. Warfare became a special calling for the nobility, and the four-horse chariot, bearing a driver, a lancer and an archer, became the predominant instrument of wars, which were rarely pressed to the last extremity. This period was followed by that of the 'warring kingdoms', as the new feudal states entered into rivalry one with another, and sought to annex neighbouring territories. From 355 BC, new armies made their appearance, comprising fast-moving light infantry and horse archers (copied from the Huns), supported by siege trains. Territorial aggrandizement took on serious overtones, for terrorism was now freely resorted to as a means of imposing political will. Eight of these campaigns, waged between 331 and 260 BC, are reputed to have led to a total of over a million executions. The Ch'u and the Ch'in dynasties were the main rivals.

From about 246 BC there began the struggles for Chinese unification. Chang, ruler of the Ch'in, a man of great political as well as military gifts, led his cavalry-based army to create the Empire of China. From 222 to 210 BC he reigned as the Emperor Shih Huang Ti. Disarming the feudal armies, he created a network of roads to link the great provinces that would form the basis of China for 2,000 years. After defeating the Hsiung-nu (or Huns), he built the Great Wall of China. Extending over 1,600 miles, standing some 20 feet high and measuring some 17 feet wide at the summit, and fortified by frequent wall towers, this monument of military engineering symbolized the power of the new Empire. In subsequent campaigns, Shih Huang Ti swept south of the Yangtse to conquer new provinces. However, the short-lived Ch'in Dynasty abruptly collapsed in 207 BC, and a period of anarchy ensued.

In terms of weaponry, from the earliest times the Chinese made great use of reflex composite bows constructed of wood, horn and sinew, to fire iron-tipped bamboo arrows. Bronze helmets may have appeared by 2500 BC, and body armour was well developed by 600 BC. Within 300 years complex siege engines had made their appearance; they were of much the same types as those used in Persia or Macedon, but with some ingenious adaptations which included extendable scaling ladders. Elaborate engines were also devised to achieve psychological impact and spread terror. These included huge paper dragons with glowing eyes and fiery breath, borne on the backs of hundreds of soldiers, and loud explosive effects employing gunpowder. Surprisingly, the ingenious Chinese were slow to adapt their 'noise powder' for firing missiles, but the techniques of flame warfare were well known to them, and eventually they developed the means for propelling fire arrows by rudimentary rockets.

Most Chinese armies were raised in the provinces, and were employed to guard the frontiers and to police the Empire. The basic unit was the

43

right
Mythical Chinese
warriors armed with
what appear to be long
whips or weighted
throwing thongs.

below
One of the outstanding
feats of military
architecture–the Great
Wall of China, which
stretches for almost
2,000 miles. It was
intended to keep out the
wild nomadic peoples of
Eurasia but proved
incapable of delaying the
Mongols in the twelfth
century.

camp of 500 men, and twenty camps formed the command of a high mandarin. Discipline was severe for both officers and men.

The chaos that followed the Ch'in was in turn replaced by four centuries of good order from 202 BC under the strong Han Dynasty, which took in the period of the 'Great Peace' (80 BC–AD 1). Forming cavalry armies of 10,000 horsemen, the emperors began to launch a series of preventive raids against the Huns. Military colonies were established beyond the frontiers, and armies of over 100,000 men were involved on occasion, as in 102 BC when the forces penetrated as far as Turkestan. Such was the military might of China under the Han, particularly under such emperors as Wu'Ti (140–80 BC) whose long reign saw one of China's most successful martial periods. The future held great fluctuations of fortune, but cataclysm would finally come in the thirteenth century at the hands of the Mongol Khans.

Meantime China had produced a great military philosopher in Sun Tsu (*c.* 500 BC). His famous treatise, *The Art of War*, was probably a composite work improved over succeeding centuries by such experts as Se-Ma and Ou-Tse–a fact which illustrates the essential continuity of Chinese military thought. The result is a work of philosophy as well as a military manual, reflecting the high culture of the Chinese mandarins as well as their practical skills. Emphasis is placed on strategy and the exercise of command, on the value of achieving surprise against an unprepared opponent, and on the significance of

organizing popular guerrilla-type operations. As for the good general, says Sun Tsu, he will be 'magnaminous, prudent, bold without being foolhardy, proud without being presumptuous, strict without being severe, precise without being pettifogging'. Above all, he must be truly superior to those he commands, and imbued with the spirit of initiative: 'to be a general requires a continual and personal intellectual effort'. Here, in sum, was a firm and coherent military doctrine the like of which would not be encountered until the nineteenth century in Europe. Significantly enough, the first translation of *The Art of War* did not reach the West until 1772.

In the Indian subcontinent, the great Aryan invasions of *c.* 2000 BC encouraged the creation of a new Hindu culture. The great mass of Hindu armies comprised foot soldiers, many of them bowmen, backed by chariots and elephants. Iron weapons only appeared about 500 BC, and cavalry seems to have been introduced at much the same time. The Indian bow measured 5 feet, and fired 3-foot arrows to an accurate range of up to 150 yards. In the fourth century BC, Chandragupta (reigned 325–297) learnt much from his brief contact with Alexander the Great, and created the Mauryan Empire, which at its peak could boast an army of 150,000 men and 3,000 war elephants. Skill at siege warfare also developed, and the *Arthasasra*, or *Manual of Politics*, contained much of military value, stressing the importance of training and discipline, and of backing the regular forces with a kind of militia. However,

this document does not approach the subtlety of the work of Sun Tsu and his collaborators, and many of its lessons were soon ignored or forgotten.

By AD 1000, a mighty new power was stirring in Eurasia. Brought up as nomadic horsemen and herdsmen, the Mongols were born warriors. The problems of survival amidst the bleak and inhospitable vastnesses of the Eurasian steppes encouraged hardihood, and the tribal activities of hunting, herding and feuding with neighbours made these fierce peoples expert with the horse and bow. The capacity of the individual Mongol for endurance was phenomenal – he could subsist for long periods on the most meagre of rations – and his lust for bloodshed and loot was insatiable. The Mongol's greatest weakness as a warrior was lack of discipline, for a Mongol resented

above
Fourteenth-century metal halberd head, dating from the Chang era.

below
Mounted soldiers of the Hindu Kush armed with scimitars, lances and small circular *targes* or shields; two also carry throwing chains with star-shaped weights, right and centre. These stone carvings form part of the Baluch Tomb at Pirpatho, Pakistan. *National Museum of Pakistan, Karachi.*

leter qui ont caquis tan tes tres z noummes. et entoles tient leur pmer usage quil nolet estul tr leur seignor. Je apestr -ij fois a loducnon delem

leur cher seignor z natu rel ne por seignone ne por neletre quil aient con quistes nont uolu changer tenir pmer usage. et pres ce q changnisen fu fautx

taking orders and was prone to leaving his comrades at the height of battle in search of plunder. Once, however, these unruly warriors were provided with stern leaders of the calibre of the Great Khans there were few opponents who could stand in their way.

The staggering scale and rapidity of their conquests place the Mongols in a unique position, and their system of war repays study. In the early days of expansion it was the combination of rapid, harassing advances, swirling cavalry envelopments and, when necessary, equally rapid and elusive retreats, that made the Mongol armies so difficult to face. The atrocities they committed against combatant and non-combatant alike – Genghis in person was responsible for the slaughter of an estimated 18 million Chinese alone during his campaigns – bred hopeless apathy and terrible fear in their opponents. Yet it was contact with the Chinese – and the assimilation of their best skills – that transformed the Mongols from warring tribes into world conquerors.

For all his elemental ferocity, Genghis Khan (1167–1227) was aware of the importance of using the ideas of the conquered. In 1212 the tactic of driving hordes of Chinese in front of his advancing columns proved very effective in overcoming the Sung armies, for Chinese ancestor worship forbade the killing of kith and kin. Thereafter, Chinese officers, artificers, engineers and scholars were forcibly incorporated into the Mongol armies, and the combination of tribal ferocity with Chinese knowledge forged a virtually unbeatable fighting machine.

The basis of Mongol warfare was unadulterated terror. Massacre, rapine and torture were the price of defeat, whether enforced or negotiated, although Genghis, in his earlier years, when he was imposing unity on the Mongol tribes, proved capable of making allies of those vanquished people he wished. Nevertheless such leniency was rare. Genghis himself explained his savage policy: 'The vanquished can never be the friends of the victors. The death of the former is therefore necessary for the safety of the latter.' The whole apparatus of terror was remorselessly applied to sap the victim's will to resist, and in practical terms this policy of 'frightfulness' certainly paid short-term dividends. Whole armies were known to dissolve into fear-ridden fragments at the news of the approach of the *toumans*. Far ahead of the armies moved a highly effective fifth column – very often operating from the trade caravans of the East – passing back military intelligence to the Khans, bribing officers and statesmen, signing secret (and usually worthless) treaties of friendship with disaffected princes, arranging for city gates to be left unlocked and sectors of fortifications unmanned. Many enemies were paralysed by such measures before an army crossed their frontiers.

Another secret of Mongol success lay in the mobility and tactical organization of their forces. At no time did the Horde which conquered almost one-third of the world's surface number more than 250,000, large numbers of Chinese, Turkish and Indian auxiliaries being included in this number. Every man was mounted, and there was no infantry arm of any kind. Even the heavy

opposite page
The Mongols were skilled at all aspects of siege warfare. Whenever possible they preferred the use of guile to force, but when compelled to attack, their feared 'perpetual storm' was rarely repulsed. Genghis Khan assimilated many Chinese techniques and experts into his army, and possessed a prefabricated siege train carried dismantled on horseback. Another Persian representation, prepared for the Emperor Akbar, of an attack on a Chinese city *c.* 1204.

Dismounted Mongol archers, from a Japanese manuscript scroll of the twelfth century. Their skill with the bow, whether at the full gallop on horseback or dismounted as at the battle of Bhamo, was legendary. Each warrior habitually carried two quivers of arrows, as on the top right, and two varieties of bow. *Imperial Household Collection, Tokyo.*

equipment required for formal sieges was made in prefabricated parts, carried piece by piece on the backs of packhorses. Every horseman was expected to carry all his own weapons, tools, rations and spare clothing. Most of these items were packed in hide or skin bags, which could be inflated to assist in the crossing of rivers. The warriors wore iron, fur-lined helmets and quilted or armoured jackets, and their weapons included scimitars, lances, murderous hooks, cleavers and axes. The chief weapon, however, carried by three out of five Mongol warriors, was the reflex bow. Each mounted archer carried two varieties: a heavy bow for dismounted use (particularly during sieges) and a light version for use from the saddle. Two quivers were carried containing three types of arrows designed for different ranges and targets; one variety had an attachment that emitted a demoralizing howl as it sped towards its target – a forerunner of the German Stuka dive bombers of the twentieth century. Great emphasis was placed on good marksmanship; practice was continuous, and the trained archer was expected to be able to hit small targets while riding at a full gallop. All were trained to be capable of endurance and extreme fortitude, and ability alone governed the selection of commanders.

The Mongol Horde was organized into *toumans* of 10,000 horsemen; generally three *toumans* formed a Horde, but there was some flexibility in higher organization. Each *touman* was organized on stereotyped lines, divided into formations of 100 units of 100, and, lastly, groups of 10. A Horde was commanded by one of eleven *orloks*. Like Napoleon's *corps d'armée* and Hitler's Panzer divisions, the *toumans* often moved at considerable distances from each other, but proved highly adept at accurate navigation over long distances and huge areas, displaying great skill at rapid concentrations for major battles. Decentralization of advance aided mobility – up to fifty miles a day – and eased subsistence. Mongol forces relied on local procurement for food whenever it was feasible, but were also capable of living off mares' milk and blood for long periods when necessary. For this purpose, each warrior generally owned two horses, one always a mare.

Intercommunication and control posed obvious difficulties, but a simple and highly effective system was evolved. The excellence of the Khan's worldwide intelligence system has already been mentioned, and great effort was expended analysing the characteristics of opponents and the events of past campaigns. Marco Polo of Venice, who visited the East at the height of the Mongol supremacy, wrote highly coloured accounts of what he heard and observed – and mentioned a wagon carrying a lodestone which aided Mongol navigation across the empty steppes. It is certain, however, that a system of couriers was in existence that was capable of passing messages at unrivalled speed. These horsemen were accorded absolute priority, and were bandaged into the saddle to enable them to sleep as they rode. For close-range use, signal flags of black and white were employed, and also messages tied to arrows. Behind everything lay a ferocious discipline; molten lead and boiling oil were liberally applied to transgressors, even senior officers.

49

Mongol strategy and tactics developed a broad pattern. Once demoralization and espionage had prepared the way, the Hordes would generally attack at several widely separated points to confuse and divide the foe. Objectives were to induce the enemy to divide his armies, to sever his communications, ravage his frontiers and terrorize the populace–all features of twentieth-century *Blitzkrieg*. Every type of deception was used, including feigned flights to procure the Mongols their big battles on favourable terrain. Battle tactics were not stereotyped but highly flexible. The Mongol philosophy of war, whether on campaign or in battle, was based on belief in the ferocious attack as the means to secure the vital initiative. Many actions were based on frontal pinning attacks followed by cloud envelopments of the flanks. Tactically, the Mongols often advanced in formation five ranks deep. The first two ranks were more heavily armoured, wielding lances and hooks, while those in front were also equipped with shields. Behind this shock force came three ranks of lightly armed bowmen. As the heavies advanced, archers would ride ahead pouring fire at the foe before wheeling to one side. Into the gaps their arrows had made charged the mailed cavalry to complete the victory.

When faced by a strong city, the Mongols would make every effort to secure its capture by treachery and intrigue. If thwarted, a blockade

was imposed and the full ingenuity of the Chinese artificers brought into play. Once a breach had been made in the walls by the heavy mangonels, the Mongols would swarm forward to carry out the feared 'perpetual storm', wave after wave of attacks flinging themselves against the defenders in ceaseless succession, day and night, until weight of numbers finally told.

Contrary to popular belief, there was also a positive constructive side to Mongol activities. Although they wrought terrible destruction and gloried in their prowess (the Khans instituted a body count after action, collecting the severed right ears of their victims), Genghis and his immediate successors were often at pains to reconstruct and absorb large areas of their conquests. The usual method was to appoint a local puppet leader, backed by a force of Mongol warriors, who was made responsible for law and order and the levying of taxation.

Nor were the Mongols invariably successful. With no political or religious motivation, the sheer professional pride and ferocity of the Mongols did not, in the long term, prove capable of warding off subversive influences exerted by the superior civilizations they overran. Their forces became increasingly hybrid as the centuries passed, and however invincible their *toumans* might prove on the open plains, they were less effective amidst mountains or forests. The Japanese in particular, with their fierce warriors (predecessors of the famous *samurai*) proved a match for the Mongols, and after the scattering of his invasion fleet by the 'Divine Wind' or *Kamikaze* in 1281, Kublai Khan called off his projected invasion of the Japanese islands. As the generations passed, Chinese influences began to absorb the conquerors, who eventually succumbed to corruption and external pressure.

Genghis (1167–1227), the Supreme Emperor, was the true founder of the Mongol Empire, and one of the greatest captains of all time. Until 1190 all his energies were absorbed in unifying the tribes, but there followed thirty-seven years of massive conquests which successively took in much of Tibet, China, Persia, southern and central Russia, north-west India and Afghanistan. After his death, his sons and generals carried on his work. The Mongol general, Subotai, expert at siege warfare, overran western Russia, part of Hungary, and Poland in 1241. However, the death of Genghis' son Ogotai the following year probably saved Western Europe from the attentions of the Mongols; as it turned out, the *toumans* were recalled to Asia to sort out the succession of power. Thenceforward their activities were largely restricted to Asia. Kublai Khan, who ruled from 1267 to 1294, completed the conquest of China and brought the Mongol Empire to its greatest physical extent. Shortly thereafter whole provinces began to fall away, and the Khan emperors of China ultimately became assimilated

م\ نزدیک شد یک ش بود که از دست بر آمده بود و بغایت آنهی در دی زا
نه نهصد و چهار بار میسره و سپهر شد سلطان ابو منلہ بکا کبرمیرزا
مراهشده بجانب اش رفته بود و بحرد و آمدن و ش ا بش و قزلیاش
و شهم چوب د سته ها که فته ضرب راست زده ز د ا و شاورد

mounted warrior. The *toumans* of Genghis Khan were amongst the most effective organizations of military force ever to be devised, and the relative simplicity of their administrative support holds lessons of great importance. For here was the concept of *Blitzkrieg* war on a scale never before encountered.

The Siege of Merv, 1221

Tolui, the youngest and possibly the most brilliant son of Genghis Khan, moved westwards from Balkh to attack the great Persian city of Merv. Crossing the Rivers Murghab and Kushk, he invaded the Persian province of Khorasan before sweeping towards the city.

The local population was in a state of dire confusion as the Mongols approached, for a vast host of defeated Turcoman refugees (recipients of earlier Mongol attention) had settled in their neighbourhood, and were making intermittent raids against the citizenry of Merv.

Typically, Tolui exploited this situation, and destroyed the Turcoman camp in a daring night attack, scattering the survivors to the four winds; the majority of the refugees, however, were drowned in the river. With their reputation for terror tactics thus reinforced, on the following morning (25 February 1221) the Mongols appeared before the gates of Merv.

Tolui in person rode around the city, seeking out the weak places in the defences, and for six days the Mongols continued their preparations. Although all reports indicated that the defences were strong and would need a lengthy siege to overcome, Tolui ordered a general assault on the seventh day. The Mongols were driven back with considerable loss, but this induced the jubilant garrison to mount two sorties from different gates – as Tolui had hoped. Once out in the open, the defenders stood little chance against the battle skills of the Mongols, and after a fierce struggle the survivors were driven back within the walls of Merv. All will to offer further resistance suddenly evaporated, and on 2 March the Governor agreed to surrender the city in return for assurances of good treatment.

As was all too often the case, these undertakings were not honoured. The Mongols ordered the whole population out of the town, and for four days men, women and children streamed out into the countryside. After selecting 400 artisans and a few children for slavery, Tolui gave the word for the rest to be massacred. Each Mongol and auxiliary were allotted the task of butchering between 300 and 400 persons.

The terrible carnage over, the Mongol Horde moved on. Then some 5,000 survivors crept from their places of concealment. To their horror, however, they discovered a small detachment of the Mongol rearguard still close to the town. These warriors, lamenting the fact that they had missed the earlier massacre, forced the survivors to come out into the open, bearing a sack of grain apiece. Tamely they agreed, and thus burdened,

Another striking scene from the *Memoirs* of Babar, showing a sortie from Samarkand during the siege of 1500. The Khanate of the Golden Horde was the last flowering of Mongol-based empires. *Victoria and Albert Museum, London.*

by their conquered millions. Nevertheless, the Khanate of the Golden Horde, extending over southern Russia, Persia and the Middle East, lasted into the fifteenth century, coming to its peak under Tamerlane the Magnificent (1336–1405). Thus for over 200 years the Mongols played a determinant role in world affairs before suddenly declining, through lack of leadership, into tribal obscurity once again.

The Mongol period marks the apogee of the

were butchered with ease. Some Persian chronicles put the death toll at Merv at over 1 million souls, and even the most conservative estimates put the figure as high as 70,000. From such events the Mongol *toumans* acquired their terrible reputation.

The Battle of Bhamo, 1277

Following the final conquest of China by the Mongol Hordes, Kublai Khan decreed that some of the neighbouring countries of South-East Asia owed him tribute. When the Mongol Viceroy of Yunnan, east of the Irrawaddy, sent emissaries to the states of Pagan and Pegu in Burma, they were sent back with a very abrupt answer by the local Buddhist authorities. As if this was not enough, when Kublai sent a personal embassy in 1273, King Narathihapate had the temerity to have the ambassadors executed on the spot. Although such acts of savagery were nothing

Genghis Khan, the Mongol genius who created his own army by uniting the Mongolian tribes, and then led them in an immense saga of conquest, rapine and destruction which eventually covered most of Eurasia.

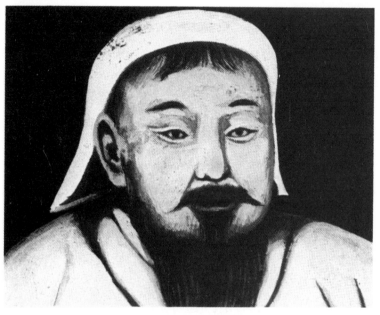

Battle of Bhamo

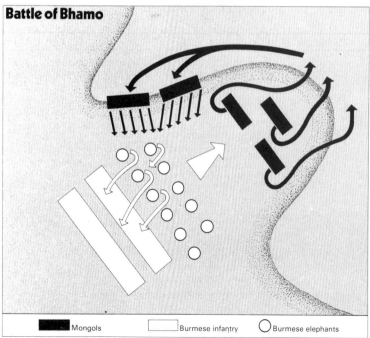

Mongols ▮   Burmese infantry ▯   Burmese elephants ○

new to Mongol politics and diplomacy, Kublai decided to exact a fearful vengeance. Once again, however, he was forestalled by Narathihapate who wasted no time in invading Chinese territory, boldly carrying the war to his enemy, though rashly, as it turned out.

By early 1277 Nasr-Uddin, Mongol Viceroy of Yunnan, had driven the Burmese out of China, and the *toumans* were ordered into Burma. According to Marco Polo, who met an eyewitness of the event, the two armies met in a long valley near Bhamo. The Burmese numbered 40,000 troops and some accounts claim that they were supported by 1,000 elephants. Nasr-uddin, on the other hand, appears to have commanded hardly more than a single *touman* of mounted warriors, perhaps 12,000 strong.

With such a numerical advantage, at first all went well for O'ho, the Burmese field commander. Catching the scent of the elephants, the Mongol horses became unmanageable, and the line was thrown into confusion. Disaster appeared to confront the Mongols, but with typical flexibility Nasr-uddin proceeded to snatch victory from defeat. Rallying his shaken horsemen at the far end of the valley, he ordered them to dismount, tether their horses inside the jungle, and then creep back to its edge on foot. This was a rare departure for the Mongol armies of horse archers, but it led to a notable success. Hidden along the fringe of the jungle the Mongol bowmen poured a murderous fire on the advancing elephants, employing the heavy bows normally reserved for siege warfare, and induced the pain-maddened beasts to turn and trample the following legions of Burmese.

Seizing their opportunity, the Mongols rapidly remounted and flung themselves against their disordered opponents, who broke and fled. During the subsequent ruthless pursuit, the greater part of the Burmese army was cut down. King Narathihapate escaped with his life but lost his dignity, and by 1283 his kingdom had been completely destroyed.

THE WEST

The Rise and Fall of Feudalism

The collapse of the Roman Empire in the West before the pressures of the barbarian hordes led to a period of chaos and confusion, and to a deterioration in the military skills. For three centuries, warfare reverted to the tribal level, in the main taking the form of raiding in search of plunder or of desperate local defence against marauders, some of whom were seeking settlements whilst others remained migratory. Thus the Visigoths and Ostrogoths settled much of the Balkan, Italian and Danube regions, whilst the Franks pressed into Gaul and the Saxons spread from Germany into England. The forces of Islam, repelled by Byzantium, swept into Spain and southern France from North Africa, and in the middle of the fifth century the terrible Attila, 'the scourge of God', led his Huns of Mongol origin deep into the West before being decisively checked at Chalons in 451. Two years later, the death of Attila led to the withdrawal of the Huns, but Rome finally went into eclipse in 476 at the hands of a Gothic leader, Odoacer.

Chaos continued, but the Franks slowly asserted their paramountcy in Gaul, and proved capable, under Charles Martèl, of rebuffing the Arab invasion from Spain in 732 at Tours. This success led, thirty-six years later, to the accession of Charlemagne and the creation of a short-lived but important Frankish empire stretching from the Elbe to Rome and the Pyrenees. Charlemagne's military system will be described on a following page, but his empire did not long survive his death, as internal divisions and new external pressures broke up his achievement.

The new threats to stability were three in number: the Saracens seized southern Italy, Sicily and Sardinia; the Magyars swept up the Danube Valley and deep into Germany, before being checked in 935 and routed in 955; and thirdly the Norsemen sailed from Scandinavia and attacked England, Ireland, northern France and Frisia, and even established a state at Novgorod deep in western Russia. Of the three, the Norsemen proved the most redoubtable. After a century of conflict—and many reverses at the hands of Alfred, King of Wessex—they established a Scandinavian monarchy in England from 1016; a century earlier, in 911, they had been granted the Duchy of Normandy as a feudal fief of France. Operating from this base, Norman conquerors, after assimilating the elements of feudalism and following conversion to Christianity, crossed the Channel to seize England in 1066, absorbed much of western France and, in 1091, completed the conquest of Sicily and southern Italy, an enterprise which they had commenced fifty years before the battle of Hastings.

There followed the period of the Crusades (see next chapter) and then, from the early thirteenth century, the High Middle Ages, which saw the decline of Rome's spiritual authority and the disintegration of the Holy Roman Empire, and included the Swiss wars of independence and the Hussite rebellion in Bohemia. In the meantime, Edward I conquered Wales (though his son failed lamentably in Scotland) and, a generation later, there began the so-called Hundred Years War between England and France (1337–1453). This struggle proved the swansong of feudalism in both countries. By the late fifteenth century, after bitter internal upheavals, England and

The 'Dark Ages' in Europe are well represented by these Vandal bronze matrices, used for decorating a seventh-century casket. Symbolic hunting scenes are represented. *National-museum, Stockholm.*

Hic pugnat dux hennras filius scē hedwigis cum thartaris in campo qd̄ dicitur wolstat

Hic decollat idē dux hencus fili scē hedwigis atharrais cui aīa susepta est mcelum ab angelis

above
Manuscript illustration, *c.* 1028, showing mounted warriors, possibly Normans. Note the conical helmets, the hauberks of chain maîl, the lance pennants, and the broad-bladed sword. The stirrup was well established by this period. Norman bands operated in southern Italy and Sicily, where they established a kingdom. *Montecassino Abbey.*

right
A scene from the Bayeux tapestry. The Norman knights of William the Conqueror fight for possession of Senlac Hill against the Saxon fyrd, or peasant militia.

France were emerging as the prototypes of nation states ruled by centralized monarchies, and a new age, both politically and militarily, was born in Europe.

This millennium of history in the West contained, from the military point of view, two strands of development of the greatest importance: first, the evolution of the supremacy of the mounted warrior, with the associated aspects of the growth of feudalism, the knight and the castle; second, the eventual overthrow of the mounted knight and his replacement by the foot soldier armed with superior pole arms and missile weapons, culminating in firearms. In other words, shock action gave place to firepower on the battlefield, and amateurism to a growing professionalism in the organization of armed forces and their strategic employment on campaign.

The supremacy of the horseman rested on several factors. His mobility made possible deep penetration raids; the combined height of horse and rider offered psychological and practical advantages in close combat with dismounted foot soldiers (until the dramatic developments of the period 1250–1350); and the advantages conferred by the stirrup–developed in the East as early as 400 BC and introduced in the West by the Goths some 600 years later–made it feasible for the mounted warrior to remain in the saddle despite his increasingly cumbersome armour, and to sustain the shock of the lance's impact in the full clash of battle.

The main problem associated with these advantages was one of cost. Sturdy horses had to be bred, fed and maintained. The equipment of the mounted warrior also tended to be increasingly elaborate and costly, especially as missile weapons improved in range and penetrating power. Only rich men could afford the necessary refinements, and the association of military role and social class soon became established as one of the pillars of the feudal system.

As the barbarian hordes were almost invariably mounted, it became increasingly important to match them with mounted troops. In Germany, in return for the protection of his arms, the peasantry agreed to perform services for the local chief. The Franks adopted this system, and under Charlemagne (768–814) carried it a great deal further. For the first time since the demise of Rome, a regular military system was devised in the West. Realizing the need for a sizeable striking force of heavy cavalry, capable of meeting such foes as the Lombard lancers, Charlemagne required all his nobles to perform knightly service in return for the tenure of land or fiefs. His knights were equipped with a hauberk of chain mail, a helmet, shield, light axe and a lance. Less reliance was placed than heretofore on mobilization of the mass of the people in times of crisis, although considerable numbers of foot were still required, armed, at Charlemagne's insistence, with bows and arrows as well as

Statue of Charles the Great at Mustair. Charlemagne symbolized the first recovery of Western Europe from the confusion and chaos of the Dark Ages during the eighth century. His empire eventually extended over much of what is now France and West Germany.

Viking runic stone from Sweden, depicting several aspects of the Scandinavian art of warfare.

right
Wolfram of Eschenbach departing for the Crusades. The Middle Ages were for long dominated by the mounted warrior. Note the twelfth-century suit of chain mail, the crested pot helm and the protective saddle. The requirements of chivalry, and of identification in battle, led to the development of heraldic devices –repeated in this case on banner, shield, helm and the horse furnishings.

below
Charlemagne was one of the first rulers to reimpose some form of order in Western Europe. His armies were the most proficient of their day. The Emperor mourns the deaths of his warriors in the chapel, top right, at his capital, Aachen.
Domschatzkammer des Aachener Domes, Aachen.

conventional tribal weapons. Rich landowners were required to provide one warrior for every four households they held.

Even more important, Charlemagne imposed discipline on his host, and thus greatly improved its effectiveness. He also developed a sound administrative base for its support. Between 803 and 813 he issued five military ordinances which spelt out his requirements in the necessary detail. He insisted on a single tactical doctrine, and established a supply organization, including a convoy system, which made possible campaigns at any time of year. He established a regular siege train as part of his forces, and a staff system was set up at Aachen which included inspectors-general and institutions for instructing young noblemen in the military profession. By these means he built up a small but highly proficient Frankish army, based upon the armoured knight, and bound to the leader by an oath of loyalty and service.

Charlemagne was an abler strategist than a tactician. Inspired by a strong sense of Christian mission, albeit of a muscular variety, which induced Pope Leo III to crown him Emperor in 800, he fought and conquered the pagan tribes of Western Europe. Tiring of Saxon raids, he

developed a proven strategy of preemptive strikes which kept his foes too occupied to invade the Carolingian Empire. Above all, to protect his frontiers, he built systems of burghs or fortresses, linked by roads of a sort, both as defensive centres and as bases for offensive forays.

Although many of Charlemagne's reforms proved transitory, the supremacy of the mounted warrior was now firmly established. Equally important were the feudal bond and the early castle. In succeeding generations these trends continued, adjusted to circumstances. As new waves of raiders swept into the Carolingian Empire, after Charlemagne's death, the focus tended to shift from the centre to the periphery. Local protection and maintenance of law and order became the primary duties of the feudal lord, and the need for local refuges encouraged the building of castles. As siege methods remained crude, these also enabled an ambitious vassal to defy his superiors with some impunity – and to that extent reduced the king to the status of 'first amongst equals'.

Anglo-Saxon England developed its armies along different lines from those of France or Germany. The feudal system developed far more

slowly, and Anglo-Saxon armies comprised thegns, the 'Companions of the King', backed by the fyrd (provincial levies) led by the earls. Like Charlemagne, Alfred the Great (d. 899) made considerable use of the burgh system not only to check Danish incursions, but also to build an effective fleet. Like the Norsemen, the Anglo-Saxons preferred combat on foot, and only used horses as a means to reach the battlefield before forming the shield wall of thegns supported by the crudely armed fyrd.

However, shortly before the Norman Conquest,

left
Thirteenth-century armourers at work, manufacturing casques and swords. Armourers worked on a local basis; there was as yet no centralized arms industry. Excellent individual craftsmanship was one result. *Trinity College Library, Cambridge.*

below
The true knight of the Norman period; note the nose-guard on the conical helmet, the loose-fitting chain-mail hauberk, the broad sword and the kite-shaped shield displayed on the battlements. Reliquary of St Mellan de la Cogolla, Spain.

feudal concepts were reaching England, and soon after 1066 the Normans had imposed the most comprehensive feudal system in Europe, bringing England back into the mainstream of European development, both social and military. Gradually the two systems and cultures merged, to produce the most redoubtable martial power in Europe. The feudal host was closely tied to land tenure. The tenant owed his lord forty days' military service a year, and according to degree was expected to bring a number of retainers into the field with him. Such armies were clearly impermanent and hard to discipline or train, but the tough fighting qualities of the Normans made them superior to the French, who only developed a full feudal system in the fourteenth century.

By that date, feudalism had already passed its zenith in England. Under the Angevin and Plantagenet dynasties the disadvantages of the feudal arrays became appreciated during their almost ceaseless wars, and this encouraged the development of the 'king's army'. As institutions of central government improved, the rulers preferred to levy a money tax, scutage, from their nobility in lieu of personal military service. With funds thus provided, they could hire professional mercenaries, or bring into the field armies largely composed of hired freemen and yeomanry – far more promising material, especially as archers, than half-armed serfs or unwilling feudal retainers. With this development, carried through in the thirteenth and fourteenth centuries, the time was approaching for the eclipse of the mounted medieval knight (whose highly developed code of chivalry encouraged him to fight as an individual rather than as a member of a team) and the re-emergence of the foot soldier.

A new professionalism accompanied this change; the Hundred Years War and the subsequent Wars of the Roses hastened the process by demonstrating the value of the hired soldier, and by encouraging the feudal nobility to tear itself to pieces. These developments were accompanied, and to a large decree encouraged, by changes in weaponry. Swords, lances and daggers remained virtually unchanged, although manufacturing processes improved, and several new pole and staff weapons appeared. These included the Franconian light axe, the redoubtable Viking double-bladed war axe, and the deadly halberd and glaive, Swiss specialities, whilst the eighteen-foot pike also reappeared amidst the Alps. Of ultimately far greater significance, however, were the improvements in missile weapons. The bow was not in great favour in Western Europe for much of the Dark Ages, although Charlemagne attempted to encourage its use, and the Norsemen certainly knew its value. However, by the eleventh century short bows were reappearing in many armies, and soon the crossbow was in widespread use. Its origins are obscure (the Romans appear to have had a 'hand *ballista*'), and the principle of torsion which provided its propulsion was far from new, but its effect was impressive. Loaded by use of a windlass or crank, the crossbow fired a short metal bolt or quarrel which could penetrate mail and armour up to a range of 100 yards. It was slow to reload, but in every other way superior to the ordinary short bow. It proved so devastating against mounted cavalry that the Pope formally outlawed its use against Christians in 1139, though the Church approved its use against the infidel.

Even this efficient weapon, however, did not long remain unsurpassed. The English longbow soon proved the most formidable missile weapon of the battlefield. Six feet four inches long, this weapon was adopted by Edward I from the Welsh, and Cheshire archers became particularly proficient in its use. Drawing the bowstring to his ear rather than his chest, the archer fired a cloth-yard shaft, which was tipped with steel and flighted with goose feathers. The yew longbow had a maximum range of over 400 yards, and could be lethally aimed at up to 250 yards. A skilled archer could fire up to sixteen arrows a minute (to the crossbowman's two or three), and even plate armour was not proof against them at close range. Seven types of arrowhead were developed for varying targets. A 'long bodkin' point could penetrate mail and plate armour to a depth of five and a half inches, or split through four inches of seasoned oak. Many a knight was pinned to his saddle by a shaft that penetrated armour, mail and the flesh and bone of his thigh. Providing the archers were properly protected by men-at-arms and pits (as at Crécy, 1346) or palisades of sharpened stakes (as at Agincourt, 1415), mounted or dismounted knights were

Count Günther of Schwarzenburg (died 1439). Note his armour, covered by a surcoat, his crested helm, emblazoned shield, and two-handed long sword. Such elaborate helms were eventually relegated to tournament use. Effigy in Frankfurt Cathedral.

almost helpless against them. When these conditions were ignored, disaster could ensue, as at Bannockburn (1314), when Robert the Bruce's Scottish army thrashed Edward II's ill-coordinated troops. Nevertheless, the scholar Roger Asche could claim as late as the early sixteenth century that 'every English archer beareth beneath his girdle twenty-four Scots', and the English proved very reluctant to discard the weapon in favour of the firearm. Not until after Henry VIII's reign did its widespread employment die out, and even in the Second World War it was in occasional use by commandos. However, its disadvantage lay in the time it took to train an expert bowman. To draw the string of a 60-pound bow required a 300-pound pull, and accuracy called for a strong left arm, good muscular coordination and a trained eye; accordingly, training started in boyhood, and practice had to be encouraged by royal edicts, which, for example, forbade any other sport on Sundays. Hence the importance of scutage, which enabled English kings to hire reliable yeoman archers for up to sixpence a day.

The damage wrought to the chivalry of France by English longbowmen was paralleled by the havoc caused to Austrian knights by Swiss pikemen and halberdiers. The Swiss formed dense *schiltrons* or 'hedgehogs' of pikemen which proved impregnable to shock attack, whilst the murderous halberd had a hook to haul a horseman from his saddle and both a spear-point and an axe-head with which to cut him down. Just as the English were slow to drop the longbow, so were the Swiss unwilling to abandon the pike in favour of firearms. The Flemings were equally

right
Wagon laagers employed by the Swiss at the siege of Laupen Castle, 1485. Note the wheeled assault wagon in the middle-ground, bristling with handguns. Such concepts were borrowed from the Hussites. *Bürger-bibliothek, Bern.*

below
A closer view of another wheeled assault wagon. Jordan von Burgistein has received a discouraging wound from the crossbowman. The penetration power of bolts of this sort was considerable. *Bürger-bibliothek, Bern.*

adept with pikes, as they proved at Courtrai (1302) when the French knights were decimated. Nevertheless, it was with firearms that the future lay. The formula for gunpowder was recorded by Friar Bacon in 1260, and sixty-four years later the first known use of the cannon took place at Metz. Rudimentary handguns–the true ancestors of infantry firearms–requiring two men to fire and carry them, were in limited use during the Hundred Years War, but these were crude and inaccurate weapons. However, once design and effectiveness improved, they became cheaper weapons to employ, in that almost any soldier could be quickly trained in their use.

During the Middle Ages, armour developed almost as rapidly as weapons. The iron cap and simple quilted hauberk of the Carolingian warrior, supplemented by a circular shield, gave place to the conical helmet with nose-guard, chain-mail shirt and kite-shaped shield of the Norman. The conical helmet gave place in turn to the pot helm early in the thirteenth century, and metal caps were added to chain mail at elbows and knees–traditionally vulnerable points. Visors appeared at the beginning of the fourteenth century, and soon after came the breast- and back-plate–the intermediate stage before the introduction of massive plate armour by about 1400. Archers never wore more than a helmet and a breastplate or hauberk, and they could find the joints in their opponents' harnesses at close range. Handguns spelt the end of armour as body protection, relegating its use to the tournament field, and from 1500 its use in armies began to decline, although some cavalry retained it late into the seventeenth century; however, full plate was soon replaced by simpler forms. Three-quarter and then half suits of plate armour became the norm.

The castle played a central role in warfare until the advent of effective artillery. Its evolution followed well-marked stages. Until Charlemagne, there were few attempts to do more than patch up what was left of Roman fortifications. Even Charlemagne's burghs were simple affairs of earth and timber, most of them comprising a rectangular palisaded enclosure, standing within a moat, with a keep or tower at one corner, besides other buildings for the garrison, sheltering peasantry and stores. By the eleventh century, many keeps were being built of stone, and sometimes a second bailey or enclosure was added. In the next century, as the wealth of the nobility increased and building mania gripped Europe, the keep became incorporated in a curtain wall of stone with gatehouses, towers at the corners, and sometimes a barbican before the gates. The final flowering of the medieval castle came with the development of the great concentric fortresses inspired by the Crusades, which will be described in the next chapter. The Angevin kings of England built the great fortress of Chateau Gaillard in Normandy, and Edward I constructed the equally impressive fortresses of Beaumaris and Caernarvon, along with others in North Wales. Cities defended their perimeters in similar ways.

The techniques of siege warfare varied little from Roman practices until the advent of bombards, although there were a number of developments. Blockade to induce surrender through starvation was frequently resorted to, but more vigorously prosecuted sieges became increasingly common as engines of war improved. The object was to make a breach through which an assault might be launched to dislodge the garrison. One means of achieving this, if the ground permitted, was sapping. Using sheds on wheels covered with soaked skins to protect them from missiles being rained down from above, the miners dug away the earth beneath the wall's foundations and shored up the masonry with timber. Once a sufficient area had been excavated, brushwood would be piled around the props and then fired, and the consequent collapse of the supports would bring down the wall overhead.

Engines of war operated according to the principle of torsion or counterweights. The siege mangonel flung rocks or other missiles, its source of power being a skein of tightly wound fibre. The *ballista* operated on the principle of the bow. Both these engines had relatively short ranges and needed to be protected by earthworks or palisades. The mighty trebuchet swung a beam by action of a counterweight to sling its missile. This might weigh several hundredweight, and ranges of up to a quarter of a mile were not unknown. Sometimes flaming matter or dead animals were flung into the beleaguered place to cause fires or spread disease, and the Moslem Turks had a habit of firing in the heads of decapitated prisoners, as a means of discouraging the garrison or townsfolk.

Other equipment included large battering rams, slung under protective roofs, and great mobile siege towers of timber, which were ponderously rolled up close to the wall until a drawbridge could be lowered on to the battlements, over which an assault party would swarm. To get such machines close enough it might be necessary to fill a moat with fascines of brushwood, and close fire support had to be provided by archers operating from behind mantelets to drive the enemy back from his ramparts during the critical stages. Or again, desperate escalades might be made with scaling ladders.

Of course, a defender could fight back. Countersaps could thwart mining attempts, huge *ballistae* mounted on towers could shoot arrows and even tree trunks to discourage the attackers and destroy their engines and fieldworks, and when a breach had been made there was often time to extemporize internal defences to seal the gap. Boiling oil, pitch or molten lead were poured through machicolations on to the heads of working or storming parties near the foot of the walls. Sieges, therefore, could be both lengthy and costly affairs.

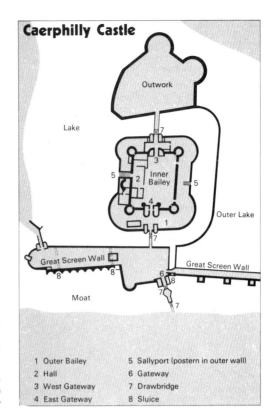

Caerphilly Castle

1 Outer Bailey	5 Sallyport (postern in outer wall)
2 Hall	6 Gateway
3 West Gateway	7 Drawbridge
4 East Gateway	8 Sluice

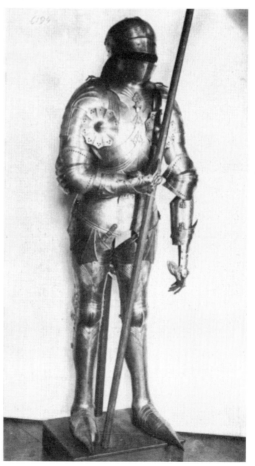

The perfection of plate armour: German full-suit of the fifteenth century. Such harness of finely tempered steel was lighter than might be expected, and was deliberately streamlined in order to deflect weapons as well as for aesthetic effect. The advent of effective handguns soon ended the practicability of such costly equipment. *Bayerisches National-museum, Munich.*

The towering walls of these castles were not, however, any match for artillery. The earliest cannon (c. 1324) was vase-shaped, and appears to have fired a bulky arrow, but iron cannon-balls were soon being manufactured in Italy. Cylindrical barrels, reinforced with hoops, were the next development. They were bulky, heavy and unmanoeuvrable, usually being mounted on a flat timber base or along a series of trestles. The earliest cannon were cast in one piece, but improved smelting methods enabled them to be cast around a wooden core, which was burnt out when the metal had solidified. Experimental breech-loaders were abandoned as too perilous.

Fifteenth-century Flemish tapestry depicting (in fifteenth-century dress) the siege of Troy (*c.* 1200 BC). The lavish decorative style and general richness of dress, armour and tents is representative of the High Middle Ages, the apogee and at the same time the swansong of warfare based on the concept of chivalry. Soon the professional soldier would take over. *Victoria and Albert Museum, London.*

The French were the first to take cannon really seriously. Charles VII owned thirty-four bombards besides numerous other pieces, many of them with a range in excess of 500 yards. The brothers Bureau were the first master artillerists of the age of gunpowder. In a single year their bombards enabled Charles VII to retake no less than forty strong towns and fortresses from the English towards the end of the Hundred Years War. A few years earlier, it would have taken between four and ten months to capture a single one, using the old methods. Cannon proved their effectiveness once and for all at Constantinople in 1453, when the Sultan, massing all of sixty-

The storming of a bridge in the Hundred Years War, late fourteenth century. The 'snout-vizored' helmets were supposed to deflect arrows or lances. *British Museum, London.*

The medieval castle reached its final development in the concentric design, represented by this aerial view of Harlech. The *enceinte* with round towers still retained an incorporated keep. Some examples of this type of castle had successive series of walls and towers.

nine pieces (including thirteen reputedly capable of firing 1,500-pound stone balls) before the famous triple walls, proceeded to capture the great city and bring to an end the long-lived Byzantine Empire. By this time, rudimentary mortars, firing explosive shells, were also in existence.

The use of cannon on the battlefield was long limited by their lack of mobility. A few rudimentary bombards were present at Crécy in 1346, but the first battle in Western Europe where artillery had a marked effect was Castillon (1453), a French victory of considerable note, in which heavy English casualties were caused by enfilade fire from a flank. However, thirty-four years earlier in Bohemia, at Sudomer, the Hussite leader John Zizka had defeated an Imperialist force by drawing up his followers within a wagon laager supported by cannon. This, therefore, was probably the very first battle decided by

the major use of cannon. There can be no doubt that the arrival of the age of artillery was instrumental in the dissolution of what remained of the feudal system in the fifteenth century. Kings were careful to keep control of such powerful weapons, which had ended not only the resistance power of the castle but also the age of the mounted knight.

It is difficult to select European commanders of truly outstanding merit from the long period covered by this chapter. Charlemagne we have already discussed, and for the later period Robert Guiscard, conqueror of Sicily, Edward I and Edward III, kings of England, John Zizka of Bohemia, and the French champion, du Guesclin, all deserve a mention. None, however, measures up to the stature of Genghis or of Alexander the Great. Most of the commanders we have listed were notable for their tactical rather than their strategic skill. As the importance of the horseman waxed and waned, and as that of the foot soldier re-emerged, important lessons were learnt, and put into practice, particularly by the English leaders, concerning the coordination of mounted and dismounted warriors, together with bowmen. Zizka was the first general to use artillery systematically, appreciating its value when deployed within the protective cover of a circle of wagons. Strategically, Charlemagne had considerable gifts, and du Guesclin was astute enough to realize that the most effective way to neutralize the English predominance in the Hundred Years War was to cut down major engagements to a minimum and concentrate on guerrilla warfare based upon surprise and ruses, and backed by good military intelligence. Joan of Arc inspired an

early example of a truly national resistance to the invader when all was almost lost again, two generations later. Although this foreshadowed future major developments in warfare, neither 'du Guesclin nor Joan of Arc were in any way typical of their period. In overall terms of leadership, therefore, mediocrity was more the rule than the exception.

Nevertheless, warfare had become far more professional by the late fifteenth century. The mercenary Free Companies were the effective link between the days of the feudal host and the era of royal and national armies.

The Battle of Hastings, 14 October 1066

Following the death of Edward the Confessor, Earl Harold Godwinson had himself crowned the King of England. Immediately two rival claimants to the throne mobilized their forces. From Scandinavia came Harold Hardrada, King of Norway, and in Normandy Duke William prepared an invasion fleet, having secured the Pope's blessing for his enterprise.

First to reach England was Hardrada, accompanied by the disaffected Tostig, sometime Earl of Northumbria. Harold, who had been awaiting the Norman invasion, at once rushed his huscarles north to meet the Scandinavians and destroyed them at the hard-fought battle of Stamford Bridge on 25 September. As was the northern custom, both sides fought on foot.

Profiting from this diversion, William landed near Pevensey on 27 September and camped his army near Hastings. Learning of this new invasion, Harold rode rapidly south with his

above
The Château of Angers, Loire valley. A view of the moat and the towered *enceinte*, or connecting wall. Note the drawbridge. Weapon slits were narrow to prevent affording an entry to a foe.

left
Aerial view of Château Gaillard, France, a fine example of a keep with inner and outer baileys, perched in a highly inaccessible position.

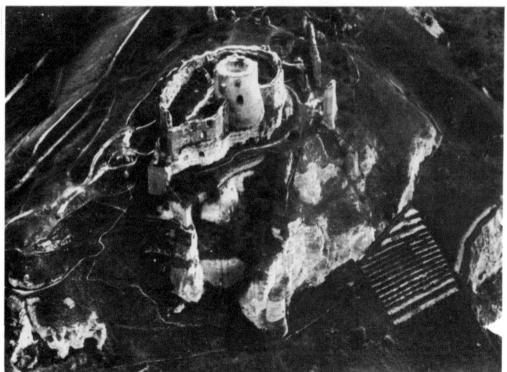

A late fourteenth-century siege: a storming is in progress, using hooked ladders, whilst the defenders hurl down boulders. *Bodleian Library, Oxford.*

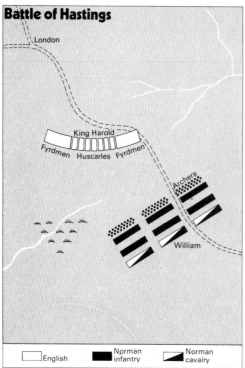

Battle of Hastings

London

King Harold

Fyrdmen   Huscarles   Fyrdmen

Archers

William

☐ English	■ Norman infantry	◣ Norman cavalry

huscarles, covering the 190 miles to London in four days, to confront this fresh invasion. Summoning the southern fyrd to join him, Harold advanced to Caldbec Hill, some seven miles from the Norman camp, on 13 October. This position commanded all the routes to London.

Early on the 14th William moved forward to attack Harold's position astride the ridge. The Norman army was divided into three sections, each including a proportion of archers, spearmen and mounted knights – the foot soldiers leading. His force totalled some 9,000 men, of whom perhaps 3,000 were mounted. Facing him along the low ridge known as Senlac Hill to the fore of Caldbec Hill stood the Anglo-Saxon army, the 8,000 fyrdmen drawn up in two bodies on the flanks of the shield wall formed by the 2,000 dismounted huscarles, above whom flew Harold's banner and the Dragon of Wessex.

The first Norman attack was led by the archers and foot soldiers but achieved nothing. The Saxon huscarles caught the arrows on their round shields, and the fyrd bombarded the Norman infantry with a shower of missiles. The Normans fled down the hill in confusion, stampeding some of their waiting cavalry in the process. Part of the Saxon fyrd pursued them, but were cut down.

An earlier investment of the thirteenth century. Note the absence of plate armour and the employment of a battering ram. The garrison appears in musical mood despite the gravity of the situation. *Trinity College Library, Cambridge.*

A wooden siege tower being prepared to overlook the enemy battlements. Such constructions would be wheeled up to within close range of the city walls, and assaults would then be launched over small drawbridges. *British Museum, London.*

Another thirteenth-century representation of a trebuchet, loaded more conventionally with a large boulder; the artillerist appears to be in some danger of sharing the fate often reserved for Christian prisoners. Note the use of the short bow and the battle mace in the skirmish depicted, which represents a sortie being pursued back within the gates of the beleaguered city. *MS 638 folio 23v (top), Pierpont Morgan Library, New York.*

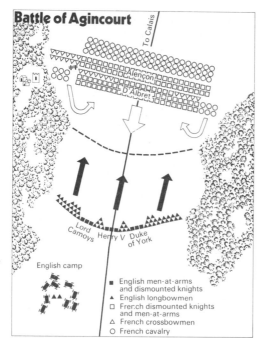

Battle of Agincourt

below
The battle of Agincourt, 25 October 1415. This manuscript illustration gives the archer the pride of place. This was symbolic of the age, for the foot soldier was fast emerging as the master of the battlefield. The long era of the mounted knight was almost over.

This was the critical moment for William; some accounts claim that this Norman flight was a deliberate lure, but it seems improbable. However, the rumour spread that the Duke was dead, and William had to remove his helmet to prove that he was unharmed. Calmly he proceeded to rally his men, and after luring more of the Saxon fyrd from the ridge, he then launched the first of a series of charges up the slope by his mail-clad knights, covering their advance by ordering his archers to fire high into the air. Traditionally, one of the plunging arrows hit Harold in the eye – but certainly many of his compatriots were laid low by this means. Gradually, the staunch shield wall began to be weakened, but it held off the Norman knights for several bitterly contested hours. A battle of attrition had developed, and both sides sustained heavy losses. However, by dusk the Normans had wrested the advantage from the Saxons, who were finally disheartened when a Norman warrior cut down and killed Harold with a sword. The thegns of his bodyguard fought to the bitter end around the body of their leader, and resistance only ended after night had fallen. Many of the fyrd managed to escape in the gloom into the nearby forest.

Victory gained William the English realm, and on Christmas Day he was duly crowned in Westminster Abbey. The battle is often represented as the triumph of the mounted continental knights over warriors fighting on foot. It certainly led to the introduction of the feudal system into the British Isles, but from the military point of view the lessons of lasting significance were the importance of archers employed in a supporting role and the resistance power of a well-disciplined infantry force, typified by the Saxon shield wall. The eventual merging of Anglo-Saxon and Norman skills and characteristics would, after a few centuries, produce a formidable fighting race.

The Battle of Agincourt, 25 October 1415
In August 1415, King Henry V invaded France and eventually captured the town of Harfleur. As the year was well advanced, he decided to march to the English fortress of Calais for the winter, postponing his projected advance on Paris until the following spring.

To reach Calais it was necessary to cross the River Somme, but the advance guard of the French Constable, d'Albret, occupied all the fords and barred Henry's way. Meanwhile the main French army was massing its strength around Rouen, before crossing the Somme at Amiens.

The English, only 5,320 strong, sought vainly for a crossing place for five days, their rations running perilously low. At last, on the 18th, an unguarded crossing was discovered near Nesle, and the army passed over, but the French were only seven miles distant. It was soon evident that Henry would be forced to fight his way through

to Calais against daunting odds, and on the 24th
his weary army camped near Maisoncelles,
within sight of the vast French camp.

Next morning, St Crispin's Day, Henry ordered
his army to advance 1,000 yards to occupy the
narrowest part of the plain, bounded by two thick
woods, having the chateau and village of
Agincourt to his left. The position he adopted
required every available soldier, so no force
could be left to guard the camp. The flanks of his
line were slightly advanced, and comprised
mostly archers placed along the edge of the
woods. In the centre he drew up the remainder of
his 4,590 archers in two wedges, placing his 730
knights and men-at-arms, all dismounted, in the
intervals. The whole front was protected by lines
of sharpened stakes known as *chevaux-de-frise*,
and extended for some 900 yards.

The vast French host of 3,000 crossbowmen,
7,000 mounted and 15,000 dismounted knights
and men-at-arms, was confident of victory, the
nobles laying wagers on how many captives they
would take. Accordingly, no steps were taken
to oppose Henry's advance to the forward
position.

The Constable gradually deployed his army in
three dense lines, each 1,200 yards wide, the
first two dismounted (with the crossbowmen and
a few bombards deployed between them), the
third mounted. Two further bodies of mounted
knights were drawn up on each flank, slightly
to the rear. The first French attack was launched
by the flanking cavalry, stung into action by
long-range archery. The hail of fire they met
caused the horses to stampede, and the knights
trampled through their leading dismounted
formations. These were having great difficulty
in advancing owing to the previous days of heavy
rain, which had turned much of the ground into

a morass. As the French struggled forward, the narrowness of the English position forced them to crowd in on the centre, and in the resulting press some were suffocated in their armour, and many more proved incapable of wielding their weapons. All the time the hail of arrows poured down, until Henry judged the moment had come for the *coup de grâce*.

Charging forward, the English men-at-arms were joined by archers wielding swords and axes. Once the first French line was routed, the well-disciplined English returned behind their stakes, and then meted out similar treatment to the second French line. After thirty minutes a wall of prostrate Frenchmen divided the two armies, and during the ensuing pause the archers advanced to take prisoners.

The battle appeared won when a French marauding party circled the woods and surprised Henry's undefended camp. In the belief that a new enemy force was attacking him, the King reluctantly ordered the prisoners to be slain, as the remaining French cavalry to his front appeared to be about to charge. The danger of a double envelopment did not, however, become a fact, and the 'cruel butchery' was stopped. The French then retired.

Half the nobility of France lay dead amongst the 8,000 slain, including the Constable, and 2,000 remained captives. The total English loss was 400 men. Henry had won his way through to Calais, and the superiority of archers and dismounted men-at-arms fighting in close coordination had been convincingly demonstrated.

Harbingers of the modern age of warfare. Fifteenth-century French bombards hurl stone cannonballs at the enemy defences. Note the elevating gear and the wooden beds for the barrels. *Bibliothèque Nationale, Paris.*

Painting of the battle of Agincourt from the St
Albans Chronicle. The triumph of Henry V and his
English and Welsh longbowmen was reversed within
two generations. *Lambeth Palace Library, London.*

The capture of Antioch, 1098, climax of the First Crusade. The Crusaders repulsed two relieving armies, and captured Antioch from Yagi Siyan on 3 June after an eight-month siege, just two days before the arrival of a third army. Note the scimitars and the extraordinary face-shields of the Syrians. *Bibliothèque de l'Arsénal, Paris.*

A stylized representation of Jerusalem at the time
of the Christian kingdoms during the Crusades.
Koninklijke Bibliotheek, The Hague.

THE EASTERN MEDITERRANEAN

Byzantium, The Arabs and The Crusaders

At this point we must retrace our steps to the fifth century, and follow the development of warfare in part of the Mediterranean world. As the Roman Empire in the West crumbled, Rome's Eastern Empire first survived and then grew strong. Constantinople became the repository and fortress of Western civilization, merging the cultures of Rome and Greece. To survive, Byzantium (as it eventually became known) had to overcome many external threats and internal perils, but in the process it evolved a complex yet highly effective politico-military organization which for a millennium had no peer.

Basically, Byzantium faced the same challenge as Rome–the attempted incursions of tough, barbaric peoples across her frontiers. Unlike Rome, Byzantium proved equal to the challenge, and rose above it. One of the main reasons for this was the combination of political acumen with the faith of the Greek Orthodox Church, the fusion giving birth to a fervent national spirit. Another was the burgeoning wealth of Byzantium, placed geographically at the hub of the known world and thus able to exploit the great commercial opportunities its location offered. Its position athwart many of the age-old migration routes also invited the attentions of migrating peoples, but the Empire's development of a highly centralized, autocratic form of government, backed by an efficient military system designed to protect the frontiers, and the emergence of a number of brilliant emperors and commanders, ensured its success and survival for many centuries.

Perhaps the most testing time came with the sudden explosion of energetic Islam in the seventh century. For a century from 632 it seemed that nothing could check the Moslem flood, which spread from Arabia to reach the approaches to Constantinople, gained the River Indus, occupied North Africa, Mesopotamia and Spain, and then thrust deep into France. Bitter religious wars were the result, but Byzantium's vast resources earned survival.

Warfare, as in the West, was to a marked degree dominated by the mounted warrior throughout the Byzantine period, and also for much of the Arab ascendancy. The Crusaders learnt the value of infantry during the twelfth century, but promptly forgot much of it–except possibly the English. However, Eastern developments in fortification design and siegecraft were assimilated. Paradoxically, it was Christian powers, particularly Venice, which ultimately did most to undermine both the prosperity and the security of Constantinople, but it was left to Sultan Mohammed II to deliver the *coup de grâce*. The collapse of Christendom in the Levant led to a new wave of Moslem expansion through the Mediterranean and into southern Europe which was only checked at Malta (1565), Lepanto (1571) and before the walls of Vienna (1683).

The Crusades demonstrated the power of the Church in its organizational and inspirational aspects. They also showed that Western Europe had emerged from the Dark Ages with a capacity to mount vast international enterprises, although a failure to appreciate how sustained an effort was required to make the Christian kingdoms of Jerusalem a lasting proposition led to ultimate failure.

Until 524, Constantinople was very much on the defensive, and her armies came to rely increasingly on mercenaries, including Hun light and Gothic heavy cavalry, together with Anatolian and Frankish foot. This was potentially dangerous–as Rome had learnt to its great cost–but the reforms of the enlightened Emperor Justinian (reigned 527–65) reduced the reliance on mercenaries before the implied peril became manifest. Henceforth the *federati* were never allowed to total more than half the Byzantine forces. After recovering from long wars on the frontiers Byzantium was able to take the initiative, inspired by the leadership of the great Belisarius and his pupil Narses.

Byzantine armies were largely recruited from the sturdy peasantry of the Empire, supported by mercenaries. The armies were generally small (approximately 10,000 men), relying on skill, cunning and manoeuvrability to defeat foes superior in numbers. Like the *toumans* of Mongolia, some were based almost wholly on mounted troops, most particularly the *cataphract* or armoured horse archer, who comprised half their forces. The horse archer combined the advantages of missile power, mobility and shock action to a very high degree. The universal use

opposite page
A depiction of the siege of Constantinople from *Voyage d'Outremer*, by de la Brocquière, 1455. *Bibliothèque Nationale, Paris.*

of the saddle and the stirrup gave these horsemen a safe seat and a wide range of operations.
The *cataphracts* were supported by mail-clad
lancers, and armoured heavy infantry served in
many of the armies, being also employed to
garrison the fortresses along the frontiers. These
garrisons in turn were seconded by reservists
– old soldiers granted a piece of land in the frontier regions by way of a pension – and between
them they were expected to be able to defend key
points and report enemy incursions until the
nearest cavalry army could be mobilized and sent
to their assistance. The cavalry was now deemed
to be the battle-winning arm.

During Justinian's remarkable reign, the
Byzantine Empire expanded until it comprised
much of the Mediterranean world and the Levant.
The Sassanid Persians, the Vandals and the
Ostrogoths were defeated in turn, and Byzantine
fleets exerted full mastery over the inland sea.
Four major offensive wars were fought and won,
but the Emperor's parsimony never permitted
his armies to top 150,000 men. He was fortunate
to possess so loyal a subordinate as Belisarius,
who, despite many slights and snubs, served his
master well.

The military system of Justinian was con-
solidated by the Emperor Maurice (reigned
582–602), who placed the defensive strategy of
Byzantium upon a firm footing. Careful organization eventually reduced costly overheads
without incurring risks. Senior appointments
were kept in the Emperor's gift, the distinction
between native and mercenary formations was
abolished, and the strategical reserves operated
around new, massive chains of fortifications
built along the frontiers. On the Danube, a
line of fifty-two fortresses were built, supported

by a further twenty-seven to the south, whilst
around Constantinople and the Golden Horn
arose the famous triple walls.

In due course, the Empire was divided into
themes (districts), each with its own army or
thema under a *strategos* (general) who wielded
full civil as well as military authority in his area.
Military roads, signal stations and courier posts
linked the *themes* with the capital. The administrative organizations were developed equally
effectively, including supply, medical and chaplains' departments.

Most important of all, however, was the fact
that from the outset the Byzantines studied
warfare, and spent much time and effort in
analysing their own and their adversaries'
military capabilities. Such thoroughness was
another major secret of their long-lived success.
Important military texts were written. Vegetius'
De Re Militari (392), Maurice's *Strategikon* (575)
and Leo the Wise's *Tactica* (c. 900), together with
the Staff Manual, produced c. 980 and attributed
to Nicephorus Phocas, provide evidence of
Byzantine analytical study, covering every major
aspect of warfare.

From the seventh century defensive strategies
predominated, the generals adopting the doctrine
of phased or graduated response. An elaborate
spy system based on merchants and missionaries
lay at the base of a cunning and devious diplomacy, which did not hesitate to employ guile,
fraud and bribery against Byzantium's enemies.
Recourse to arms generally came only as a last
resort when every other deterrent had failed.
Military campaigns were carefully adjusted to
suit the particular challenge in a given case.
Huns were to be attacked in winter, or Arabs
in wet weather – when the Byzantines knew that

82

their effectiveness was greatly reduced.

Byzantine organization of formations and general tactics merit further attention. The equivalent to the later battalion was the *numerus* of some 400 men; between five and eight of these units formed a *turma* (division), and two or more *turmae* were grouped in a *thema*, of which there were at one time thirteen. These formations were commanded by counts, dukes and *strategoi* respectively, all of whom were appointed by the Emperor personally. Variations in the composition of *turmae* and *themae* were deliberate attempts to confuse enemy intelligence, in much the same way as Napoleon employed flexible *corps d'armée* in a later century.

The tactics of these armies were highly flexible, and were based on launching a crescendo of coordinated blows against the foe. Ahead of the army, and on its flanks, moved a screen of cavalry; in the centre were two lines of infantry; these were supported by two flanking forces of cavalry on each wing, and as many more were held in central reserve. If the opponent was a mounted force, it was lured to attack the Byzantine centre before being outflanked with cavalry from the inner wings, whilst the outer launched a major attack on the rest of the army. If the first line of infantry found itself under pressure, it could retire through the second line, which again could be sustained by a double envelopment carried out by the reserve cavalry. If the foe was basically a dismounted army, the Byzantine army would seize the initiative, its infantry advancing in a deep formation, sixteen ranks deep (much like the Greek phalanx), covered by archers and slingers, whilst the cavalry also moved forward in *numeri*, some ten horsemen deep. This proved an effective formation.

There were variations on these tactics, but the *themae* all practised a standard tactical doctrine. Similarly, officers were trained from youth, and had to move up the chain of command in a logical manner. Cadets served on campaign in menial positions, and for promotion, experience and recommendation were necessary. Above all, warfare was regarded as an intellectual challenge. In direct contrast to the situation pertaining in Western Europe, the calling of arms was highly professional, based on scientific analysis, both on land and at sea. Ultimately, however, the professionalism began to fade, dating from the defeat of Manzikert (1071), which forced Byzantium to abandon most of Asia Minor (formerly its most important ground) to the Turks. Recourse had to be made, once more, to reliance on mercenaries, and ironically the consequent

The great Byzantine Emperor, Justinian, whose long reign saw the Eastern Empire consolidate and expand its position in southern Europe and the Levant. From a plaster cast of a gold medal. *British Museum, London.*

The ruins of the famous triple wall, built to protect Constantinople by the Emperor Theodosius. The advent of cannon in the fifteenth century rendered these defences obsolete.

prolonged decline in Eastern military professionalism and dedication coincided with the first hesitant re-emergence of these characteristics in the West.

However, the seeds of decline had been sown several centuries earlier. The Moslem challenge was indubitably a major solvent of Byzantium's supremacy. Mohammed succeeded in uniting many of the Bedouin Arab peoples before his death in 632, and in providing them with the inspiration and physical means to challenge the empires of Byzantium and Persia. Inspired by the words of Mohammed, Arab camel troops penetrated deep into Persia, and overwhelmed the *themae* of Asia Minor. Rather surprisingly, the *cataphracts* and mailed lancers found the volatile and fast-moving Arabs more than a match. The skirmish battle was the Arab speciality; fighting in loose groups of skirmishers suited their character, which resented tight discipline but laid great stress on personal valour. Battles of attrition, involving paring down their opponents' strength by days of minor but highly aggravating and exhausting action, were the norm. Eventually, following their final overthrow of Persia in 651, the Arabs were mounted on horses.

The architect of the Arab Empire, which in extent came to rival that of Byzantium itself, was Khalid-Ibn-al-Walid (fl. 636), who did much to transform the dash and cunning of the Arab peoples into instruments of empire building. His first weapon was manoeuvre; his second, the reduction of administrative requirements to the barest minimum. The tough life of the Arabs amidst the semi-arid and desert areas required

them to subsist on the bare minimum of supplies, as did the Mongols, and as desert fighters they had no equals. Khalid's horsemen could live for weeks on a diet of dates, salt and water, and their mounts were no less hardy.

After a full century of great successes, which included the overthrow of the Persian Empire and the conquest of Asia Minor, the impetus of Moslem expansion slowed down as Byzantium mobilized its full resources to meet the new menace, and as grave internal dissensions fragmented the Arab world. Although they assimilated many organizational and tactical practices from Byzantium, the Arabs never fully mastered the imperial *themae*, which earned Constantinople a few more centuries of survival. Thwarted in one direction, the Moslems turned south and west, and concentrated their efforts along the northern and eastern littorals of Africa, into Spain and (briefly) France. Of great importance, however, was the conversion to Mohammedanism of the redoubtable Seljuk Turks, whose military skills would eventually secure the capture of Constantinople itself. Between them, the Arabs and the Turks formed a devastating aggressive force, inspired by religious fanaticism.

A declining Byzantium could summon neither the will nor the energy to attempt to stem the Moslem flood. Instead, the task was undertaken by the Christian powers of the West under the aegis of the spiritual authority of Rome. Between 1096 and 1270 a total of eight Crusades of varying size and type were mounted in repeated attempts to free the Holy Land from the Moslem yoke, with the alternating aid (on a limited scale) and obstruction of Byzantium.

The Tetrarchs, a sculptured group of local Byzantine princes on the façade of the cathedral of St Mark's, Venice. These Tetrarchs were military and civil governors of the *themes* or regions of Byzantium.

The Crusades were important on several counts. First, they marked an immense change in the wealth and power of Western Europe; for the first time since the days of Ancient Rome the West was strong enough to mount an offensive against the East. Secondly, the men who took service in the armies of the Cross were all volunteers. Their motives varied from the altruistic to the profane and bloodthirsty, but there was no denying that Crusader armies were multinational in composition and represented a great expansion of European interests.

Growth of population, particularly in France, was one major incentive, and the Church deliberately encouraged the Crusades as a means to provide a safety valve and a distraction. The organization of at least the first three Crusades was masterly, given the problems of the period, and offered a genuine demonstration of international effort, although rivalries between armies, and between Crusaders and Byzantium, were a constant factor.

To regain the Holy Land posed the strategic tasks of defeating the Saracens and Turks, and above all of securing key points from which the conquered areas could be supervised and controlled. It is estimated that, to achieve the first object, a total of some 100,000 people, half of them warriors and half of them non-combatants, were involved in the four armies engaged in the First Crusade launched by Pope Urban II in 1096. Their organization was typical of the period – one mounted knight for every six or seven foot soldiers. In operational terms difficult marches over near-waterless areas, pitched battles and bitterly contested sieges, such as those of Nicea

and Antioch, were of equal importance. After three years, Jerusalem was occupied and four Latin kingdoms were established. Highly vulnerable to Moslem counterattack, these small principalities built massive fortresses along the frontier areas to serve as refuges in times of Turkish incursions, and as centres for political and economic control at other times. But constant Turkish attacks regained area after area, and made necessary fresh Crusades to make good the damage. Thus Saladin's capture of Jerusalem in 1187 led to perhaps the greatest effort of all, the Third Crusade, effectively led by Richard Cœur de Lion after the death *en route* of the Emperor Frederick Barbarossa and the return to France of Philip Augustus.

Exposure to Byzantine and Arab ways of making war had a number of important effects on Western European military ideas, some lasting, others transient. First, they learnt from the Arabs the importance of psychological preparation for battle. The Arabs used cymbals and drums to produce a growing crescendo of noise as they moved to contact, slow at first, then ever faster, and this enhanced the terror of the situation. Secondly, the Crusaders came to appreciate the significance of manoeuvre and carefully coordinated action, with cavalry and foot working as a team. The experience of many an ambush or enveloping attack by the Arab and Turkish cavalry drove these lessons home. Thirdly, the inhospitable terrain of the Holy Land soon convinced them of the importance of logistics and military administration, and by the Third Crusade an elaborate supporting base had been established in Cyprus. Furthermore, the study

of Byzantine military architecture and siege methods led to major changes in Western design and practice. Towers became round rather than square (proving less vulnerable to undermining) and the great concentric castles came to consist of successive lines of turreted curtain walls in place of the former keep and bailey tradition. So strong did these mighty fortresses become that even the development of massive trebuchets and other sophisticated engines of war proved insufficient to overcome them, and an attacker had scant choice but to resort to extremely costly direct stormings (these became a speciality of the Turks, whose 'perpetual storms', wave after wave, became justifiably feared) or to lengthy blockades meant to starve the garrisons into surrender. However, the great Krak des Chevaliers (completed 1140), placed between Homs in Syria and Tripoli in Lebanon, which could hold a garrison of 2,000 Hospitallers and shelter some 8,000 local peasantry, fell to the Arabs in April 1271, after a siege of only five weeks (it was undermanned at the time). On the other hand, Kerak of Moab, east of the Dead Sea, defied Saladin for many months in 1188 before succumbing.

The Crusades also provided the inspiration for the creation of the Military Orders: the Hospitallers of St John of Jerusalem and the Templars. These warriors, half-monk and half-soldier, entered their respective Orders after taking vows to protect pilgrims, to liberate the Holy Land from the infidels, to convert the heathen and to defend Christian territories from Moslem attack. Their influence encouraged the spread of the concepts of chivalry in the West,

The siege of Tunis in 1535, showing a strange mixture of Moslem and Christian troops. The Arabs were notable horsemen. Note the Christians 'dicing' for possession of the unfortunate damsel, right. *Kunstsammlungen Veste Coburg.*

Rumelahisar, situated on the hills dominating the Bosporus, a castle built by Mehmet II two years before the conquest of Constantinople.

The scene was then set for the second great surge of Islamic expansion, dating from the capture of Constantinople in 1453. Led by the Turks, who based their army upon the redoubtable corps of Janissaries, both horse and foot (originally recruited from Christian slaves), supported by vast provincial levies of the faithful, this period of expansion would only be halted before the gates of Vienna in 1683, although Christendom would finally triumph in Spain over the Moors following the capture of Granada by Ferdinand and Isabella in 1492, and Moslem naval power would be similarly destroyed by the great battle of Lepanto in 1571. It would not be until the second quarter of the eighteenth century, however, that the Moslem Turks would fall into a steady decline.

It remains in this chapter to describe briefly the main attributes of the great commanders of this lengthy period of military history. Two soldiers stand out, namely Count Belisarius of Byzantium and Khalid-Ibn-al-Walid of Arabia, but two more merit passing attention – the great Saladin and Richard Cœur de Lion.

Belisarius was the great general of the golden age of the Eastern Roman Empire. He substituted strategical cunning and tactical skill for mere numbers. To conquer the Vandals in North Africa, he needed an army of only 15,000 (including 6,000 horse archers); the greater part of Italy was wrested from the Ostrogoths by a mere 11,000 troops, eventually reinforced by another 15,000. Belisarius perfected the stratagem of the indirect approach (Napoleon would use the same method in his strategy of envelopment) and associated it (unlike Napoleon) with the tactical defensive action. At the battle of Daras (530) he lured a strong Persian army into making an unwise attack by feigning weakness and asking for peace negotiations on the eve of battle – a trick that would be repeated before Austerlitz in 1805 by the great French Emperor. Three years later, Belisarius defeated a reputed 100,000 Vandals with 15,000 troops, and captured Carthage. In 535, after seizing Sicily, he invaded southern Italy, and smuggled a force of men into the heart of Naples via a disused aqueduct. Shortly thereafter, he defended Rome with only 10,000 troops against Vitiges' 150,000 Ostrogoths, and by a subtle combination of harassing sorties, campfires lit to give a misleading impression of the size of his forces, and a number of brilliant raids which led to the capture of the enemy's food depots at Tivoli and Terracine, Belisarius contrived the complete rout of his superior adversary, and went on to capture his base at Ravenna. The year 540 saw perhaps his greatest military achievement, when he foiled Chrosoes' invasion of Palestine by bluffing his way into contact with his stronger adversary before winning the crushing victory of Carchemish. As Liddell Hart commented: 'Never was an invasion, so potentially irresistible, so economically defeated.'

with its stress on the knightly virtues of honour, valour and help for the oppressed.

In later centuries, the Order of St John of Jerusalem in particular became the bulwark of Christianity in the Mediterranean world, earning international acclaim for its stout defence of Rhodes (ultimately lost in 1522) and Malta (successfully held in 1565) against massively superior Moslem forces.

Further lessons learnt on the Crusades related to personal equipment. The fine quality of Damascus steel, of which the Saracen scimitars were made, increased the effectiveness of Crusader swords and spearheads. Many improved techniques were learnt from Syrian arms smiths: ring mail was transformed into linked chain mail, and entire suits of this strong material weighing as little as thirty-one pounds could be manufactured. The Saracens wore tight-fitting conical helmets with vertical nose-guards, sometimes with crests of feathers, loose strips of mail hanging down to protect the neck, and flowing cloaks. The Crusaders soon learnt the need to wear white surcoats over their mail to reduce the discomfiting effects of the sun's rays on the metal.

For their part, the Saracens came to respect the European crossbow, and ultimately to devise tactics capable of defeating the Crusaders in battle, based upon the concept of dividing the Christian knights from their foot soldiers, a speciality of the great Saladin. However, considerations of supply, internal political rivalries and soaring costs ultimately doomed the Crusades to failure.

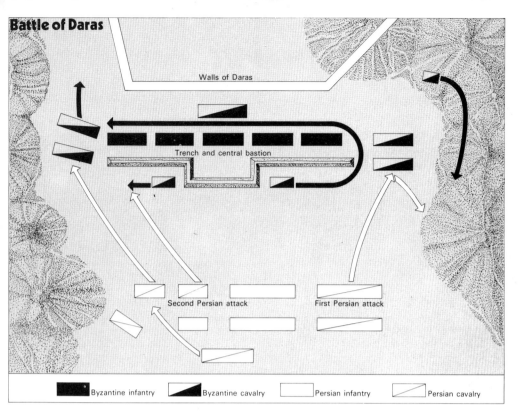

Battle of Daras

Walls of Daras

Trench and central bastion

Second Persian attack

First Persian attack

■ Byzantine infantry   ◣ Byzantine cavalry   ▢ Persian infantry   ◿ Persian cavalry

The Emperor Justinian was indeed fortunate to possess such an outstanding general. Even after the Count's death his good work was carried on by his former pupil, Narses, who earned great fame by destroying Totilla's Gothic horde at Taginae (552).

Khalid-Ibn-al-Walid filled the same role for Islam as Belisarius had for Byzantium. A string of impressive victories redound to his credit, all displaying his keen grasp of strategy. In April 633 he destroyed a Persian army at Oballa, after ambushing its rearguard. A few months later, he routed a mixed force of Greeks, Persians and hostile Bedouin at Ain Al Tamr. This was followed by an epic march through the Syrian desert which ended with the infliction of a telling defeat upon the Byzantine Emperor Theodore at Ajnaidan in July 634. Next year the Arabs besieged Damascus itself, and in 636 Khalid destroyed a major Byzantine army at Yarmuk. Here was a great master of manoeuvre, ambush and surprise in a desert setting, as cunning as the 'Desert Fox' of the Second World War, Erwin Rommel.

The Battle of Daras, 530

The battle of Daras was fought in northern Mesopotamia between a Byzantine army, 25,000 strong, led by the great Belisarius, and a vast host of Sassanid Persians numbering some 40,000 warriors. Determined to prevent the frontier fortress of Daras from being besieged, Belisarius took up a position close to the city and prepared for battle. Well to the fore he drew up

his staff slingers and light archers, supported by two bodies of Hunnish horse, with orders to harass the Persian approach. On each flank he drew up his heavy cavalry in two equal bodies, half of them riding armoured and half of them riding unarmoured horses. These mounted troops projected towards the enemy, Belisarius having decided to refuse, or hold back, his centre, which comprised some cavalry and the mass of his heavy infantry, archers and javelin troops. A reserve of *clibanari*, or cuirassiers, was placed behind the centre. A broad ditch, provided with crossing points, was dug in front of the whole position. Finally, hidden away behind a hill, a party of Huns lurked beyond the Byzantine left wing. Having drawn up his army, Belisarius awaited the enemy.

The Persian host advanced in two dense lines

The great Saracen leader, Saladin, opponent of Richard the Lionheart during the Third Crusade, 1189–92. Saladin's empire, based on Egypt, of which he was Sultan, did not survive his death in 1193, but he had effectively fought the Crusaders to a standstill.

Affin quil ne sēble
que par enuie
ennuy ou faulte
dauoir assez veu
listoire doultre mer Je naye de
laisse la conqueste de consta
tinople faicte par les francois
Je la toucheray mais en tres
bresf en ces ptis passures aus
quelz elle nappartiet directemt

par ce qle sut faicte par cpi
ens sur epiens. En la cite de
Jadres assegnee ou prochaim
precedent article aruineret
mahieu de mont moreny
et plusieurs autres seignez
et pelerins francois. Et en
celle mesmes cite bint par
deuers les pelerins Alexis
filz de surfac Jadis empeur

of units, with cavalry formations at the extremes of each line and a number of war-elephants in the rear. The infantry in the centre comprised mercenary slingers, archers and javelin throwers, backed by Persian peasant levies. On the left were the Immortals, élite Sassanid Persian heavy cavalry, backed by a formation of *clibanari* and supported by a cloud of light horsemen. This pattern was repeated on the Persian right.

Once the light screening troops had fallen back, the Persian wings (but not their centre) came into contact with the Byzantine cavalry forces. On the Persian right some progress was made, but once the ditch had been crossed the Sassanids were suddenly taken in their flank by 600 Huns from the left centre and simultaneously assaulted in their rear by the concealed auxiliary force, which came galloping out of the hills. Soon the Persians were in retreat on this sector, but they managed to rally well to the rear of their own line.

Meantime, on the further flank, the Byzantine heavy cavalry was also borne back by the attack of the Immortals and their auxiliaries. Indeed, the Byzantine line, commanded by Count John, was only able to rally close to the gates of the city. However, the watchful Belisarius realized that his moment had come. The Persian left was now wholly separated from its centre, which was indulging in intermittent exchanges of archery fire with the Byzantine centre. To make the most

of his opportunity, Belisarius summoned the 1,200 Huns from the area of his centre and hurled them against the rear of the victorious Persian left wing. At the same time, Belisarius launched his élite reserve against the Sassanid flank. Attacked on three sides, the Persians were lucky to escape away beyond the city. There was no question of their taking any further part in the battle.

Leaving the rallied horsemen of his original right wing to pursue the discomfited Persian cavalry, Belisarius led his bodyguard and the Huns against the unprotected left flank of the Persian centre. This soon reduced the whole Persian formation to a mass of fugitives, shattered beyond recall. After a brief pursuit, Belisarius rallied his men. Eight thousand Persians were left dead on the field.

In this manner Belisarius demonstrated his great skill at tactics. His infantry, it should be noted, played scant part in the battle; it was the mounted arm, with its variety of types and weapons, bows, twelve-foot lances and throwing darts, that was the key arm of the Byzantine armies. By clever positioning of his men Belisarius had dictated the type of battle he wished to fight; he had successively defeated one flank, routed the other, and then scattered the centre of his far more numerous opponents, demonstrating the greatest control and flexibility. This decisive victory, his first, so delighted the Emperor

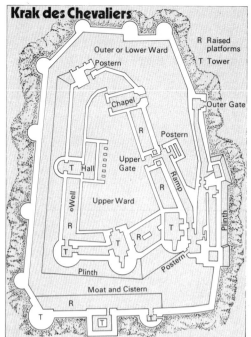

Krak des Chevaliers

R Raised platforms

T Tower

Outer or Lower Ward

Postern

Chapel

Outer Gate

R

Postern

R

Upper Gate

Hall T

Well

Upper Ward

Ramp

R

R

R

Plinth

R T

T

T R

T

Postern

Plinth

Moat and Cistern

R

T T

One positive result of the Crusades was a great advance in Western military architecture. This fortress, Krak des Chevaliers, was a major link in the protective system of the Christian kingdoms in Palestine.

Justinian I that he appointed Belisarius his chief commander in the East.

Two Battles of the Crusades: Hittin, 1187 and Arsouf, 1191

Saladin had moved with his allied Egyptian, Mesopotamian and Syrian army, perhaps 20,000 strong, to besiege the Crusader fortress of Tiberias on the Sea of Galilee. The Christians at once drew forces from other garrisons to form a relief force. These troops gathered at Saffaria, sixteen miles west of Tiberias; they numbered 6,000 mailed cavalry, 18,000 foot and a large detachment of light horsemen. Somewhat unwisely, the Crusader generals, King Guy of Jerusalem and Count Raymond of Tripolis, decided to advance directly on the besieged town through the intervening desert, which Saladin had rendered completely waterless. After covering ten miles on the first day, with no sign of Saladin, the Crusader host camped for the night on account of the exhaustion of the infantry.

Throughout the night, Turkish archers kept up a harassing archery fire, and next morning (4 July) the troops were only too glad to move on,

fedecif postulauit.
naldus de castelli
contunctiose rel
t modum leuis
aut teuge ad
10 certamen. Quod
de populatur

hac clade comes tripolitanus licet omnibus suf
pectus dns reginaldus fydomis patronus atq;
dominus taliamus cum paucis fratribus milicie
templi. facta est autem hec misera belli congsi
suo quinto scilicet & quarto nonas iulii infra
octauas aplozr petri & pauli. Cuasit etiam ab
hac clade theodoricus magister milicie templi.

Battle of Hittin

Raymond of Toulouse

Sea of Galilee

Hittin

Saracen trap

Tiberias

Overnight camp

| ▰ Crusader infantry | ◣ Crusader cavalry | ◹ Saracen cavalry | ○○○○ Saracen archers |

below
Suleiman I, The
Magnificent, Sultan of
Turkey. His long reign
(1520–66) saw many
triumphs for Islam on
land and sea, and its
influence was widespread.

opposite page
The siege of Rhodes in
1480 by Mohammed II,
which was repulsed with
severe Turkish losses.
Rhodes was finally
evacuated in 1522, after
a siege by Suleiman I in
which he is said to have
lost 90,000 men out of an
investing force of 200,000.
*Bibliothèque Nationale,
Paris.*

despite their thirst. Eventually the sweltering columns reached a stream – and discipline disappeared as the parched foot soldiers broke ranks and flung themselves into the water. It was for this moment that the shadowing Saladin had been reserving his 10,000 mailed cavalry and an additional force of horse archers. Sweeping forward, the Turks succeeded in driving a wedge between the Crusader cavalry and infantry. The latter refused to make any attempt to force a way through to rejoin their mounted comrades, but instead formed up on the hill of Hittin, where they were rapidly cut down.

Saladin next turned his attention to the Crusader cavalry, which soon found itself surrounded. So many horses had been wounded by arrows that the whole force became immobilized. Realizing that safety could only be attained by boldness, Raymond and the advance guard charged the Turks to their front and broke through. They were not followed by the rest, however, and after a few hours of desultory fighting, the main body of Crusader knights, sweltering in their hot equipment and nearly mad with thirst, were compelled to surrender. King Guy was captured, and the kingdom of Jerusalem never recovered from this blow.

Four years later, Richard Cœur de Lion, King of England, inflicted a heavy defeat on the brilliant Saracen commander at Arsouf, south of Acre. Richard was preparing a drive against Jerusalem with probably as many as 100,000 troops under his command. His staff and medical services were carefully organized, even including a corps of laundresses to keep the clothing clean

THE BATTLE OF DARAS, 530

The disposition of the forces at the outset of the battle will be found on the double-page spread overleaf, accompanied by a key. The captions below describe the crucial moments in the battle, which are to be found, in chronological order, on the page opposite and on the final page of the colour section. A full description of the battle will be found on pp 89–92.

1. The Persians and Arabs, left, open the battle by attacking both flanks of the Byzantine army. On the right flank, bottom, they are taken in flank and rear from behind the shielding hill by a concealed party of Herule cavalry.

2. On the Byzantine right flank, the Immortals, supported by horsemen, drive back the Byzantine right-wing cavalry. Belisarius orders his Huns to mass near the flank of the main cavalry battle, right.

3 and 4. The Immortals drive the Byzantine right wing back to the gates of Daras, but are separated from the rest of their army and are suddenly attacked in flank and rear by the Byzantine reserve and the Huns. The Persian left is thus driven off the field.

5. Belisarius dispatches part of his cavalry to pursue the discomfited Persian horsemen, rear left, and leads the remainder of his right-wing cavalry and reserve against the unprotected flank and rear of the Persian and Arab centre, which breaks and flees.

Daras is an illustration of the consequences attendant on the failure of a double envelopment, the effects of a force attacking from a concealed position in a tactical outflanking move, and the use of entrenchments to 'refuse' part of the battle line; by keeping his infantry virtually out of the battle, Belisarius largely neutralized the Persians' overwhelming strength in the centre. Finally, it illustrates the advantages to be gained by fighting from a strong defensive position, which enabled Belisarius to place all the onus on his crack cavalry army in first checking the Persian attacks and then repulsing and routing them, before falling upon the isolated and tactically unprotected Persian centre to achieve a decisive victory.

1

2

Byzantine Forces
1. The city of Daras
2. Belisarius, commanding cavalry reserve
3. Byzantine centre – heavy infantry, archers, javelin troops
4. Cavalry supporting centre
5. Trench and embankment raised to protect and 'refuse' the Byzantine centre
6. Hunnish light horse
7. Byzantine heavy cavalry, protecting flanks
8. Staff slingers – the wings of the advanced skirmish line
9. Light archers
10. Auxiliary cavalry

Sassanid Turks and Arab Allies
11. Kavadh I with reserve of Persian war elephants
12. Peasant levies with, in front, mercenary light javelin throwers
13. Persian cavalry
14. Screen of Persian and Arabian light horse
15. Persian heavy cavalry (Immortals)
16. Mercenary slingers and bowmen

3

4

5

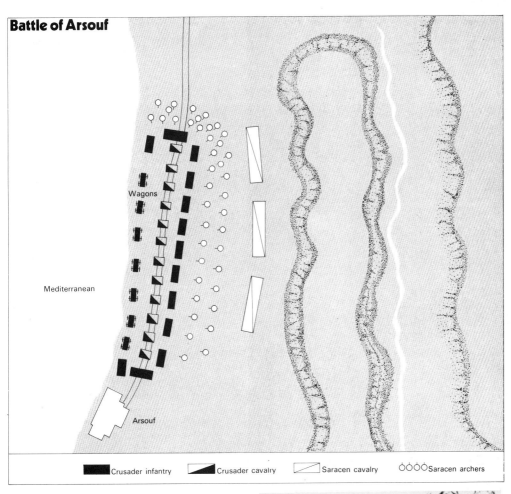

Battle of Arsouf

Wagons

Mediterranean

Arsouf

■ Crusader infantry ◢ Crusader cavalry ◺ Saracen cavalry ○○○○ Saracen archers

and thus reduce the danger of epidemics. Richard was nothing if not thorough.

On 7 September, as this mighty array moved south from Acre to build a forward supply base, Saladin descended upon the marching column. The Turks paid special attention to the rear of the column, hoping to induce it to halt and turn about to face its tormentors, thus creating a gap in the line of march which Saladin could then exploit. Thanks, however, to Richard's prudence and the discipline of his men, the opportunity was never offered. He had drawn up his infantry on all sides of his main column, and these troops covered the continued march of the army with their bows. The knights were under strict orders not to charge until they received Richard's trumpet signal, no matter what the provocation.

Shortly before the dogged column reached Arsouf, the right moment came. The ferocious Moslems became too bold and disorganized; the trumpet rang out and the Crusaders launched a crushing charge. For a loss of 700 men, the Christians cut down ten times that number. Infantry and cavalry, working in close coordination, had won a great victory. Saladin never again attempted a full-scale battle against Richard Cœur de Lion. Next year Richard made a treaty with Saladin, who died in 1193.

The fervour of the Crusades gave birth to several religious orders of celibate knights. This picture probably represents a thirteenth-century Hospitaller taking his vows. *British Museum, London.*

THE EMERGENCE OF MODERN WARFARE

The true transition from feudal to modern warfare came in 1494, 'that most unhappy year', as many Italians lamented. It saw Charles VIII of France invade Italy at the head of an army that was more professional, more national and better equipped than any of its immediate predecessors, and its success over the *condottieri* forces of medieval Italy proved the harbinger of immense changes over the next two centuries. In due course, the struggle for power became a bitter contest between the French house of Valois and the mighty Habsburg families of Austria, and, above all, of Spain. Armies were still the 'playthings of kings' for much of the period, but there was a growing fusion of royal and national interests.

These interests became partly absorbed in the mighty religious fervour unleashed by the Reformation, and from the 1540s to 1643, various countries, and ultimately the whole of central Europe, became enmeshed in a series of bitter and near-total ideological wars. They wrought so much havoc in the United Provinces, France and the states of Germany in turn during the Eighty Years, Civil, and Thirty Years Wars respectively, that a widespread revulsion against the horrors of such wars spread throughout Europe, with profound effects on the conduct of warfare and policy during the succeeding 150 years. Not until the Napoleonic era would struggles on such a wide scale recur. At the close of the period covered by this chapter, the onset of limited war was already in evidence, as Louis XIV battled against successive coalitions in pursuit of France's territorial aggrandizement – the quest for the natural frontiers of the Rhine, the Alps and Pyrenees. This era also saw the building of the first great overseas empires by Portugal and Spain. In the years of rivalry that followed, Spain would become bankrupt, and new colonial powers – the English, the Dutch and the French – would emerge. Although there would be colonial wars fought in the Americas and the Indies, and although great fleets would contend for command of the oceans, the focal point of all struggles, and the centre of military development, remained Europe.

From the point of view of weaponry, the sixteenth and seventeenth centuries were dominated by the development of firearms and cannon. The medieval handgun had been prohibitively weighty, but the development of the lighter arquebus was to revolutionize warfare. The arquebus possessed a shaped butt and, in the earlier models, a hook intended to reduce the recoil – hence the German word *Hakenbüchse* or 'gun with hook'. *El gran capitan*, Gonzalo de Cordoba of Spain, adopted increasing numbers of arquebusiers at the expense of crossbowmen and men-at-arms, backing them with more lightly armed troops wielding sixteen-foot pikes. His victory over the French at Cerignola in April 1503 effectively established the firearm-bearing infantryman as the most important soldier on the battlefield.

The arquebus was still a difficult weapon to employ, but it played a central role at Pavia in 1525 (see below), one of the last major land engagements fought for several generations. However, as the sixteenth century drew on, the matchlock musket came to the fore. A weighty weapon, requiring a forked rest to sustain the weight of the barrel, and rarely capable of more than one shot every two minutes (the arquebus had a rate of almost a shot a minute), its advantages lay in its longer range and greater reliability. The transition was gradual; in the third quarter of the century the Spaniards only armed fifteen per cent of their musketeers with the matchlock, but by 1600 the proportion was almost fifty per cent. By this time there was also one soldier bearing a musket to every one 'trailing' a pike. Many still regarded the latter weapon as the more honourable to bear, but increasing numbers came to favour the musket. 'I know not whether it be to take more wages, or to be lighter laden, or to be further off', as one contemporary remarked.

The Spaniards rapidly surpassed the French, and became the military leaders of the sixteenth century. By 1540, the Spanish *tercio* (originally one third of an army) of highly disciplined pikemen and matchlock musketeers had become the envy and terror of Europe. By the end of the century the earliest, massive *tercios* had been refined to a force of 3,000 foot, subdivided into three columns or *colunellas*, each commanded by a colonel. Originally (*c.* 1505), each *colunella* of

opposite page
The land-based campaigns of the Moslem Turks took them to the gates of Vienna. From 27 September to 15 October 1529, the Austrian capital was closely besieged. The active defence by the garrison gravely hampered the Turkish operations, and with the onset of winter Suleiman gave up the attempt. This was only one of several sieges of Vienna, that of 1683 being probably the most famous, as it led to the final repulse of Islam from the mid-Danube basin. *Osterreichische Nationalbibliothek, Vienna.*

the first twenty created by Ferdinand of Aragon had comprised a mixed force of pikemen, halberdiers, arquebusiers and sword-and-buckler men in five companies, 1,250 men in all. These later became exclusively made up of pikemen and musketeers (or arquebusiers), and Cordoba employed his firepower element on wide frontages behind field fortifications, using his pikemen to protect the musketeers whilst they were in the open or reloading, and to add the traditional shock element, 'at push of pike', to exploit the effect of fire action.

The French developed along different lines, Francis I creating the first regiments on a ten-company basis. Henri IV trained the front ranks to fire from the kneeling position, thus doubling the rate of fire by enabling two ranks to fire at once. The French also developed the first chain of command running down from the monarch to the Constable or Lieutenant-General, and thence to the Serjeant-Major-General charged with overseeing supply, organization and the lines of battle. The French had also hit upon the idea (soon copied by Spain and Austria) of maintaining a nucleus of permanent regiments, which were expanded into armies by hiring mercenaries when needed, the main types being Swiss (for pikes), German *Landsknechts*, and Italian adventurers. The Swedes and the Dutch, however, employed almost wholly native armies.

If the changes in hand-held firearms were one important development, the improvements in artillery were of equal significance. One reason for Charles VIII's initial predominance in Italy was his possession of the first true field artillery – the creation of Jacques de Genouillac. His guns were lighter than their predecessors; cast in bronze, drawn by horses in tandem (an 18-pounder culverin needed nine), they could keep up with an army on the march. Gun carriages, trunnions for elevation and metal cannonballs were other developments of the greatest significance.

Once again, however, the French surrendered their early lead, this time to the German gun founders, and ultimately to the Spaniards. Types of guns proliferated – the Emperor Charles V tried to restrict them to seven calibres, but Henri II of France's similar restrictions had no effect. Nevertheless, by 1600 the major types had emerged that would last three centuries – culverins, demi-culverins, 6-pounder sakers, smaller falcons, not to forget early forms of mortar, *pedreros* and *grands canons*, which in the extreme case produced 'Mad Margaret', 15 tons dead weight with an 18-foot barrel and a 33-inch

Spanish Infantry Formations

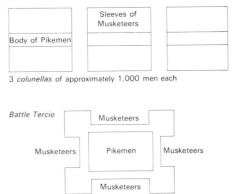

A diagram showing the *colunella* and the battle *tercio*, the basis of Spanish infantry method in the sixteenth century.

The crossbow, key missile weapon of the late Middle Ages. These weapons shot a 'quarrel' or bolt with considerable force, capable of penetrating plate armour. However, they were slow to reload, being capable of no more than one shot a minute. Note the ratchet device for drawing back the bowstring to the notch half-way up the stock. Such a weapon was decidedly inferior to the arquebus, and soon died out in the early 1500s; a detail of The Martyrdom of St Sebastien by Hans Holbein. *Bayerische Staatsgemälde-sammlungen, Munich.*

bore. Artillery remained the perquisite of boards of ordnance and guilds of gunners, and did not form part of the developing regular military hierarchy. Nor had the trains been subdivided into distinct field and siege trains at this stage, but the development of faster-burning coarse powder improved effectiveness from 1530 onwards. These guns were still immensely bulky pieces, difficult to deploy for battle and virtually irrecoverable in the event of a defeat leading to a retreat from the field; however, they were an immense improvement on the massive bombards of the previous age.

Artillery, however, effected a far more significant change as the sixteenth century progressed. The first experiments with the forcing of major engagements, between 1500 and 1525, had led to a more conservative and defensively based approach to war, and the importance of the siege as the central operation of most conflicts became greatly enhanced. The new guns proved so devastating against castle walls that they compelled a major development in the science of both offensive and defensive military engineering.

During the latter years of the previous century, the art of siegecraft had transcended the science of fortification, as the great bombards had torn down the towering walls and towers of castles and towns alike. The fall of Constantinople in 1453 had heralded the end of an age of military engineering as surely as it signalled the demise of the Byzantine Empire.

By the middle of the sixteenth century, designers had revolutionized the aspect of regular fortification. The architects of the Italian Renaissance were the first to conceive designs capable of defying the new power of siege cannon. In place of the ancient walls, they sank their fortifications into the ground; instead of massive piles of masonry, they constructed low-lying earthen banks of immense thickness, sometimes facing them with stone, which were capable of absorbing the hammer blows of solid shot, and of standing the recoil of their own guns; the old circular towers were replaced by four-sided angular works named bastions, which were designed with mathematical precision to command all approaches towards the position, and to eliminate all dead ground at the foot of towers or curtain walls.

These bastions were intended to serve as gun platforms, for the principles were that fire should be met with fire, and that defending fire should be mutually supporting in carefully devised patterns. The many tons of earth needed for the bastions and *enceinte* were provided by digging a deep ditch around the outer side, which was itself protected by a covered way, and by an outlying area of completely open ground (or glacis) leading up to it, a veritable killing ground which could be wholly swept with fire from the defences. To protect lengths of curtain wall or gateways, further recourse was had to *ravelins*, *demi-lunes*, *redans* and hornworks – all these being varieties of defensive works built within the ditch area.

In many cases, these new fortifications were merely added to existing medieval defences, at least in the first instance. In other cases, wealthy monarchs or potentates erected custom-built fortresses of the latest design. That of St Angelo in Rome is one example, as are the artillery castles still standing at Deal and Camber in England, built by Henry VIII before 1540 (the former mounting no less than 145 cannon in successive tiers of circular bastions). In France, the defences of Le Havre, amongst others, date from this period. Circular bastions, however, soon gave way to angular bastions, as any circular design inevitably affords a measure of cover in dead ground to an attacker immediately at the foot of the wall. In the Mediterranean world, the defences of Rhodes (overwhelmed by the Turks in 1522) were less practical and modern than those built by the knights of St John to protect the Castile at Valletta, which proved impregnable. In Holland, the Dutch adopted the Italian bastioned *enceinte*, but, for reasons of economy and speed of construction, built them almost exclusively of packed earth, interseamed with coarse grass and osiers to increase solidity. They

proved highly effective during the dire Eighty Years War (1566–1648), fought to achieve independence from Spanish rule, as earth bastions, properly provided with stout timber palisades, were every bit as difficult to breach or climb as those built of masonry.

These improvements outclassed the power of available siege guns, and the defensive again became the predominant form of war. After 1525, campaigns accordingly became increasingly dominated by sieges. The development produced a number of great masters of siegecraft, including Alexander Farnese, Duke of Parma, and his Dutch opponent, Prince Maurice of Nassau. Moreover, in 1546 the means for scientific alignment of cannon by use of a quadrant and rudimentary ballistic tables was devised by a Venetian mathematician, whilst the German development of siege mortars enabled an attacker to lob simple bombs over the new-type defences to explode within.

A besieging army first built itself a strong defensive position (as the French had done at Pavia–see below) to provide a refuge against relief attempts or sorties by the garrison, creating lines of contravallation and lines of circum-vallation (towards and facing away from the town). Next, after redoubts had been established towards the target, a series of zigzag trenches would be driven forwards, forming a continuous parapet of earth-filled *gabions*. As these approaches crept ever closer, the besiegers' guns and mortars would pound the palisades and defences to distract the garrison and make a breach. The main pieces used for this task would be 24-pounder *demi-canons*. Mines would be driven below any strongpoints, ready to be

above
Detail of a Flemish tapestry, depicting the battle of Pavia, 25 February 1525. The armoured knights of France and their armoured steeds proved no match for the German arquebusiers and Spanish pikemen, harbingers of the new form of warfare in which the foot soldier proved superior to the mounted warrior. The Age of Chivalry was dying; modern warfare was in the process of being born. *Palazzo di Capodimonte, Naples.*

left
The design of fortifications gradually adapted to the menace of heavy cannon. The Castel San Angelo in Rome, guarding the Tiber bridge of that name, was essentially a gun platform superimposed on earlier medieval fortifications.

Guard, blow and open your pan.

Present

Give Fire

Dismount your musket.

Unhook your match.

Return your match

Clear your pan.

Prime your pan.

Shut your pan.

blown when the sap-heads of the trenches approached close to the hostile ditch.

Troops would mass, ready to storm into the town through the breach, but it became unusual for a garrison to hold out to the bitter end. Indeed, the rules of war enjoined that a besieger, put to the cost and effort of a full-scale storm, could, if successful, butcher the defenders with no more ado and wreak havoc on the townsfolk into the bargain. Rather than court this fate, most garrison commanders surrendered on negotiated terms when they judged a storming imminent. Sieges and all the preparatory work involved could take up a great deal of time and effort. Parma, a great master of siegecraft, took fourteen months to capture Antwerp (1585–86), and only succeeded by constructing a fortified bridge over the mouth of the Scheldt. The Dutch had already proved their skill in defence at Alkmaar (1573), when a small patriot garrison held off 16,000 Spanish veterans until the Prince of Orange authorized the breaking of the dykes to flood out the besiegers. The most celebrated siege of this long struggle between Dutch and Spaniards was that of Ostend, which lasted three years (1601–04)–the garrison having access to the sea–and it required all of General Spinola's skill to gain a capitulation, for an aggregate cost of 70,000 casualties.

Prince Maurice of Nassau was famous for lightning blows. In two years (1590–92) he took eight major fortresses in the Low Countries in a series of campaigns that drove the Spaniards from the Waal/Lower Rhine regions. Such a record would not be equalled until the days of Marshal Vauban during the wars of Louis XIV. Using improved methods, Vauban conducted 55 successful sieges, built 33 new fortresses, and improved some 300 more, along the frontiers of

above
The slow rate of fire of the matchlock – one round a minute at the best – was largely due to the complicated reloading drill, which required all of twenty-four separate evolutions. The weapon's effective range was no more than 100 yards, but it was simpler to train raw soldiers in its use than to turn them into adequate bowmen.

right
Hans Holbein's depiction of Swiss infantry, armed with their redoubtable pikes. The *schiltrons*, dense masses of pikemen fielded by the cantons, were often hired by other armies as mercenaries. For many years the Swiss scorned firearms, preferring the 'queen of weapons'. *Kunstmuseum, Basel.*

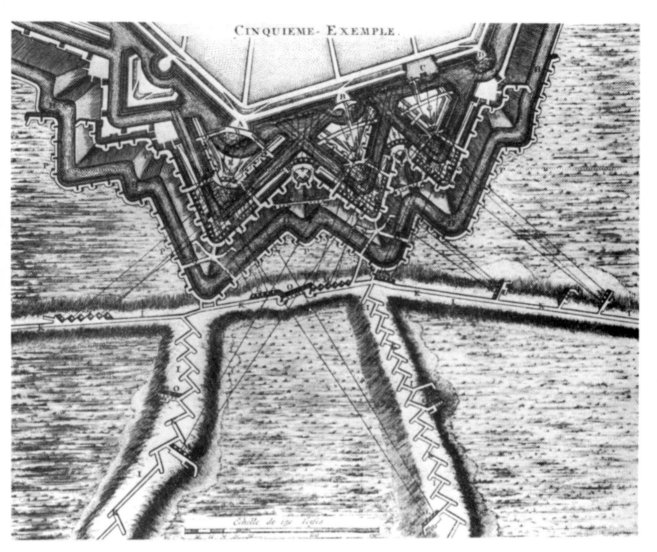

France. This was the golden age of siege warfare.

It would, however, be erroneous to believe that wars diminished notably in ferocity because of the decrease in the number of pitched battles. Spanish soldiers butchered Dutch women and children in the name of a Catholic God, as at Haarlem (1572), and sixty years later the infamous sack of Magdeburg by Count Tilly horrified the conscience of the age. During the Thirty Years War it is estimated that the population of parts of central Germany dropped by a third due to the interaction of sword, famine and pestilence. The days of limited warfare only began in the latter half of the seventeenth century.

Armies were still relatively small, few surpassing 40,000 men in the field, but governments were becoming better organized for their maintenance and support. There was also a small but select number of theorists at work. Machiavelli's *The Prince* and *The Art of War* set new standards of ruthless opportunism. 'Success is based on force', was one of his main sayings. He continually stressed the importance of seeking the decisive battle. 'If a general wins a battle, it cancels all other errors and miscarriages . . . The battle is the end for which all armies are raised.' He also pointed out the perils of defeat: 'But, if you lose it, everything you have achieved previously goes up in smoke.' Machiavelli also stressed the need for armies of citizen-patriots in place of mercenaries, foreseeing the emergence of the nation state, the growing totality of warfare, and the role of the cunning and ruthless Prince. He appreciated that all diplomacy was based on force, and regarded war as a natural condition for mankind. Behind everything he taught lies the principle of expediency, replacing both ethics and morality. The end justifies the means, in politics as in war, and the essential end, as he saw it, was the realization of Italian nationhood. Albrecht Dürer wrote on fortification, Tartaglia on artillery and the Huguenot, de la Noüe, in his *Political and Military Discourses*, clearly defined the dividing line between strategy and tactics. To this extent, therefore, the foundations were being laid for truly professional armies.

The French religious wars saw a considerable

Siegecraft reached a new peak in the second half of the seventeenth century. The French specialist, Vauban, wrote famous treatises on both the attack and defence of fortresses. Note the approach trenches leading to the forward parallel or lateral trench, which holds the siege batteries as the sappers dig forward into the fortress ditches and ravelins. *Traité de l'Attaque des Places.*

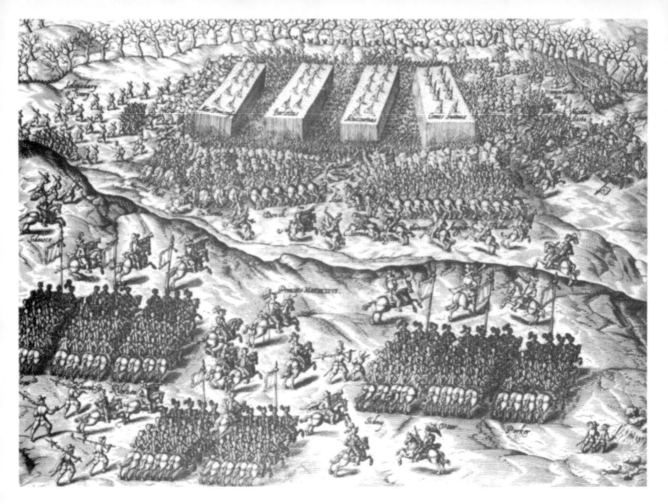

above
Prince Maurice of
Orange leads the Dutch
and their allies against
the Spanish at Zutphen,
22 September 1586.
British Museum, London.

below
Gustavus Adolphus
inspecting his armoury
while a siege is in
progress.

cavalry commander in Henry of Navarre. The typical cavalry trooper was now armed with the horse arquebus, the ancestor of the pistol, which was fired by the action of a wheel-lock. Cavalry formations tended to be used in firepower roles, rank behind rank, the greatest experts being the German *Reiters,* who performed the *caracole* with great regularity. Henry of Navarre, however, retained movement and shock action as the basis of his cavalry manoeuvres, concentrating on breaking the enemy's lines with sword and pistol, using formations six ranks deep. Under

Maurice's inspiration the Dutch horse was greatly improved and won the victories of Turnhout (1597) and Nieuport (1600).

The Spaniards remained the military leaders of Europe, with their Imperialist allies, until the beginning of the seventeenth century. Overseas, small bands of adventurers led by Cortes and Pisarro conquered great empires in Mexico (1518–39) and Peru (1531–33) respectively, with the aid of their firearms and the first horses to appear in Aztec and Inca lands. In Europe, however, the day of Spain was almost over, and a new power was about to emerge, equipped with the first truly modern army. That power was Sweden, led and inspired by Gustavus Adolphus, the 'Lion of the North'.

If Maurice was the first luminary of the 'Military Revolution', with his interest in the mathematical and scientific basis of warfare and his introduction of the first linear tactical system, Gustavus was in effect the father of modern warfare. His reforms covered practically every aspect of seventeenth-century armies, and his influence and example eventually spread to almost every European country. Above all, he concentrated on improved firepower on the battlefield, in terms of both improved weaponry and organization and tactical doctrine. In most

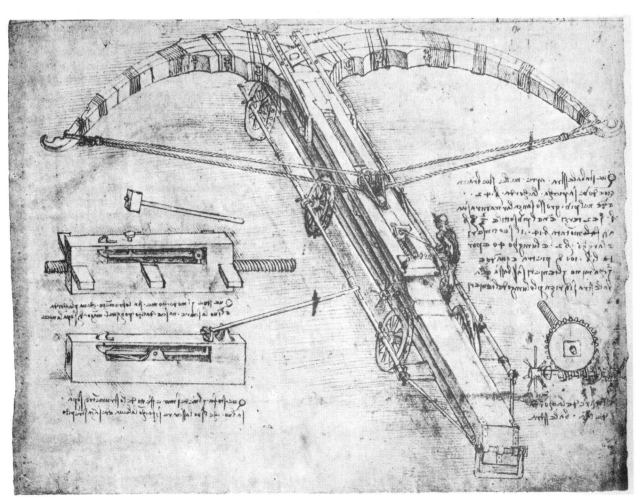

instances he began where Maurice had left off.

The Swedish infantry received an improved, lightened musket fired by the wheel-lock principle and supported by a less cumbersome, dual-purpose rest. The introduction of paper cartridges (ten per man) containing powder charge and shot, was a further refinement, speeding reloading. Gustavus still believed in 'push of pike' (indeed his 'squadrons' contained 192 musketeers to 216 pikemen, whereas the Dutch battalions held 250 and 240 respectively), but his flexible tactics made greater use of firepower potential, and the pikes themselves were reduced to a length of eight feet. Swedish reforms affecting artillery were even more significant. Clear distinctions were drawn between siege, field and regimental guns. Improved casting methods, carriages and trained crews gave Gustavus the most mobile artillery in Europe. By 1630, his train of 80 pieces required only 1,000 horses and 100 wagons, whereas just five years earlier the Swedish train, only 36 cannon strong, had needed over 1,000 horses and 220 carts to support and operate it in the field. Battle tactics were based upon a complex and flexible fire-plan, involving salvo firing by the three permitted calibres, 24-pounders (mostly reserved for sieges), 12-pounders, and small 3-pounders. The last were revolutionary weapons. Developing out of the often hazardous leatherguns (a thin copper barrel wound in rope and plaster within a leather cover), *la pièce suèdoise* of 1630 was an all-metal weapon, firing a 3-pound ball, yet was light enough to be drawn by a single horse or three men. For the first time, cannon could accompany formations anywhere and one was habitually attached to each squadron. It was further provided with pre-packaged rounds, each ball being attached to a box containing the powder charge, and this made possible a rate of fire slightly superior to that of the

average musketeer. Close fire-support of infantry was thus made possible for the first time.

Where cavalry was concerned, Gustavus admired the *élan* of Polish horsemen, and modelled his tactics on the charge rather than the *caracole*. For the attack his horsemen were drawn up three lines deep. Only the first was permitted to employ pistols, before joining the remainder in a charge home with cold steel. Body armour was reduced to a minimum in the interests of mobility, and parties of musketeers and light guns were brigaded with the horse to increase its security.

In terms of organization of fighting formations, Gustavus rejected the *tercio* as too inflexible and cumbersome, and in its place instituted the brigade, formed of three or four squadrons apiece. These formations were subdivided into platoons, and drew up for action six ranks deep: 36 files of pikemen in the centre, supported by two sleeves of 96 musketeers apiece, each with a frontage of 16 men. Gustavus was always experimenting with new tactical combinations, varying the positioning of the elements within the brigade to achieve better firepower and mutual support. As

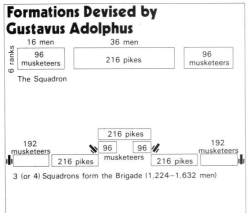

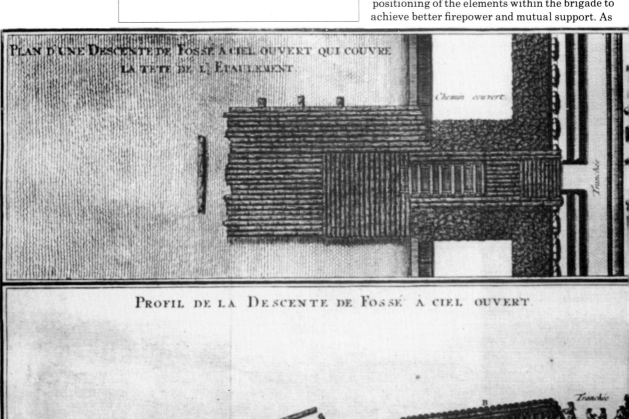

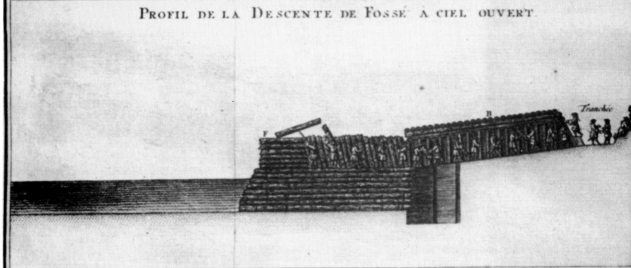

a result, infantry became a force of greater flexibility than ever before. Linear tactics had been born, and from Breitenfeld (1631) onwards they proved superior to the mass formations of conventional warfare.

Gustavus' ideas did not stop with weapons or tactics. He introduced good-quality, standardized uniforms as a means to induce high morale and better health. He insisted on regular pay, provided chaplains, banned women from the camps and imposed a severe but just discipline on officers and men alike. He preferred native troops to mercenaries, and would only employ the best of the latter to fill his ranks. Great attention was paid to supply and reinforcement. The result was a revolutionary army of a calibre that none could match. Aided by Axel Oxenstierna, the patriotic, far-seeing and eminently practical Swedish Chancellor, who virtually governed the state for a dozen years following Gustavus' death at Lutzen in 1632, Gustavus also created a national basis capable of supporting his army. Commerce was expanded, the fiscal system reformed, industries developed, resources exploited. The government operated on a regular annual budget. Manpower for military purposes was based on a national militia formed by conscription; drafts from the regular units were regularly drawn from the militia, for which all able-bodied men of fifteen and over were liable. A strong national *esprit de corps* was the result, and Swedish arms swept to great successes during the Thirty Years War.

Other powers could not surpass this example, but they could emulate it. Cardinal Richelieu launched the reform of the French army by hiring the entire army of Bernard of Saxe-Weimar into the service, and sending young officers to study and serve on the staffs of the great Swedish generals. Applied in turn by Turenne, Condé and Luxembourg, this system of war was one of the factors leading to French martial predominance between 1643 and the 1690s (the skills of Vauban providing the other). Another to copy the example of Sweden was Oliver Cromwell, whose small, élite New Model army of 1645, 21,000 strong, proved more than a match for the less disciplined forces of Charles I and his allies at

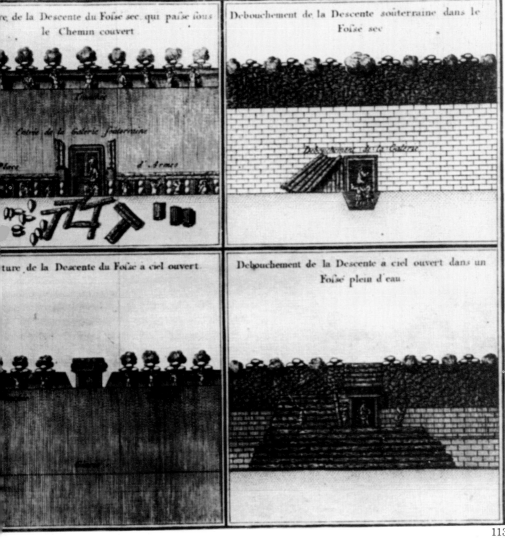

re de la Descente du Fossé sec qui passe sous le Chemin couvert.

Debouchement de la Descente souterraine dans le Fossé sec

ture de la Descente du Fossé a ciel ouvert.

Debouchement de la Descente a ciel ouvert dans un Fossé plein d'eau.

A detail from Vauban's work, *Traité de l'Attaque des Places*, illustrating the critical stage of the descent into the enemy fortress's ditch. Whilst musketeers give covering fire, centre, sappers and miners break through the counterscarp (or outer) wall of the ditch, using underground galleries. This task, conducted very close to the enemy's main positions, was immensely complicated if the ditch was filled with water. Note the use of overhead cover against enemy grenades and mortar bombs; fascines and timber were the main trench materials.

An etching by Dürer of sixteenth-century German cannon. The early French superiority in this field was soon surrendered to the German gunfounders. Note the trail attached to the fore-carriage by a spike secured by a restraining chain; also the form of elevating gear and the lifting handles above the trunnions. Such guns could weigh several tons, and often broke down on the rough roads of the period. Although such weapons restricted the movement of armies, they also spelt the doom of the walled city or castle. *Kupferstichkabinet, Staatliche Museen Preussischer Kulturbesitz, Berlin.*

opposite page
Plundering of a Convoy by Vrancx. An all too typical scene of the Thirty Years War, when mercenary armies ran riot over much of central Europe, earning the military profession a debased name. *Bayerische Staatsgemäldesammlungen, Munich.*

Prince Maurice of Orange (1567–1625) the principal military inspiration in the struggle led by the Dutch Protestants against the power of Catholic Spain during the latter half of the Eighty Years War. He served the United Provinces as Stadtholder from 1585 until his death. A master tactician specializing in lightning attacks, he was also a great expert at siege warfare. Together with Gustavus Adolphus of Sweden, he was the dominant influence on the development of modern land warfare.

such battles as Naseby and Dunbar, and ultimately defeated a Spanish army at the battle of the Dunes near Dunkirk (1658). But the experience of the English Civil War, though grim enough, was only a microcosm of the continental wars of the same period.

This chapter ends with long years of French military superiority, based upon larger armies than had been seen for many ages. Louis XIV commanded 400,000 men in his various armies, and enjoyed fifty years of almost unalloyed success. His early wars were characterized by campaigns of manoeuvre punctuated by frequent minor actions; from 1672 ponderous campaigns based upon sieges became more frequent as Louis pursued his ambitions by the ruthless combination of diplomacy and armed might. Latterly, his generals proved less able than Condé or Turenne, the principles of Sweden were forgotten or misapplied, and it was left to Marlborough, Eugène of Savoy and Charles XII to redevelop Gustavus' doctrines.

Nevertheless, France's contribution to military administration was vast by any standard. Le Tellier and Louvois (1641–91) did for the French army what the great Colbert achieved for the French navy. They instituted rigid centralization under civilian ministers, imposed close inspections of formations to enforce minimum standards (the name of one inspector-general, Martinet, has entered the English as well as the French language), and closely supervised the allocation and expenditure of public funds. However, they never defeated corruption or banned the sale of commissions, and the strictly worded regulations were often flouted in practice. Nevertheless, the supply system based upon civilian *intendants de l'armée* and frontier depots proved effective.

Armies had come a long way since 1494. Modern warfare had been born.

The Battle of Pavia, 25 February 1525

The long rivalry between France and Spain for mastery in north Italy came to a grim climax north of Pavia in 1525. King Francis I, with a mixed Franco-Swiss force of some 28,000 men and 53 cannon, was besieging the city (garrisoned by 5,000 Imperialists), when Ferdinando Francesco

above
The great siege of
Ostend, 1601–04, was
really more of a land
blockade than an all-out
investment, for the Dutch
Sea Beggars were
generally in contact with
the garrison from the
North Sea. The scene
shows the bustling
activity in the Spanish
camp of the besiegers,
whose commander,
Archduke Albert of
Austria, is shown left
foreground. Note the
type of tents, the military
transport, and the
activities of the sutlers
and *vivandières*. Over the
three years, the Dutch
lost some 30,000 men, the
Spaniards perhaps twice
as many, the great killer
being disease engendered
in the insanitary trenches
and camps. *The Prado,
Madrid.*

right
Gustavus Adolphus at
the head of the Swedish
cavalry at Lutzen. His
death in action was a
severe setback for the
Protestant cause in the
Thirty Years War.
*Statens Museum for
Kunst, Copenhagen.*

above
The battle of Pavia,
25 February 1525. Note
the diminution in the
amount of body armour,
and the weaponry of the
early sixteenth century.
*Museo di Capodimonte,
Naples.*

left
The last flowering of
chivalry in the late
Middle Ages in France
was marked by struggles
for power between the
great magnates and their
supporters, who were
generally stronger than
their unfortunate
monarchs. At the battle
of Nancy, 5 January 1477,
Charles the Bold of
Burgundy was defeated
and killed by a Swiss
army which had invaded
Burgundian territory
during the protracted
struggles for control of
parts of Burgundy and
Alsace. Louis XI of
France financed the
Swiss, whose reputation
for invincibility and
ferocity was at this time
second only to that of the
Turks. *Musée Dobrée,
Nantes.*

Part of a series of paintings depicting the *Triumphs
of Maximilian*. Holy Roman Emperor from 1493 to
1519, Maximilian I was involved in incessant wars
with France and Italy. Trains of artillery were
becoming highly organized and well equipped by this
period; here we see several types of equipment
besides a massive siege gun. The horses are
harnessed in pairs; in much of Europe they were
placed in tandem until well into the eighteenth
century. *Graphische Sammlung Albertina, Vienna.*

d'Avalos arrived with 23,000 German, Spanish and Italian troops and 17 guns, to attempt its relief. Ferdinando's army was on the verge of mutiny over pay, and the entrenched French camp was dauntingly strong, but he had no alternative but to force battle on his superior opponent.

Realizing that his best chance of success lay in luring the French to fight outside their position, the Imperialist commander decided to set a trap. During the stormy night of 24 February the army marched along the eastern side of the enclosed Mirabelle Park and made three breaches through the wall. Through this his army filed, and by dawn was drawing up within. Alerted by their pickets, the French army soon came pouring into the park, led by their 2,000 light cavalry accompanied by small cannon. Behind them advanced 5,000 German halberdiers drawn up in a vast square, together with a party of the Swiss contingent. By this time Ferdinando had completed his array, placing his heavy armoured cavalry on his western flank near the River Vernavola, three squares of Spanish and German troops in his centre, and his light horse on his left, with several thousand skirmishers deployed to the fore of the line.

Without hesitation, the French light guns opened fire on the Imperialist squares (which lay on their faces for cover), whilst the lance-wielding light cavalry charged for one of the gaps in the wall through which the Imperialist

artillery was still being moved. Simultaneously, Francis I led his heavy cavalry to attack the Imperialist cuirassiers, whom he repulsed with some loss.

It appeared that both flanks of the Imperial army were about to give way, but the initiative was regained by Ferdinando when 1,500 Spanish arquebusiers, with the famed Spanish pikemen

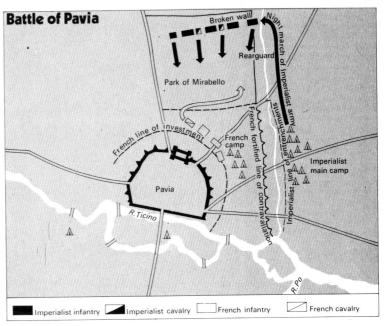

Battle of Pavia

Imperialist infantry   Imperialist cavalry   French infantry   French cavalry

Axel Oxenstierna (1583–1654), Swedish statesman and administrator. As Lord High Chancellor, he provided much of the drive behind the Swedish war effort. Like the later French Revolutionary figure, Lazare Carnot, he deserved the title, 'Organizer of Victory'. Like Carnot, he lived to see his life's work in near ruins. *Kungl Vitterhets Historie och Antikvitets Akademien, Stockholm.*

Gottfried Pappenheim (1594–1632), a celebrated cavalry general, who served under Wallenstein's command.

Albrecht von Wallenstein (1599–1641), perhaps the dominant figure in the Thirty Years War before the Swedish intervention.

in support, were rushed from the centre to take the near-victorious French *gendarmerie* in the rear. This move coincided with a rally by the Imperialist horse, and the French cavalry were entirely routed. Seeing this, the 5,000 German troops in French pay surged forward against the Imperialist centre, only to be encircled by two formations of Habsburg halberdiers, numbering 12,000 in all, who proceeded to hack them to pieces. Similar treatment was meted out to the Swiss in turn.

Profiting from these distractions, the garrison of Pavia sortied out in strength to fall upon the remaining Swiss and Italian troops holding the siege lines. After scattering these weak contingents, the garrison fell on the rear of the exhausted survivors of the French army.

It is estimated that in this two-hour engagement some 550 Imperialists were killed, but the French lost probably as many as 13,000 killed and half as many prisoners, together with all their guns. This disaster (which included the capture of Francis I) ended French pretensions to power in northern Italy and inaugurated the long period of Spanish and Habsburg control of the region.

The tactical flexibility of this battle highlights the importance of infantry in an offensive role and the relegation of the cavalry to a relatively secondary position. The Spanish infantry's firepower had proved notably superior.

The Battle of Lutzen, 16 November 1632

After his partial conquest of Saxony during the summer of 1632, the Imperialist general, Count Wallenstein, decided that serious operations were over for the year, and ordered his men into winter quarters. He established his headquarters at Leipzig and sent a large detachment of troops under Count Pappenheim to Halle, more than a day's march away.

Such a move was exactly what Gustavus Adolphus, leader of the northern Protestants, had been anticipating. He at once ordered his 14,000 foot and 5,000 horse to march on Leipzig from Naumburg, intending to catch Wallenstein's Catholic army scattered. That experienced commander, however, managed to gather much of his army before the blow fell and, marching north of the city, he selected a strong position facing south and overlooking the road the Swedes were reported to be using. The front extended for some 3,000 yards, from a canal to Lutzen, further protected by marshes, whilst the highroad's ditches to the fore gave good cover for the musketeers. To the rear ran the road to Halle, from which Wallenstein had summoned aid, but at the outset his force numbered only 8,000 infantry and 4,000 cavalry. However, his position was strong and would compel the Swedes to mount a frontal attack. Accordingly he drew up four *tercios* in oblong formation, pikemen in the centre (ten ranks deep), arquebusiers at the angles, and seven cannon to the fore of the

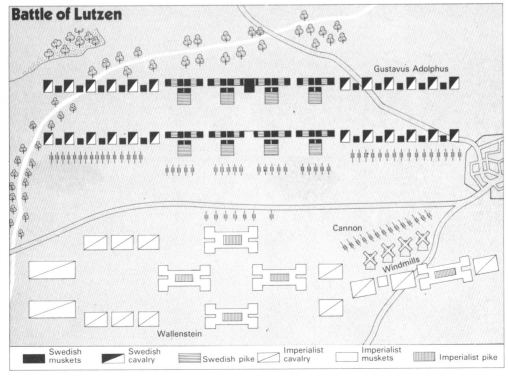

Battle of Lutzen

Gustavus Adolphus

Cannon

Windmills

Wallenstein

| ▆ Swedish muskets | ◢ Swedish cavalry | ▤ Swedish pike | ◿ Imperialist cavalry | ▭ Imperialist muskets | ▥ Imperialist pike |

123

army. Near Lutzen he drew up his fifth *tercio*, some cavalry and fourteen guns on Windmill Knoll. On his left he placed much of his cavalry, but relied on Pappenheim to reinforce this flank, which constituted a weakness.

Gustavus appeared on the afternoon of the 15th, after being delayed by an Imperialist force on the River Rippach. This delay gave Wallenstein time to summon aid from Pappenheim, although this could not reach him until the next day. The Swedes drew up for battle in two lines. In the centre of each were four brigades of foot, and on the flanks were two equal bodies of cavalry, supported by interleaved small detachments of musketeers. Forty light regimental cannon were divided between the wings, and the twenty larger pieces were established before the centre. As the hour was so advanced, however, and as dusk was falling, the main engagement had to be postponed until the following morning. Every hour that passed was to Wallenstein's advantage.

The delays continued even the next morning – a thick mist shrouded the battlefield until 11 am, and it was only at that hour that Gustavus ordered the advance into action. His aim was to turn the weak Imperialist left, where a gap existed, and so stalwart were his men's efforts that by midday it seemed they were on the point of succeeding. At this moment, however, Pappenheim rode up with his cavalry from Halle and managed to check the Swedish advance, although Pappenheim himself fell mortally wounded. This was the signal for a near panic in Wallenstein's army, and a Swedish success again seemed close. It was thwarted, however, by the redescent of the fog, as the Swedish centre, with superb discipline and tactical coordination, swept over the road, clearing the ditches, and captured the seven guns drawn up beyond.

On Wallenstein's right, meanwhile, the forces on Windmill Knoll were more than holding their own against Bernard of Saxe-Weimar and the Swedish left. The firing of Lutzen forced the

The battle of Lutzen, 16 November 1632. This struggle ended in a notable Swedish success, but was, in fact, mostly fought in a dense fog. However, the death of Gustavus Adolphus in action proved a grave blow to Swedish long-term chances in the war. This picture gives some idea of the appearance of the Imperialist *tercios*, foreground centre, and the Swedish brigades, background centre. Cavalry still operated in dense formations. An engraving by Matthaus Merian.

Swedes to mount a direct frontal attack on the knoll, and the cannon took a heavy toll. Gustavus Adolphus, who until this time had been commanding on the left, brought over a cavalry regiment to support his subordinate and charged. Almost instantly the King of Sweden was killed.

The Swedish dismay can be imagined, but the thickening fog earned a respite which enabled Bernard to reorder the left wing and assume control of the whole battle. Meanwhile, the Imperialist general, Piccolomini, was leading a series of charges with heavy cavalry to re-establish Wallenstein's left wing–with such good effect that he rescued the seven captured cannon and regained the line of the road.

Thus at 2 pm the Swedish fortunes seemed at a low ebb, but Bernard of Saxe-Weimar, against the advice of his staff, decided to mount one last desperate attack against Windmill Knoll. By 4 pm this attempt had succeeded despite heavy losses, taking the main Imperialist battery, and only stout fighting by the *tercios* prevented a Swedish breakthrough in force. So matters rested at 5 pm when the arrival of Pappenheim's infantry redressed the balance. Wallenstein, however, afflicted by gout, had decided to retire on Halle, and proceeded to extricate his men. The Swedes were too exhausted to pursue, and were out of both ammunition and reserves. They took all the Imperialist guns and baggage, and had inflicted possibly 10,000 casualties for a loss of some 7,000.

Although tactically indecisive, this battle illustrates the contrast between Swedish and Imperialist armies. Strategically, moreover, it had very important effects, as it totally disrupted the Imperialist strategy, which was to drive a corridor between the Swedish field forces and their Baltic bases. Nevertheless, the death of Gustavus Adolphus was a major setback for the Protestant cause.

right
The siege of Vienna,
1683. This was probably
the most famous siege
operation of the century.
The Turks, hitherto with
an unsullied reputation
for success in siegecraft,
were defeated. Vienna
was saved by the arrival
of King John III Sobieski
of Poland and a multi-
national Christian army.
His victory below the
Kahlenberg on
12 September ended the
two-month siege. This
setback marked the
checking of the Moslem
tide in the Danube.
*Historisches Museum der
Stadt Wien.*

below
The battle of Pavia,
25 February 1525. The
destruction of the French
army of King Francis I
inaugurated the period
of Spanish control of
Italy. *Kunsthistorisches
Museum, Vienna.*

THE EIGHTEENTH CENTURY
The Age of Limited Warfare

At the beginning of the eighteenth century European attitudes towards warfare were again changing. The religious partisanship that had so embittered the Thirty Years War had largely subsided, save in areas affected by the Habsburg-Turkish struggles, and the dawn of the Age of Reason urged the virtues of military moderation on rulers and generals alike. Nationalism in its true sense still lay ahead, although the desperate French war effort after 1709, and the conduct of Sweden throughout the Great Northern War (1701–22) against Russia, were early manifestations of wars involving whole populations, as opposed to dynastic struggles waged between monarchs. In the decades intervening between the eras of religious and national wars, the conduct of military operations became limited in the sense that the objectives were usually restricted to territorial, commercial or colonial ambitions. This did not mean that there were fewer wars, but it did encourage humanitarian and more moderate attitudes towards the problems associated with warfare. There were still occasional atrocities–as in Marlborough's ravaging of Bavaria in July 1704, or Louis XIV's two devastations of the Palatinate–but there were fewer than in former times.

Many factors contributed to the limitation of warfare at this time. In addition to the psychological revulsion from military excesses, there were the physical limitations–above all the appalling state of the roads and the shortage of fodder and fresh rations during the winter months–which made it extremely difficult for the slowly growing armies and their increasingly heavy cannon to move operationally between October and April. The campaigning season, therefore, lasted only six months a year. A further restraining factor was the social structure of the period, closely reflected in the military hierarchy, where high command was often regarded as the perquisite of the nobility alone, a class still imbued with a few traces of medieval chivalry. Only artillery and engineer officers received any formal training; the rest learnt the 'bless'd trade' literally 'at the cannon's mouth', so amateurism was not unknown. The rank and file came from the lowest strata of society, kept in some form of order by draconian discipline, but liable to desert or loot, given a chance. Conscription in its true sense still lay in the future, and armies were made up of 'volunteers' from the depressed classes. As Defoe observed, '. . . the poor thieve, turn soldier or starve'. There was also, however, a leavening of adventurers and professional mercenaries who served alongside the freed criminals and depressed peasantry, but the military life was far from popular and this made recruiting difficult. These factors had the effect of keeping field armies relatively small, averaging between 40,000 and 70,000, and in consequence the direct effects of wars left the greater part of the populations of Europe comparatively undisturbed.

The inadequate administrative and supply systems of the age further checked the intensity of warfare. Most armies relied on pre-stocked magazines, and were tied to the distances they could carry their bread, as the troops could rarely be trusted to forage for themselves unless they were rigidly supervised on account of the danger of mass desertions. Field armies could rarely move for more than four consecutive days without halting to bake. The relatively low state of agricultural productivity at this time further restricted the size and scope of armies in the field.

The Netherlands were the scene of many campaigns because of their relatively high agricultural yield, their strategical position between France and the German states, and their rich towns and well-developed waterways. The region's many protective fortresses, however, made it a theatre of limited, inconclusive war–dominated by sieges and manoeuvres. Elsewhere in Europe, warfare centred around the Po, Danube and Drave valleys, the hot plains of eastern Spain or the great marshes and waterways of Poland and western Russia.

Certain advances in military science encouraged this form of largely defensive warfare. The artillery remained very cumbersome and short-ranged until the 1770s, and its impact as an offensive weapon was largely vitiated by the work of Vauban and his military engineers. The measure of impregnability that the 'three orders' of military architecture conferred on fortresses and towns compelled generals to concentrate on

A map showing the defence fortresses on the western sector of the north-east frontier of France. Two hundred years later, many of these place names were to become familiar to the Allied and German soldiers of the First World War.

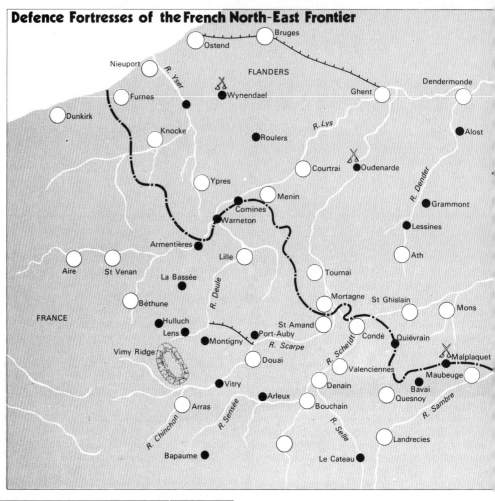

Defence Fortresses of the French North-East Frontier

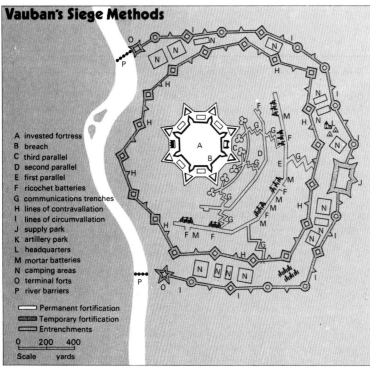

Vauban's Siege Methods

A invested fortress
B breach
C third parallel
D second parallel
E first parallel
F ricochet batteries
G communications trenches
H lines of contravallation
I lines of circumvallation
J supply park
K artillery park
L headquarters
M mortar batteries
N camping areas
O terminal forts
P river barriers

☐ Permanent fortification
▧ Temporary fortification
☐ Entrenchments

0   200   400
Scale   yards

sieges and the operations in support or in relief of them. In the simplest of terms, Vauban's system was based upon enfilading fire, defence in depth, and an aggressive conduct of the defence. At the same time he perfected the techniques of the siege itself by regularizing the laborious sapping forward by means of approach and parallel trenches, and the clever siting of batteries and mines. Vauban's celebrated volumes became essential reading for all senior officers. All-out stormings were discouraged; capitulations on terms after forty-eight or more days became the norm. Thus, sieges came to dominate European warfare.

Taken together, these factors resulted in a marked limitation of war. The ultimate aims of most generals were taken up with the disruption of the foe's communications and the capture of his cities, rather than with the destruction of his field armies. Pitched battles were almost deliberately avoided as being too expensive in irreplaceable manpower and material, and campaigns often hinged upon elaborate manoeuvres designed to compel the foe's retirement from some strategically important or economically vital area.

In the years following Rocroi (1643), Turenne

The Vauban fortress of Mont-Louis, as it appears today. Note the successive lines of low-profile defences–ditches, *ravelins* and bastions. It still serves as a French army barracks. *Yan, Toulouse.*

below
Key
A bastions–artillery positions situated to sweep the *glacis*
B ditch–stone-faced
C sally-port bridges (temporary)
D *demi-Lune*–designed to cover the wall connecting two bastions (or curtain)
E *ravelin*–designed to cover the vulnerable angle of a bastion
G covered way and traverse–used to protect the ditch and enfilade the *glacis*
H *glacis*–an area of levelled, sloping ground, affording the clear field of fire
I counterscarp gallery–designed to cover the ditch and for the opening of mining galleries
J palisades–of sharpened stakes; used when the ditch was unflooded.

taught Europe how to fight wars of movement and small engagements with the minimum cost, but in the hands of mediocre French commanders his concepts were replaced by a hidebound approach leading to abortive forms of warfare. Only a handful of great leaders of the calibre of the Duke of Marlborough, Prince Eugène of Savoy, Marshal Villars and (later) de Saxe, Charles XII of Sweden and Frederick the Great of Prussia, were willing or able to break away from the deadening military customs of the day and restore some measure of activity, movement and decision to the conduct of war. For the rest, it was an age of mediocrities.

On the field of battle, success or defeat rested on two chief factors: discipline and firepower. Discipline implies control, and Marlborough's trusted aides and staff were trained to serve as his eyes amidst the smoke of battle, enabling him 'to ride the whirlwind and unleash the storm'. By 1700, the standard infantry firearm in the English forces was King William's Land Musket, later replaced by the famous Brown Bess, both of them far more reliable flintlock muskets than the cumbersome matchlock they replaced.

A second important development was the growing employment of the socket bayonet. The

Fortification

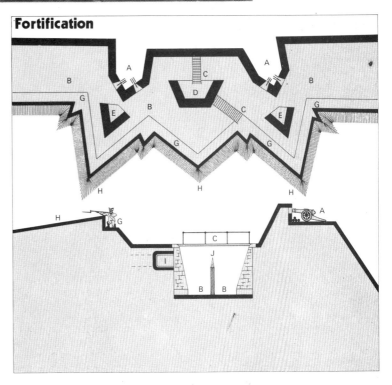

English and Dutch were the first to be completely re-equipped with this refinement of the earlier plug and ring bayonets which had not been successful, particularly the former which fitted into the musket's muzzle and thus made firing impossible while it was fixed. The French were rather more reluctant to abandon their cumbersome eighteen-foot pikes than their adversaries, and although these had all but disappeared from the battlefield by 1703, the heirs of Turenne clung on to the outmoded five- or six-rank-deep linear formations which had won France fifty years of martial predominance. The main effect of the improved musket was a higher firepower potential. Under Marlborough, the English army was trained to make the fullest use of this factor. His line infantry fired in three groups of six platoons instead of files, ranks, companies or whole battalions, as was still the practice of the French and their allies. This tactical innovation (in fact a development of Swedish practice in the 1630s) gave the English the advantage of a higher and more accurate rate, based upon more effective fire control by the platoon officers and sergeants. The true significance of the socket bayonet was that it made every man capable of using a musket, enabling him both to fire and defend himself in hand-to-hand fighting without delay. Once again, it was the English who made the fullest use of this development to adopt a more aggressive

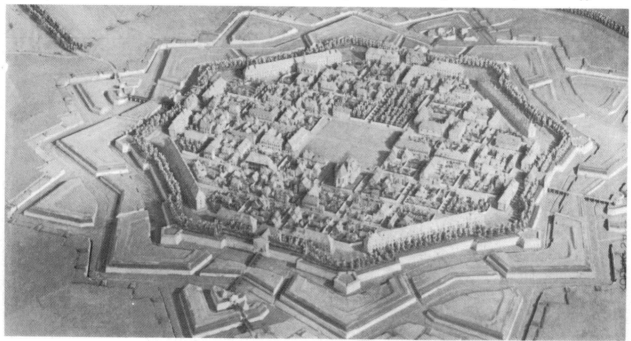

far left
Henri de la Tour
d'Auvergne, Vicomte
Turenne (1611–75), one of
the greatest soldiers of
the first half of Louis
XIV's reign. He helped
train the young John
Churchill, later the
scourge of the French
army as the Duke of
Marlborough.

left
Sebastien le Prestre,
Seigneur de Vauban
(1633–1707), master of
siege warfare. He
published three
celebrated volumes which
have become classics:
*Traité de l'attaque des
Places, De la défense des
Places* and *Traité des
Mines*. His influence on
fortifications lasted until
at least 1870. He also
wrote a penetrating
analysis of the French
economy. *Projet d'une
Dixme Royale*, which
earned Louis XIV's
displeasure.

and flexible use of the infantry arm on the field of battle. Thus was born the modern method of 'fire and movement'.

The French employment of infantry remained conventional. Its primary role continued to be the provision of a firm base for the cavalry and a force for the occupation of ground. This mainly static role contrasted most strongly with the employment of Lord Cutts' battalions at Blenheim in 1704 (see below), who contained several times their own number within Blenheim village, enabling Marlborough to mass superior forces against the French centre, ready for the *coup de grâce*.

New weapons and tactics inevitably required new formations; the deep, phalanx-like *tercios* of Lutzen did not survive the supersession of the pike on the battlefield. In their place came linear formations between three and six lines deep, and the development of the hollow square to repel the charges of cavalry. Strict drill and firm fire discipline made a redoubtable foe out of the English foot, and it was with good reason that Louis XIV specifically enjoined Marshal Villeroi 'to have special attention to such part of the line which will endure the first shock of the English troops', although in the event it was the adoption of this advice that substantially contributed to the loss of the battle of Ramillies (1706). Linear tactics were wholly designed to

far left
John Churchill, Duke of
Marlborough (1649–
1722), arguably the
greatest soldier produced
by the British Isles.

left
Prince Eugène of Savoy,
listed by Napoleon
amongst his seven great
commanders of all time.

exploit this new, far more deadly firepower of the infantry. However, the development of formalized tactics to meet the new conditions undoubtedly restricted the potentialities of most field armies, and the casualty rates soared alarmingly. Armies still fought in elaborate battle arrays which consumed precious time when being drawn up, and as a result battles could often only take place by what amounted to the mutual consent of both commanders. Armies were particularly hard to deploy, as no formation higher than the brigade was in existence until the latter half of the eighteenth century. The heavier losses likely to be incurred further encouraged great caution, and no small part of Marlborough's success was due to his ability to force action upon an unwilling foe by means of rapid marches under cover of darkness, leaving the enemy with no option but to accept battle. The rapid advance from Lessines to Oudenarde in 1708 is one example: 'If they are there, the Devil must have carried them – such marching is impossible'. This was Marshal Vendôme's reaction to reports of the Allied army's rule-defying crossing of the Scheldt on 11 July.

The administration of most eighteenth-century

Infantry Battle Tactics

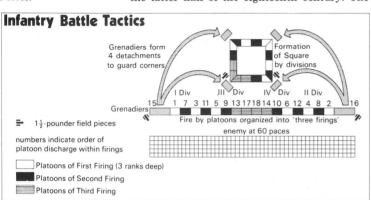

Grenadiers form 4 detachments to guard corners

Formation of Square by divisions

I Div III Div IV Div II Div

15 1 7 3 11 5 9 13 17 18 14 10 6 12 4 8 2 16
Grenadiers

Fire by platoons organized into 'three firings'
enemy at 60 paces

= 1½-pounder field pieces

numbers indicate order of platoon discharge within firings

☐ Platoons of First Firing (3 ranks deep)
■ Platoons of Second Firing
▤ Platoons of Third Firing

Cavalry Tactics

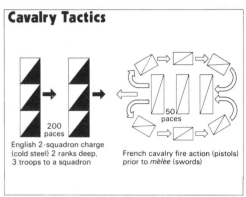

200 paces

50 paces

English 2-squadron charge (cold steel) 2 ranks deep. 3 troops to a squadron

French cavalry fire action (pistols) prior to *mêlée* (swords)

European armies left much to be desired, and nothing is more revealing in this respect than the contrast between the French and English armies. In 1704, Tallard lost one third of his force through desertion and sickness as he marched to reinforce Bavaria, and at Blenheim a part of his cavalry was rendered ineffective by an epidemic of glanders. Marlborough's longer and more difficult march from Flanders the same year presents a vivid contrast. By dint of careful advance planning, ranging from the opening of new lines of communication up the River Main, to the provision of spare boots and saddlery at Heidelberg, the Duke covered some 250 miles in under five weeks, passing across the front of powerful enemy forces with the aid of feints and deceptions, and brought his men to the Danube fit enough to fight the hard struggle for the Schellenburg Heights. His concern for his men was one reason for the high morale prevalent in forces under his command, (the men nicknamed him 'the old corporal'), and this in turn enabled him to make calls on their endurance, when need arose, that few contemporaries dared contemplate. Unfortunately the same high standards were not to be found in the English forces serving in Spain under Peterborough, Galway and Stanhope; terrible privations did much to undermine

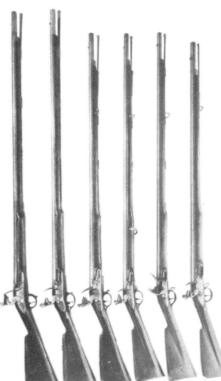

left
Examples of the Brown Bess musket, the standard British infantry weapon from about 1720. Firing a one-ounce ball perhaps twice or three times a minute, its range was about 250 yards, although for accurate shooting not more than 100 yards was attempted. *Tower of London Armouries.*

below
The battle of the Dvina, 9 July 1701, one of Charles XII's notable victories over the Russians. The Swedish infantry, left, some in four-deep line and others in square formations, are routing a Russian cavalry attack in the foreground and discouraging the Russian infantry in the centre, who are beginning to thin out and flee. *Drottlingholm Castle, Sweden.*

The battle of Wynendael, September 1708, from another of the Blenheim Palace tapestries, which provide us with the best detail of early eighteenth-century armies. The light, two-wheeled supply wagons were introduced by Marlborough in his capacity as Master-General of the Board of Ordnance. The horses were still harnessed to them in tandem. The Sergeant of the Royal Scots (the 1st Regiment of Foot) is armed with a halberd, with which he is encouraging the civilian driver to continue to do his duty whilst the action rages in the background. *Blenheim Palace.*

their effectiveness, as did the hostility of the population.

Although infantry was becoming steadily more important, the cavalry retained its ancient prestige. The French continued to regard their mounted arm as a sophisticated instrument of firepower, employing pistols or carbines, but Marlborough and Eugène favoured the doctrines of Gustavus Adolphus and Rupert of the Rhine, and insisted on the shock tactics of weight and cold steel. Cavalry charging home at the fast trot, properly supported by infantry and guns, clinched each of Marlborough's victories, and substantial numbers of horsemen were habitually retained as a reserve for the *coup de grâce*. Body armour, however, was fast becoming obsolete.

All guns were heavy and bulky, and little distinguished them in terms of accuracy or range. In all armies the trains constituted a vast and complex organization, embracing engineers, pioneers and munition services besides gunners, all owing loyalty to quasi-independent departments like the English Board of Ordnance rather than to the army authorities. As Master-General of the Ordnance from 1702 on, Marlborough

happily could ensure that these functions were properly coordinated and carried out, and he took great pains to gain increased efficiency—even siting his batteries in person, and insisting on the adoption of a light, two-wheel munitions cart to improve mobility. Of great tactical significance was the practice of attaching two light guns to each infantry battalion to provide close support. On the whole, the French made less imaginative use of their guns, but the massacre of the Dutch Guards at Malplaquet (1709) was achieved by a well-sited battery.

With a maximum effective range of little over 1,000 yards, a profusion of types, and their deadening weight, which restricted an army's advance to at best ten miles a day, the guns were a considerable liability on campaign. Entrusted to civilian contracted drivers, and drawn by hired horses in tandem, they often caused delays on the march. The situation began to improve with the foundation of what were to become regular regiments of artillery from 1716 onwards –a step that ensured proper integration within the armies–but many problems remained intractable until the 1770s.

By the time of Frederick the Great, several

major improvements had been incorporated into European armies. An iron ramrod for the musket replaced the fragile wooden ones of yesteryear. Artillery horses were now harnessed in pairs, better gun limbers were introduced, and, after the Seven Years War, the reforming work of the Frenchman, de Gribeauval, would substantially reduce the weight and number of types of field artillery. Greater use of horse artillery and howitzers also developed.

In the realms of organization and military theory, Marshal Maurice de Saxe experimented with *légions* comprising detachments of all arms, and this foreshadowed the development of mixed divisions and *corps d'armée*. His writings, *Mes Rêveries*, were a substantial advance on earlier military treatises, which were little more than complicated drill books.

Frederick the Great enjoyed one great advantage over both Marlborough and de Saxe; as ruler of an autocratic state, he could enforce the implementation of his decisions. His reign marks the emergence of both the Prussian state and Prussian militarism. Frederick was an opportunistic strategist, as he demonstrated when he seized Silesia in 1740. In fact his high-handed action in

'sowing the wind' caused him to 'reap the whirlwind'. Frederick was virtually declared an outlaw, and both he and Prussia were fortunate to survive (with British financial aid from 1757) the international reaction to his original occupation of Habsburg territory. Most of his wars were therefore fought against large coalitions, and he demonstrated the use of interior lines to perfection during the Seven Years War (1756–63). Faced by French, Swedish, Russian, Austrian and Saxon armies, he was able to reduce the odds against him by dealing rapid blows at each enemy in turn (as in 1757), and Prussia's survival is one of the finest sustained achievements in military history.

Four principles dominated his military philosophy, and were embodied in his *Instructions* issued in 1748. First came discipline of the most rigid type. 'The men must fear their officers more than the enemy.' Second, he placed great stress on subsistence. 'Understand that the foundation of an army is the belly', he wrote, devoting much space to the provisioning of depots, safeguarding of convoys, and to the disruption of enemy communications. Third, he taught the importance of offensive action. 'War is only

Cavalry preparing fascines of branches and brushwood. Some horsemen still wore vestiges of armour (breast- and backplates), see centre, but most wore coats. Fascines were needed in vast quantities during sieges for lining trenches. Flemish tapestry *c*. 1720. *Victoria and Albert Museum, London.*

right
Frederick the Great, King of Prussia. Not a soldier by inclination, a combination of circumstances and his own policies doomed Prussia to a series of huge wars against surrounding enemies between 1740 and 1763. However, his superb military gifts brought victory to his arms on many occasions, and earned him the accolade of Napoleon.

below
Maurice de Saxe, Marshal of France, depicted at the battle of Laffeldt, 1747. His military innovations, including his *légion*, were forward-looking developments, and his book, *Mes Rêveries*, set new standards in writing on the art and science of warfare. *Versailles*.

left

The siege of Malta, 1565, ended in the defeat of militant Islam by Grand Master de la Valette and his knights of the Order of St John. In the long siege, however, the Turks had a number of successes, including the capture of Fort St Elmo, depicted here, on 23 June. Note particularly the Janissaries in their tall, conical caps. These élite troops of the Sultan, originally recruited from Christian slaves, bore an immense reputation for ferocity and courage. *National Maritime Museum, Greenwich.*

below
A series of panels depicting stages of the battle of Blenheim, 13 August 1704. *National Army Museum, London.*

The Lion of the North, Gustavus Adolphus, King of Sweden, portrayed by Jean Walther at the battle of Breitenfeld, 1631. The Swedish intervention in the Thirty Years War rallied the flagging Protestant cause, and marked the emergence of Sweden as an important power. Her remodelled army set new standards and became the model for most European armies of the seventeenth century. *Musées de la Ville de Strasbourg.*

The battle of Fontenoy, 11 May 1745, by Lenfant.
The victor, Marshal de Saxe, reports to King
Louis XV at the climax of the battle. His opponent,
the Duke of Cumberland, several times came close
to victory, but French guns, placed in concealed
redoubts, clinched victory. *Versailles*.

above

A group of Prussian soldiers *c.* 1726. Drums and fifes were still the prevailing forms of martial music, but the former also served to transmit orders during the din of battle.

left

Rossbach, 1757, was one of Frederick the Great's most dramatic successes. He routed a large French and Allied army under Soubise. It would be forty years before French arms regained their reputation. The print shows the Prussians taking the massive French columns in flank, whilst their head is pulverized by the Prussian cavalry under Seydlitz.

141

The principles of interior and exterior lines. Frederick the Great was a past master at the use of interior lines, as he demonstrated during the Seven Years War.

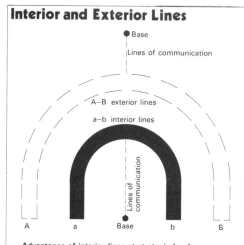

Interior and Exterior Lines

● Base

Lines of communication

A–B exterior lines

a–b interior lines

Lines of communication

A   a   Base   b   B

Advantages of interior lines at strategic level
1 opportunity to divide opponents by faster concentrations
2 opportunity to achieve local superiority of force against one
sector of a divided opponent, gaining a local (non-decisive)
victory.
Conditions for success: time and space to manoeuvre and
retention of initiative.

Advantages of exterior lines at strategic level
1 opportunity to envelop enemy if sufficiently strong.
2 opportunity to gain total victory.

decided by battles', he declared, in marked contrast to earlier generals. His last principle was that of practicability, and the application of rationalism to matters of strategy and tactics. This was based upon his study of military history. Thus harsh discipline was needed if his men were to perform the intricate manoeuvres which confounded the slow, stiff tactics of his foes. The oblique order of attack was designed to offset his numerical inferiority. Instead of attacking all along the line, he used a small force to engage the attention of the enemy and massed his attack, wave after wave, against a single flank to gain local superiority and roll up the enemy line. His preference for howitzers was also utilitarian; noting that the Austrians often adopted positions in dead ground behind ridges, he used this weapon, originally mainly restricted to sieges, to hit at his invisible opponents.

From 1759, the aggressiveness that hallmarked his earlier wars was transformed into more typical offensive/defensive concepts, and by the end of his reign he had even reverted to reliance on massive fortification systems and wars of manoeuvre, rather than brute force, to protect

One of the celebrated Potsdam Giants, a formation of élite grenadiers raised by Frederick William I of Prussia. Minimum height was six feet six inches, and monarchs vied in sending volunteers of this size as gifts to Frederick the Great's father. Frederick, however, disbanded the formation in 1740; it had never seen action.

142

his possessions. This regression shows that Frederick was not really an innovator, but rather the perfector of the concepts of eighteenth-century warfare. A supreme rationalist, he recognized his limitations and set out to achieve his goal by the best available means.

His army – its drill, uniforms, tactics and mentality – caught the imagination of Europe, and was slavishly imitated everywhere except in France. Frederick had inherited an army of 80,000 men in 1740; by the 1760s he was leading all of 150,000, many of them mercenaries. To support his armies he had recourse to ferocious taxation, and a high proportion of his budget had to be devoted to the forces. This bred unpopularity, but Frederick never allowed opposition to crystallize. War, in effect, became Prussia's first industry.

France, after a brief period of success, highlighted perhaps by de Saxe's victory over Cumberland at Fontenoy (1745), slipped into a further period of decline which led to the humiliating defeats of the Seven Years War. Over-officering and excessive recourse to the marketing of military rank lay at the root of her troubles.

By the 1770s, however, inspired by Guibert and Gribeauval, great reforms were being developed, which by the eve of the Revolution had substantially transformed the French army in terms of its artillery and tactical doctrine. Lafayette's expedition to the United States was also not without its influence.

The British army remained remarkably unchanged and unruffled by the setbacks it sustained in the former American colonies. The inadequacies of formal linear tactics showed up against the sniping fire of American patriots and in the later humiliations suffered at the hands of the Continental Army backed by the French expeditionary force. The British also tasted the problems of trying to sustain a major war over 3,000 miles of ocean.

One lesson that did emerge was the need for a reinstatement of light infantry, and by the end of the century Sir John Moore would be laying at Shorncliffe the foundations of what would become the Light Division. This type of soldier, trained to fight as an individual rather than as a 'walking musket', had already been reintroduced into several European armies. As early as 1690,

De Saxe's triumph at Fontenoy, 1745, crowned his military career and applied a severe check to British military aspirations in Europe. British captives and colours are being presented to the victor, who, however, spent most of the day in a sedan chair, being far more corpulent and diseased than appears here. *Versailles*.

The battle of Blenheim, 13 August 1704. The village of Blenheim is left centre, near the Danube, that of Oberglau in the right centre. The French infantry in the centre is being eliminated. In the foreground, Marlborough has just placed the captive Marshal Tallard in his coach. In fact there is no such hill near Blenheim, which is in a largely flat plain.

The battle of Leuthen, 5 December 1757, Frederick the Great's second great success of that year. It was notable for his use of the oblique-order attack against the Austrian forces of General Browne. By this method, maximum pressure was applied against the Austrian left, which collapsed.

Austria had used Croatian irregulars against the equivalent Turkish Arnauts, and by the 1740s the Regiment of Pandours had become part of the regular army. In France, Marshal de Saxe's insistence saw the introduction of Grassin's Legion in 1744, and by 1748 there were sixteen formations of so-called light infantry in the service. Also in 1744, the Prussians introduced a *Jägerskorps*, initially of 300 men, but this type of unit tended to be employed as conventional infantry by Frederick. It took the experience of colonial wars against Indians or American farmers to convince European powers of the value of such troops, and the lesson was best learnt by France whose *tirailleurs* and *voltigeurs* would play an increasingly important role from 1792 onwards.

The armies of the period were almost identical in terms of weapons, grand tactics and methods of supply. Everything turned on the ability of the commander, still in personal command of every part of his army. Success was won through ability to overcome the current limitations, and the ability to make the most of the increased firepower now available. In some ways the conduct of war was less barbaric (although there were exceptions) than it had been in the previous centuries and less total than it was to become in the immediate future. Indeed, the eighteenth century was a period of military transition and general mediocrity enlivened by a few men of genius, but it held the seeds of future developments in both equipment and tactics, and proved that the prosecution of war and the profession of arms could still be relatively civilized as well as honourable.

The Battle of Blenheim, 13 August 1704

Following his brilliant march to the Danube from the Netherlands, the Duke of Marlborough and his Austrian allies proved incapable of forcing the Elector of Bavaria to make peace or to fight. By August, Marshal Tallard had reinforced the Elector to a strength of some 56,000 men and 90 guns, and moving north of the Danube they threatened to trap Marlborough south of the river by severing his communications. By dint of fast marching, however, Marlborough retrieved the situation and regained the north bank, where he joined Prince Eugène's small covering force. Between them they mustered some 52,000 men and 60 guns.

Tallard, meanwhile, had camped near Blenheim with 4,000 more men and 90 guns. He never anticipated an attack as his position was strong, with secure flanks and a marshy stream to his front, and with three villages for use as strongpoints. A generation of French successes in the field also made him underestimate his opponents.

Great was Tallard's surprise, therefore, on 13 August, when the rising mists revealed the Allied army marching to offer battle. Although it was not until midday that Eugène and the right wing were in position, Tallard made no attempt to attack Marlborough's forces, but merely drew up his men. On his right he placed twenty-seven battalions of infantry, eleven of them within Blenheim itself; a further fifteen held Oberglau in the centre, the intervening area being filled with cavalry and nine battalions. Away to his left, the Elector and Marsin drew up a virtually independent array to face Eugène. The morning passed in bombardments.

Battle of Blenheim

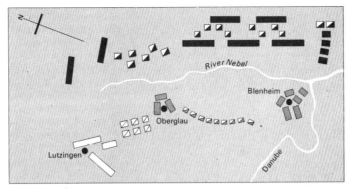

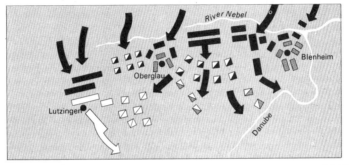

Legend:

◪ ◪	British and Allied cavalry
▬▬	British and Allied infantry
◨ ◨	French cavalry
▦	French infantry
◇ ◇	Bavarian infantry
▭	Bavarian cavalry

About 1 pm the Duke ordered his left wing to attack Blenheim. The troops failed to break in, but the local French commander was induced to pack all of Tallard's reserve infantry into the village without reference to his superior. Very soon, all twenty-seven battalions were sealed in by only fifteen Allied battalions, and Marlborough's left wing was secure.

Attempts to take Oberglau were at first unsuccessful, but Marlborough arrived to rally the troops and force the garrison back into the defences. By 3 pm the Allies had neutralized both Blenheim and Oberglau, whilst to the north Prince Eugène was pinning down foes twice as numerous as his own forces. At the crisis near Oberglau, he had at once sent over his final cavalry reserve at Marlborough's request. Co-operation between the two generals was excellent.

As Marlborough's centre—four lines of horse (eighty squadrons) and twenty-two battalions—deployed over the Nebel marshes, the time for the *coup de grâce* was fast approaching. Tallard's virtually unsupported cavalry repulsed the first wave of horsemen launched against them at a fast trot, but when Marlborough launched a second onslaught at 4.30 pm Tallard's cavalry were exhausted and broke under the impact. The nine battalions died where they stood, and many French horsemen were drowned trying to swim the Danube.

The battle ended three hours later, when the virtually unused garrison of Blenheim was induced to surrender. Meanwhile, the Elector and Marsin were in full retreat for Hochstadt, and Tallard was himself a captive. By nightfall, no less than 40,000 of Tallard's army were casualties or prisoners, whilst the Allies had lost some 12,500 men.

This famous engagement marks the emergence of Marlborough as a great commander and the beginning of the decline in French martial fortunes. Allied boldness in forcing action on an overconfident Tallard, together with their superior tactics and cooperation, had won them a major victory.

The Battle of Leuthen, 5 December 1757
Napoleon called this battle '. . . a masterpiece of manoeuvre and resolution. It would suffice by itself to immortalize Frederick and rank him amongst the greatest generals.' In many ways this battle is the epitome of the eighteenth-century concept of linear tactics.

After his victory over Soubise at Rossbach (5 November), Frederick was still in a position to field 35,000 men but a large proportion of these were of questionable morale owing to their involvement in the defeat of Breslau. On the other hand, Frederick had 71 heavy cannon.

The Austrians, under command of Prince Charles of Lorraine and Marshal Daun, were around the town of Leuthen; they were 60,000 strong, with some 65 artillery pieces.

Frederick approached the enemy in four columns from the direction of Neumarkt, and the early skirmishes against Austrian outposts near the village of Borne went in his favour. Later in the morning he carried out a close inspection of the Austrian position from the Scheuberg. Daun's army was drawn up in a defensive position, stretching for five miles, from the woods

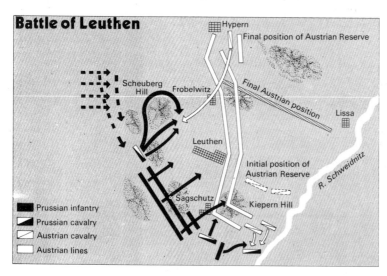

Battle of Leuthen

Hypern

Final position of Austrian Reserve

Scheuberg Hill

Frobelwitz

Final Austrian position

Lissa

Leuthen

Initial position of Austrian Reserve

R. Schweidnitz

Sagschutz

Kiepern Hill

■ Prussian infantry

▨ Prussian cavalry

▨ Austrian cavalry

▢ Austrian lines

sheltering reverse slopes – to attack the left of the enemy army around Kiepern Hill and the village of Sagschütz.

By noon, the heads of the Prussian columns were in contact with the Austrian left, and Ziethen's cavalry repulsed an Austrian counter-attack on the extreme flank. Then, under Frederick's personal control, the main attack went in, preceded by a heavy bombardment from the Prussian howitzers. Moving his infantry forward in echelon from the right, Frederick mounted a crescendo of telling attacks against the angle formed by the Austrian left, and forced it back beyond Frobelwitz in great confusion. Prince Charles tried to re-form a line near Leuthen itself, but his confused army was already incapable of rallying.

In a last effort to reverse the fortunes of the day, the Austrian right wing cavalry, supported by foot, charged down against the weak Prussian left, but the Prussian cavalry closed in on them from three sides and routed them before they could reach the exposed left of the Prussian infantry. Their whole army in ruins, only nightfall saved the Austrians from total destruction as they fled towards Breslau. They lost some 21,000 men, including some 13,000 prisoners. For their part the Prussians lost 1,150 killed, 5,100 wounded and 200 prisoners.

This defeat gave further evidence of Frederick's genius as a commander in battle, and confirmed Prussia's possession of Silesia. Frederick was not, however, able to pursue his defeated enemy to the uttermost, as further crises demanded his attention in other sectors.

and marshes near Nypern in the north to the marshes around the River Schweidnitz in the south. Although outnumbered, Frederick felt he could master his overextended opponents through the use of guile and speed of manoeuvre.

Following their setback at Borne, the Austrians believed that the Prussian main attack would come against their right wing, which they strengthened accordingly. To maintain the illusion, Frederick ordered his advance guard and part of his cavalry to attract the attention of the enemy right and centre, whilst the remainder of his army moved boldly across the front of the Austrian array – a most hazardous manoeuvre which went undetected thanks to the use of

A contemporary representation of the battle of Leuthen.

148

FRENCH REVOLUTIONARY AND NAPOLEONIC WARFARE

As a direct result of the French Revolution, the art of war underwent a considerable transformation, leading to the era of total war. In marked contrast to the preceding period, whole populations became engaged in struggles for national survival and entire economies and societies were geared to the maintenance of armed forces. Thus was born the concept of the 'nation in arms', first in a France desperately trying to preserve the principles of the Revolution, then progressively throughout continental Europe, as French proselytizing zeal forced power after power to adopt military reforms of a similar nature or accept oblivion, and twenty-three years of almost continuous wars shook the very foundations of the *ancien régime*. A degree of ideology returned to increase the doggedness and ferocity with which wars were fought, and armies ceased to be 'the playthings of kings'. In Spain (from 1808) and Russia (in 1812) guerrilla and partisan wars strengthened the commitment of the common people to these nationalistic struggles.

As countries mobilized their societies for war, larger armies came into existence. In 1792, faced by a hostile Europe, Revolutionary France set about creating armies totalling over 600,000 men to protect her frontiers, and under the administrative genius of Lazare Carnot, the 'Organizer of Victory', the first citizen armies of modern times made their appearance. Finding that reliance on volunteers alone could not provide the necessary manpower, recourse was had to the *levée en masse*, and a form of conscription was adopted from 1798 whereby the entire male population between eighteen and forty-five became liable for military service in annual classes. Within a generation Prussia, Austria and, to a lesser extent, Russia would be driven to adopt similar measures.

The new type of conscript soldier was noted for his zeal and higher level of intelligence. A revised tactical system was introduced to make the most of these characteristics and at the same time make allowance for the general lack of experience. The troops were trained to fight either in skirmishing order or in columns of attack, and the bayonet charge was accorded higher priority than volume of musketry fire.

Casualties were less important than formerly, and horde tactics designed to overwhelm the opponent were frequently employed. The earliest Revolutionary armies were noted for their disorganization and indiscipline, factors not improved by the exodus of many of their former officers, and it became necessary to amalgamate two *fédérés* or new battalions with one regular formation, the former operating as often as not in rough columns, the latter in line, so as to combine the effects of shock and firepower. The Cannonade of Valmy in September 1792 proved the turning point, and thereafter the new armies began to achieve successes.

The title *demi-brigade* replaced that of regiment, and at the instance of Dubois Crancé numbers of three-battalion *demi-brigades* were formed into mixed divisions, containing a proportion of cavalry and guns as well as infantry. These divisions became standardized from February 1793, comprising two more *demi-brigades* of ordinary infantry, another of light infantry, and a *demi-brigade* of cavalry, two *compagnies* or batteries of artillery, a divisional park and a staff—perhaps 8,000 men in all.

The flexibility of these new major formations was enhanced by a new doctrine of subsistence, that of living off the countryside. Originally a measure of sheer desperation, when the administrative machinery proved totally incapable of feeding the new armies, the idea of leaving the troops to fend for themselves (after central provision of only the most basic rations of bread and wine) was found to be feasible, and became a hallowed feature of French warfare. The reduction in wagon trains and in reliance on prestocked depots enabled the French armies to move faster than their convoy-bound foes, and this superior mobility became an important factor in their success.

Coordination and leadership posed great problems. With the flight abroad of many experienced officers, the first experiments with the election of replacements proved unsatisfactory, but gradually the principle that promotion would be based solely on professional competence took root. The able could look forward to rapid advancement. At a higher level, Carnot instituted a rudimentary new general staff in his Bureau

Topographique, and used the services of Representatives of the People – or political commissars entrusted with absolute powers – to enforce the orders of Paris on the armies at the front. The development of a signalling system based upon the Chappe visual telegraph further assisted the exchange of orders and reports, assisting the coordination of efforts on the various fronts. The degree of centralization still left something to be desired, however, for Carnot at one time had no less than thirteen separate armies in existence.

Nevertheless, the new arrangements encouraged talent and natural leaders began to emerge. Outstanding amongst these was a captain of artillery, Napoleon Bonaparte, but other talented generals preceded him, notably Moreau, Jourdan and Pichegru.

Napoleon from first to last was an adventurer. Although his martial talents amounted to genius, he was fortunate in being born in 1769 into the Corsican *petite noblesse*, for these circumstances enabled him to make the most of the opportunities the Revolution offered. On the one hand he was born sufficiently noble to be able to benefit from a state education under the *ancien régime*; on the other, his antecedents and social position did not hinder him from grasping the personal advantages offered by the new order for those able and unscrupulous enough to seize them. Thus in 1793 he rose from the rank of captain to that of brigadier-general in a matter of eight weeks, due to his conduct at the siege of Toulon. Three years later, he had attained the position

of army commander, through a combination of military skills and political opportunism. But four years on, and he was First Consul and *de facto* ruler of France. In 1804 he was crowned Emperor, at the age of thirty-five. Ahead of him lay eleven years of great military achievements and, ultimately, disaster. Not since Alexander the Great had a man enjoyed such a meteoric career.

Napoleon was no great innovator as a soldier; rather, his genius lay in the practical field. As has been well said, 'he added nothing to the armies of France–save Victory'. He found a weapon ready to hand in the army, which he inherited from a double source–the *ancien régime* of the Bourbons, and the Revolution. His debt to both was considerable. The reforms in the French army after the Seven Years War had been considerable. Gribeauval had transformed the artillery arm by lightening the cannon, organizing regular batteries, standardizing the field pieces to four calibres (12-, 8- and 4-pounders, and 6-inch howitzers), and many more improvements, including a comprehensive peacetime training programme from which the young Bonaparte had himself benefited. Guibert had produced a philosophy of total war, and at the tactical level had helped along the evolution of the *ordre mixte* formation of infantry drawn up in columns and line in mutual support. Marshal de Broglie had conducted experiments based on de Saxe's concepts with mixed divisions, and at the technological level the arms foundries had produced the musket of 1777–destined to

left
Napoleon Bonaparte, perhaps the greatest soldier since Alexander the Great and Genghis Khan.

below
Napoleon is hailed at the battle of Jena, 1806, by a member of the Imperial Guard.

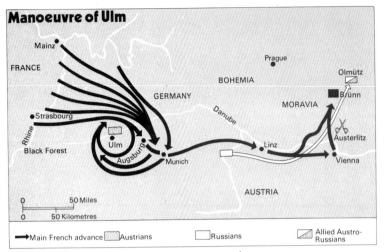

Napoleon's brilliant manoeuvre of Ulm, one of the finest examples of his wide strategic envelopments, in which he trapped 60,000 Austrian troops under General Mack.

new armies of citizens, and for establishing the principles of conscription (to provide the manpower), living off the countryside (the secret of logistical support), and the overall concept of the nation in arms. The Revolutionary armies had also evolved most of the tactical and organizational forms, including the all-arms divisions and the rudiments of a staff system based upon the earlier ideas of General Bourcet. Apart from the cavalry, which had suffered most from the emigration of officers, Napoleon thus inherited a generally battleworthy army.

His inherent military conservatism is indicated by his decisions to disband the balloon companies (*Aerostiers*) of the Republican army, and, later, to reject the American inventor Roger Fulton's offer of submarines and naval mines. He thus tended to be suspicious of new ideas. His genius was essentially practical, and was directed towards improving important aspects of his military inheritance. First, he greatly developed the staff organization. Besides categorizing the functions of each branch of the *Grand-Quartier-Général* (aided by his chief of staff, Alexandre Berthier, whom he half-seriously underestimated as the perfect chief clerk), he insisted upon the creation of simpler but more effective staffs at corps and divisional level, and thus established a proper chain of command. At the level of army

remain in use until the 1830s. Equally important, the old Royal Army contained a fine generation of junior officers and NCOs, including Augereau, who started as an ordinary cavalry trooper, Lannes, an infantry sergeant in 1789, and Masséna, a sergeant-major.

His debt to the Revolution was even more profound. Besides his own rapid preferment, he owed Carnot much for creating and training the

organization, he effected the adoption of the *corps d'armée* as the standard major formation. This was a logical development from the mixed divisions of the Republic, and indeed experimental corps had existed from at least 1798 in Moreau's army of the Rhine. But the system reached its greatest development between 1804 and 1806.

The advantages it conferred are of great importance to any appreciation of Napoleon's strategic methods in the years of his prime. First, the subdivision of his army into large self-contained formations meant that it could move in a number of widely spread columns rather than in a single dense mass. This facilitated living off the country and spread the load on the available roads, each corps having its own line of advance and subsistence area clearly allocated. Speed of movement was consequently enhanced, and the fact that each corps was a miniature army in itself, with its own infantry, cavalry, guns, trains and headquarters, meant that it could if necessary take on several times its own number for a limited period, before the end of which neighbouring formations could have been brought up by forced marches to its assistance. Napoleon calculated that a division on its own could hold out for a number of hours; a corps for up to a day. The flexibility this made

possible was one major secret of Napoleonic success. The army could march dispersed until the target was in view, and then rapidly concentrate for battle. What this system could achieve was demonstrated in the manoeuvre of Ulm in 1805, and even more convincingly in the movement of the *bataillon carrée* before Jena-Auerstadt the next year. In the former case, 210,000 men in eight columns swept from the Rhine to the Danube in a matter of eleven days; in the latter, 140,000 troops moved inexorably into Saxony and Prussia in a lozenge-shaped formation of corps, and proved capable of altering the line of advance by ninety degrees, without the least confusion or delay, when the main Prussian army was discovered to be to the west of the Saale, instead of north towards Leipzig. Such mobility and flexibility had not been known since the *toumans* of Genghis Khan. The army corps may be considered the French secret weapon of these wars, and by 1812 all major powers, with the exception of Britain, had adopted similar organizations.

Napoleon also expanded the practice of massing much of the heavy cavalry and many of the guns into reserves, to be retained under army command for use at the critical moment in a campaign or battle. As might be expected, he continued the work of reforming the artillery arm as a whole. As First Consul he effectively

militarized artillery drivers, deploying them in battalions. As the wars progressed, Napoleon steadily increased the proportion of guns to men until they had reached four or five for every thousand troops. His predilection for massed batteries of up to 100 pieces is also evident from the large batteries he employed at Eylau, Borodino or Waterloo. He also created a *corps d'élite*, in the form of the Imperial Guard, which grew from the size of a small division in 1806 to a miniature army of 112,000 by 1812, but until the last years of the Empire he proved very wary of sending it into action. Ultimately divided into three sections–the Old, Middle and Young Guards–it comprised cavalry, artillery and trains as well as infantry.

Amongst the generals of the period, Napoleon was supreme. As a grand strategist his preference for short, sharp wars led to a series of crushing victories; none more so than his rapid conquest of Prussia in 1806. On the other hand, the declaration of all-out economic warfare against Britain in later 1806, with the institution of the so-called 'Continental System', led directly to two long and disastrous struggles, namely the Peninsular War (1807–14) and the invasion of Russia (1812). These two catastrophes doomed France to defeat.

As a strategist, however, Napoleon had no peer. This was pre-eminently his realm. Setting himself to make the most of the superior mobility and enthusiasm of his armies, he devised two main strategical systems. If the foe were stronger in numbers, he habitually organized his force into an advance guard, two wings and a reserve, and advanced to seize a central position, thus dividing the enemy into parts. By adroit timing and manoeuvring of the reserve, he then fought a series of small battles with local superiority of force against each part in turn, using corps to pin down all opponents within range, however strong, until the reserve could be manoeuvred to achieve local supremacy. He first employed this method along the Ligurian coast in April 1796; it was also the basis of the Waterloo campaign nineteen years later.

If the enemy was inferior in strength to the French, Napoleon time and again adopted variations of his strategy of envelopment. After inducing the foe to make the first move, Napoleon left a small force to hold up the enemy and deceive him into believing that he was facing the complete French army. Meanwhile the mass of the army executed forced marches to sweep into the enemy's rear so as to cut his communications with his bases. This manoeuvre was particularly effective against convoy-bound opponents, who found their supplies interrupted. His morale shaken, the foe's first thought was to fight his way out of the trap, and the result would often be a reversed-front battle fought out on ground of Napoleon's choosing. First used (with only partial success) during the manoeuvre of Lodi, May 1796, this concept lay behind the Marengo,

The siege of Breslau, 1806. After the double defeat of Jena-Auerstadt, Prussian morale crumbled away overnight. Great fortresses were surrendered almost without offering opposition to the French. Here we see a battery of Bavarian artillery moving up to bombard the town of Breslau. *Residenzmuseum, Munich.*

Napoleonic Grand Tactics

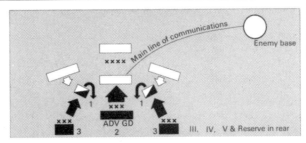

First Phase

CONTACT AND PINNING ATTACK

1 Cavalry screen reports contact

2 Advance guard immediately engages enemy

3 Nearest corps move forward to support advance guard and extend front. More enemy troops are drawn into the engagement.

Second Phase

BATTLE OF ATTRITION COVERING MAIN MOVES

1 Frontal attack builds up: enemy throws more troops into battle

2 Cavalry screen, which conceals . . .

3 . . . Enveloping force moving up to take enemy flank adjacent to his left of centre

4 Reinforcement of front attracts last enemy reserve forces

5 *Masse de décision* assembling behind right flank

Third Phase

ENVELOPMENT, BREAKTHROUGH AND PURSUIT

1 Renewed frontal attack pins down enemy

2 Revealed enveloping attack persuades enemy to weaken his left to form the line x–y

3 *Masse de décision*, after a violent artillery bombardment, breaks through weakened enemy lines

4 Light cavalry surge through gap to commence pursuit

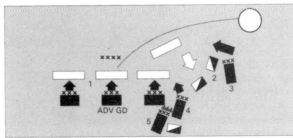

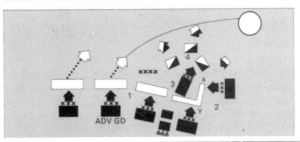

below
Occasionally, from 1809 onwards, Napoleon could make blunders, as at Aspern and Essling in April of that year, when he crossed the Danube without taking precautions and was defeated by the Austrians. However, he could still learn from his errors, and when he recrossed the great river in July 1809, immediately prior to the battle of Wagram, he had taken all necessary measures to protect the vital bridges to his rear. *Victoria and Albert Museum, London.*

THE BATTLE OF WATERLOO, 18 JUNE 1815

The disposition of the forces at the outset of the battle will be found on the double-page spread overleaf, accompanied by a key. The captions below describe the crucial moments in the battle, which are to be found, in chronological order, on the page opposite and on the final page of the colour section. A full description of the battle will be found on pp 167–169.

1. The attack, at about 1.30 pm, of d'Erlon's I Corps launched against Wellington's left centre, east of La Haye Sainte, top left. The massed French formations, presenting marvellous targets, are met and repulsed by Picton's redcoats.

2. At 4 pm Ney, believing that the Allies are beginning to fall back, unleashes a series of massive cavalry charges–unsupported by infantry or horse artillery–against the Allied line between La Haye Sainte and Hougoumont. They founder against the coolness and cohesion of Wellington's squares.

3. The arrival of the Prussians from the northeast precipitates a bitter struggle for the village of Plancenoit on the French flank. At one famous moment, shown here, the French temporarily recapture the village as two battalions of the Old Guard charge the Prussians with fixed bayonets through heavy rain.

4. Shortly after 6 pm, Ney finally launches a coordinated attack against La Haye Sainte, forcing the Allies to abandon it. Guns are rushed forward to pound Wellington's fragile centre, but the Guard, occupied at Plancenoit, are not available to exploit this success.

5. Shortly after 7 pm, Napoleon releases nine battalions of the Middle Guard for the final attack. Marching in two columns towards the crest of the ridge which the Allies have held all day, they are halted, taken in flank, and thrown back.

Overconfidence and lack of originality cost Napoleon the battle. The Allies used his own methods against him with telling effect, turning his flank at the crisis of the day. Moreover, the French army was numerically too weak for the enormous task which it undertook. Napoleon was no longer the master of Marengo or Austerlitz, and though he was by no means a total physical wreck, at Waterloo his strength was certainly impaired by illness; injudicious appointments of subordinates also cost him dear. Another crucial factor in the final outcome was the loyalty of Blücher to his ally, and the consequent appearance of the Prussian army. Finally, one must acknowledge Wellington's superb handling of his mixed army, and the steadfastness of the British troops and the King's German Legion.

2

3

1

The French
1. Napoleon and his staff
2. Cavalry corps of General Milhaud
3. The infantry of d'Erlon's I Corps
4. Massed 12-pounders of the Grand Battery
5. General Reille, commander of II Corps
6. Light infantry screen
7. General Foy's division
8. Part of Kellermann's cavalry corps supporting the French left

The Allies
9. Château of Hougoumont, containing thirteen companies of British Guards and Byng's brigade (in walled garden and orchard)
10. Brunswickers
11. British light infantry
12. British and Allied artillery
13. The mass of the Allied I Corps
14. The farm of La Haye Sainte, defended by the King's German Legion
15. The Gravel Pit, held by light infantry
16. General Bylandt's brigade
17. Part of Picton's division of the Reserve
18. The famous elm tree, Wellington's hq
19. Wellington and his staff
20. The ridge of Mont St Jean
21. A concealed re-entrant leading from the ridge to Hougoumont
22. The Charleroi–Brussels highroad.

Note that only the centre and western half of the battlefield are depicted here.

4

5

Ulm and Jena campaigns of later years. In all he used it in one form or another almost thirty times.

The battle was of central significance to Napoleonic warfare, and the siege almost disappeared. Napoleon's grand tactics were closely linked to his envelopment strategy, and indeed his greatest contribution to the art of war lay in his fusion of marching, fighting and pursuit into one continuous and remorseless process. Frontal attacks would be pressed to attract more of the enemy's reserves; then a pre-positioned force, hidden away towards one enemy flank, would, at a signal, reveal its presence, thus creating a new threat; and once the foe had weakened part of his battle line to face the new menace, Napoleon would unleash the reserve for a massive attack against the weakened enemy sector and carve a corridor, through which the massed light cavalry would pour, to convert the enemy's defeat into a full rout.

Variations of this plan were carried out at Castiglione, Austerlitz, Jena-Auerstadt, Bautzen and on many other occasions, but at Waterloo the situation was reversed, and Napoleon suffered the fate he had so often meted out to others. Here lay one weakness in the French strategical and grand tactical systems: they became stereotyped and predictable after a decade of constant

above
Napoleon's 'manoeuvre of envelopment' led to some amazing successes. Perhaps the most celebrated was the surrender of General Mack, with over 20,000 Austrian troops, at Ulm, 21 September 1805. Napoleon is shown interviewing the Austrian general, who reputedly introduced himself with the words, 'Sire, here is the unhappy General Mack.' *Versailles*.

left
Prince Golenischev Kutusov (1745–1813) was the Russian Commander-in-Chief at the hard-fought battle of Borodino in September 1812. Although defeated, and forced to abandon Moscow to the French, he preserved much of his army, and led it to success in the subsequent winter campaign.

The capture of Moscow availed Napoleon nothing, as Tsar Alexander refused to negotiate a peace treaty. Eventually the French were forced to retreat, and appalling weather increased the scale of the disaster. In all, the campaign of 1812 cost them 500,000 casualties.

use, and lost much of their old terror. The enemies of France became capable of working out countermoves which called Napoleon's bluff time and again from 1812 onwards.

Success in battle depended in large measure on securing and retaining the initiative, and on achieving properly coordinated all-arms attacks. The French sequence was as follows: after a heavy bombardment from a massed battery, the light infantry would advance to skirmish and reconnoitre the enemy position. Then cavalry attacks would be launched to defeat the enemy's horsemen and force his infantry to form squares – ideal targets for the horse artillery batteries accompanying the cavalry. Under cover of these actions the French infantry columns would hasten forward, either deploying into line for fire action or crashing into the enemy position in mass formation, and achieve a local victory with bayonet which would be exploited by more cavalry. When this tactical sequence was observed, great successes could follow; when it was neglected or mismanaged (as at Waterloo) failure could be equally dramatic.

Under the guidance of such men as the Archduke Charles, Baron Barclay de Tolly and the great Scharnhorst, the armies of Austria, Russia and Prussia adopted broadly similar organizations and tactical sequences in the years after 1807, and thus slowly made their armies more battleworthy. One of France's enemies, however, proved resistant to change and, paradoxically,

above
Austrian cavalry attack French infantry at the battle of Kulm, 30 August 1813. This engagement was a serious defeat for the French.

left
The superiority of the British line formations over the French columns was demonstrated many times in Spain, and finally at Waterloo, where d'Erlon's infantry, and even the Middle Guard, were routed by disciplined fire followed by a determined bayonet charge.

Sir Arthur Wellesley, Duke of Wellington; after Marlborough the greatest British soldier. He was a brilliant tactician with an eagle eye for administrative detail. *Victoria and Albert Museum, London.*

General Sir John Moore, 'father of modern British infantry training'. He trained the first British light infantry at Shorncliffe, and later commanded in the Corunna campaign of 1808–09, being mortally wounded in the moment of victory. His reforms underlay many of Wellington's later successes. *National Portrait Gallery, London.*

was the most successful–Great Britain. Led by the great Arthur Wellesley, Duke of Wellington, the British army clung on to Frederickan concepts of linear tactics, though reducing the battalion battle line to a depth of two ranks. In the 1790s, under Sir John Moore, a form of advanced light infantry training had been introduced for some formations; the Baker rifle they used, although slower to reload than the 'Brown Bess', had a longer range and was more accurate, especially in the hands of formations like the 95th (later the Rifle Brigade).

Wellington had four great strengths as a commander-in-chief. First, he refused to be frightened by the French systems, and soon saw ways to counter them. Second, he realized that in Spain his main role was to assist the Spanish guerrillas by mounting diversionary attacks to draw off French forces, leaving the guerrillas free to operate. Thus the Talavera campaign of 1809 was designed to make the most of the French preoccupation with Austria. Thirdly, he appreciated that the great French weakness lay in supply. In 1810, having taken great pains to build up a sound system of his own, based upon rear and forward depots and supplied by river boats, ox carts and mule trains in a carefully regulated organization, he deliberately lured Masséna's army towards the impregnable Lines of Torres Vedras, before which he had laid waste a vast tract of countryside. The lines had been commenced late in 1809, and were designed and built under conditions of great secrecy by Colonel Fletcher, Major Jones and sixteen engineer officers, aided by 10,000 local Portuguese. By September 1810 the position comprised three lines of defences, the first extending for twenty-nine miles from the Tagus to the Atlantic, the second (main) line set a few miles further back, and the third (evacuation perimeter) some two miles long, being placed near Fort St Julien. Taken together, these defensive works included 50 redoubts (smaller ones holding 50 men and 2 guns, the larger holding 500 men and 6 guns), mounted a total of 947 guns, and required 28,490 troops (mostly militia) to man them. Good lateral roads ran behind the works, with signal stations, to enable Wellington to deploy his main fighting force held in reserve against any threatened sector. In fact the lines were never fully tested, for Masséna was so daunted by the appearance of the outer fortifications that he never dared to launch a serious attack. The French army was eventually starved into retreat. This scorched-earth policy, incidentally, was operated against the French equally effectively in Russia. And fourthly, Wellington developed great skill in minor tactics. On many an occasion (although not invariably) he chose to fight tactically on the defensive. He would habitually choose positions with secure flanks and affording as much cover as possible; the troops, drawn up out of sight on the reverse slopes, missed much of the effect

of the French cannonade, only the British guns – some of them firing shrapnel, or hollow shells packed with explosive and musket balls – being in action along the crest, with the light infantry pushed well forward down the front slopes to hold up the advance of the enemy light infantry. This often confused the foe as to Wellington's exact position, and when his columns stumbled to the crest, they found themselves facing a torrent of fire, followed by a bayonet charge. Thus was many a Peninsular battle decided. Wellington also proved adept at training Portuguese troops to a high standard; only his cavalry, with its tendency to over-enthusiasm in the charge, proved a disappointment.

Waterloo, the confrontation of Napoleon and Wellington, respectively the masters of strategy and tactics, was a fitting climax to the period. Perhaps of the most lasting importance, however, was the growth of widespread guerrilla warfare in Spain and partisan warfare in Russia. In Spain, the French lost an average of 100 men a day to the guerrillas over seven years. Here was a foretaste of the things to come, which would challenge the accepted conditions of conventional war 150 years later.

The Battle of Austerlitz, 2 December 1805
Following the capitulation of the Austrians at Ulm in November, Napoleon still faced the problem posed by the approaching Russian forces.

Through the bungling of Prince Murat and the cunning of General Kutusov, the French failed to catch the Russians south of the Danube, and the Emperor was forced to follow his prey northwards from Vienna towards Brünn and Olmütz in Moravia, where Kutusov and the remaining Austrian forces successfully linked up with more Russian troops. By late November, Napoleon had some 53,000 men near Austerlitz; his lines of communication were very exposed, and over 100,000 men were by this time dispersed to guard them. The Allies had all of 90,000 men near Olmütz.

The Emperor Francis I of Austria was not eager to give battle, but Napoleon knew that the French could advance no further. If he halted, his men would starve in bleak, winter-bound Moravia, and there were signs that Prussia was about to join the Third Coalition. Consequently, he decided to lure the enemy into launching a major attack against him. To achieve this he feigned total weakness – requesting an armistice on the 27th, retreating from the approaches to Wischau in apparent disorder on the 30th, and finally abandoning the town of Austerlitz and the neighbouring Pratzen Heights to the enemy. As he had hoped, the hotheads in the Allied army were taken in by this display, and despite the caution expressed by Kutusov the Tsar Alexander ordered an attack.

Once Napoleon learnt that the enemy had

The Lines of Torres Vedras – a triple line of defended forts and other positions – were prepared in great secrecy by the British army not far north of Lisbon. When Marshal Masséna came up against them in 1810 he soon concluded that they were too strong for the French to attack.

snapped up the bait, he summoned by forced marches the outlying corps of Bernadotte and Davout, building up his strength by 1 December to 66,000 men and 139 guns. Davout's corps was still on the road from Vienna, but would arrive at least in part during the morning of the 2nd. Outnumbered as he was, the Emperor had no troops to spare for an outflanking movement, so he resorted to a bold stratagem to induce the foe to attack his right wing in great force, at the expense of the Allied centre's security. To this end, Napoleon placed only a weak force on his right (although it would be sustained eventually by Davout), thus apparently uncovering his lines of retreat on Vienna. Marshal Lannes commanded from the Santon Hill on the left, with Murat's cavalry to his right, and the rest of the army was massed in dead ground around the Zurlan and near the Goldbach stream. As he had hoped, the Russians massed almost 60,000 men under Buxhowden with orders to roll up the French line from Sokolnitz.

On 2 December the early moves were hidden by a dense fog, but by 8 am Napoleon was confident that his plan was working, and Davout's footsore troops were in contact with his hard-pressed right. Waiting until the Pratzen Heights were almost clear of Allied troops, at 9 am he launched Soult with two divisions against the summit to capture the centre of the enemy line. The Allies were astounded by this bold move, and by 11 am the Pratzen Heights were practically in French hands. Meanwhile, Lannes had stoutly resisted the advance of Bagration against the Santon, and Murat's cavalry reserve had mastered Prince Lichtenstein's more numerous cavalry, whilst Legrand was narrowly holding his own on the southern flank.

About 1 pm the Russian Guards almost regained the Pratzen Heights, but Soult was sustained in the nick of time by the Guard cavalry and Bernadotte's corps, and the crisis passed. Napoleon at once launched the *coup de grâce* by sweeping on to the flank and rear of the massed Allied left wing, now wholly sundered from the rest of the Russo-Austrian army. By 3 pm the Russians were being driven back towards the frozen Satschan meres, and although Buxhowden extricated one column, the rest were doomed. A number were drowned when the ice gave way under French bombardment.

By 4 pm the Tsar, the Emperor Francis and the Allied right were in full retreat. The Allies had suffered some 27,000 casualties; the French only

The Eve of Austerlitz by Baron Lejeune. Napoleon interrogates local peasants, whilst his troops prepare for the great battle on the morrow. In the background, the Santon mound is being turned into a strong artillery position. *Versailles*.

166

Battle of Austerlitz

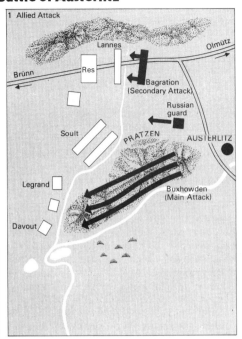

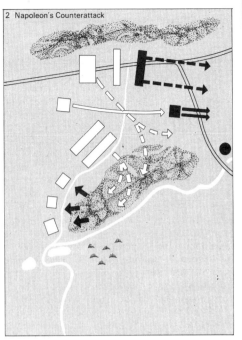

8,500. Next day Austria sued for peace. The Third Coalition lay in ruins, and Napoleon had won possibly his greatest battle. His daring had paid off handsomely.

The Battle of Waterloo, 18 June 1815

Napoleon's final campaign in Belgium got off to a brilliant start, surprising the Allies on the 15th, defeating the Prussians at Ligny and containing the Allies at Quatre Bras on the following day. It seemed that nothing could save Wellington's 68,000-strong mixed army from destruction.

However, through an extraordinary oversight, Napoleon failed to launch an effective pursuit of Blücher's Prussians until midday on the 17th and consequently was unaware that they were retiring on Wavre instead of Namur. They were thus still within supporting distance of Wellington. Similarly, Ney failed to keep the Duke pinned down at Quatre Bras until Napoleon could bring over the reserves from Ligny, and this enabled the Allied army to fall back to Mont St Jean, on the Brussels road.

Wellington, relying on Blucher's promise to march to his aid, took up a position along a low ridge, backed by a forest and with three strong-points to the fore. Most of his men were concealed behind reverse slopes, with only 185 guns along the crest. Here he determined to hang grimly on until Prussian aid materialized.

Owing to a wet night, and his underestimation of his opponent, Napoleon had not deployed his 74,000 men and 266 guns until 10 am; Marshal Grouchy, with 33,000 men, was in the meantime pursuing the Prussians towards Wavre.

The Emperor placed one corps, backed by cavalry, on each side of the highroad, and held VI Corps and the Guard in central reserve. A large battery of eighty guns was sited to the east of the road. After indicating the broad lines the battle was to follow – an unsubtle major blow against the Allied centre supported by a diversionary attack against Hougoumont – Napoleon handed control of the battle over to Ney.

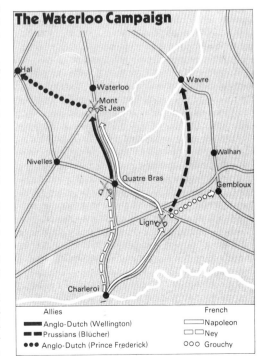

The Waterloo Campaign

Allies
- ■■■ Anglo-Dutch (Wellington)
- ■ ■ ■ Prussians (Blücher)
- ●●● Anglo-Dutch (Prince Frederick)

French
- ☐ Napoleon
- ☐ ☐ Ney
- OOO Grouchy

The Waterloo campaign. Napoleon gambled on penetrating between the forces of Wellington and Blücher and defeating them in turn. He managed to force the withdrawal of Blücher at Ligny, whilst Wellington evacuated Quatre Bras. However, he failed to pursue the retreating Prussians and did not ascertain their line of withdrawal.

The Château of Hougoumont, set before Wellington's right wing at Waterloo, proved a stalwart island of resistance against the French throughout 18 June 1815. Although over two French divisions were hurled against it, the defenders never relinquished their posts.

From the very start matters went awry. The diversion at 11.30 am eventually led to the engagement of half of Reille's II Corps, and distracted few of Wellington's troops. Indeed Hougoumont remained in British hands all day. Similarly, the preliminary bombardment caused little damage to Wellington's troops in their concealed position owing to the sodden ground. Next, at 1.30 pm, when Ney launched d'Erlon's I Corps in the main attack, he neglected to support it with cavalry or artillery, and although it took Papelotte, the attack came to grief on the ridge itself. Repulsed by Picton's tough division, the check was turned into rout by the charge of the Union Brigade. Unfortunately the horsemen, after routing d'Erlon, charged on to the great battery, and were then caught in the flank by fresh French lancers, and decimated. Nevertheless, Wellington's position was still secure, and from 1 pm, as Napoleon had soon become aware, signs of the approaching Prussians had become clearer to the north-east.

Ney's repeated attempts to take La Haye Sainte, to the fore of the Allied centre, foundered in turn, but the fiery Marshal believed he had detected signs that the Allied army was beginning to give ground. He at once ordered up 5,000 unsupported cavalry, and began a series of charges against the twenty squares hastily formed by Wellington's right centre. All attacks failed, and Napoleon ultimately had to send in his remaining cavalry to extricate the survivors. By 5.30 pm, moreover, a heavy battle for possession of Plancenoit to the east of the French position had opened as Bülow and Pirch came into action. Soon all Lobau's V Corps was in action, and an hour later most of the Guard had to be sent in.

Meanwhile, at about 6.30 pm, Ney had at last launched a combined attack against La Haye Sainte, and taken it. French cannon were now firing at point-blank range against Wellington's wavering centre, and Ney sensed victory. His appeal for reinforcements was, however, rejected by Napoleon. His attention was wholly absorbed by Plancenoit, which was changing hands with fearsome regularity.

This respite enabled Wellington to move disengaged forces from his left and right to reinforce his centre, whilst the arrival of Ziethen's Corps from Wavre greatly strengthened his left wing.

Shortly after 7 pm, Napoleon released nine battalions of the Guard for a last major blow in the centre. It was already too late. The Middle Guard rolled majestically forward up the ridge,

split into several columns, and attacked. Faced by Maitland's Guards Brigade, taken in the flank by more troops, and pounded by every Allied gun that would bear, the Guard paused, halted – and then retired. The French were astounded by this repulse. The cry '*Sauve qui peut*' went up, and soon the mass of the French army had dissolved into a mass of fugitives. The Old Guard covered the flight with great skill and devotion, but the battle of Waterloo was over, and Napoleon's last great gamble had failed.

A combination of factors – strange appointments of subordinates, underestimation of Wellington (dubbed a 'sepoy general'), fits of lethargy brought on by sickness, and above all the greater tactical skill of Wellington and the loyalty of his Prussian ally – these were the main factors in Napoleon's final eclipse. It is also noticeable that the Allies at Waterloo produced a grand tactical outflanking manoeuvre which reflects Napoleon's system at his prime. It was a case of 'the biter, bit'. It was also the end of an era.

Napoleon left most of the fighting at Waterloo to Marshal Ney's control, and lived to regret it. Only when all was lost did he take a personal part in the struggle, ordering the attack by the Middle Guard about 7.45 pm, which ended in failure.

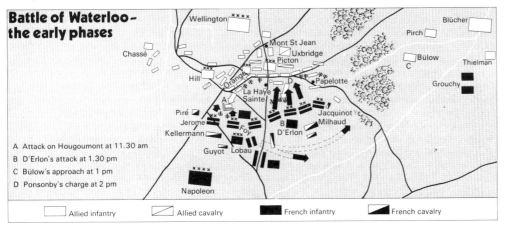

Battle of Waterloo – the early phases

A Attack on Hougoumont at 11.30 am
B D'Erlon's attack at 1.30 pm
C Bülow's approach at 1 pm
D Ponsonby's charge at 2 pm

Wellington · Blücher · Pirch · Chassé · Mont St Jean · Uxbridge · Picton · Bülow · Thielman · Hill · Orange · Papelotte · La Haye Sainte · Grouchy · Piré · Jacquinot · Jerome · Milhaud · Kellermann · Foy · D'Erlon · Guyot · Lobau · Napoleon

Allied infantry · Allied cavalry · French infantry · French cavalry

169

THE NINETEENTH CENTURY

Between 1815 and 1914 stretched a century of relative quiescence. This is not to say that there were no armed conflicts, nor that there was a halt in technological developments of military significance, but there was nothing like the Napoleonic Wars, involving numbers of powers in far-reaching alliances, and nothing to compare with the scale and horror of the struggle that would begin in 1914. Wars became localized rather than general. From Waterloo to the Crimean War, a sense of military exhaustion and disillusion gripped Europe. Apart from the occasional colonial venture (as for instance the French struggles in Algeria in the 1830s or Britain's involvement in Burma in 1823), and apart from various struggles for national independence in South America, two generations of mankind experienced little of the direct effects of war. This same period saw genuine attempts by the great powers to outlaw wars, or at least to restrict their scale and frequency. All armies, save that of Russia, were cut back to a shadow of their former size, and statesmen tried to iron out international problems by discussion and negotiation.

Their efforts, however, ultimately proved disappointing. The decline of Turkey created a power vacuum in the Middle East which led to the Crimean War (1853–56). This found Britain, France and Turkey allied against Russia. Meanwhile the reactionary states of Europe had been shaken and in part transformed by the liberal-inspired upheavals of 1832 and 1848. The growth of industrial power in the developed countries led to more aggressive attitudes, and struggles around the issue of national unification affected Italy and Germany, whilst Britain and France became variously involved in growing numbers of small imperial wars as the century wore on. Many of these took place in Africa and the Far East. In the case of Britain they included a number of short, punitive wars against China, the suppression of the Indian Mutiny (1857–58), and, from 1870, a whole series of colonial campaigns in Africa. As for France, her energies were largely directed towards North and West Africa, together with Indo-China.

Two wars in the second half of the century were of great significance. The American Civil War (1861–65) threw the United States into turmoil as a number of States tried to secede from the Union. This struggle did not spread beyond the confines of North America, but its implications in terms of new techniques, weaponry and tactics, once assimilated, were of great importance to Europe. Then, in 1870–71, Bismarck set the seal on the unification of Germany (a cause which had already involved a brief war against Austria in 1866) by fighting and defeating the France of the Second Empire. This struggle awoke Britain to the need to modernize her army, and also sowed the seeds of the two major wars of the twentieth century.

The last years of the old century and the first of the new held three more struggles of importance. The Spanish-American War of 1898 saw the United States involved outside her own boundaries in the Philippines. The Boer War (1899–1901) did much to shake British complacency and marked a turning point in the history of the British Empire. Above all, the Russo-Japanese War (1904–05) held many significant developments, not least of which were the emergence of a new power to world status and the decline of Tsarist Russia. The scene was almost set for the return of total war in 1914, as a series of international rivalries, arms races and crises (particularly in the Balkans, which remained in a state of near-constant upheaval throughout 1912 and 1913) aggravated tension and prepared the way for a great cataclysm.

The period from 1815 to 1914 saw a series of varied struggles after a lull extending over much of its first four decades. Great empires reached their fullest extent and new powers arose, Germany in Europe, Japan in Asia. The American giant set its house in order and began to flex its muscles, whilst three former powers–Turkey, Austria and Tsarist Russia–slipped into decline. Soon after 1815, military philosophers began to analyse the elements of Napoleonic warfare, and from their conclusions they distilled a general philosophy of war. Two writers were of the greatest importance in this respect–namely the Prussian soldier von Clausewitz and the Swiss-born Baron Jomini. Between them they did much to found the modern analytical approach to war, contributing greatly to its scientific study.

above
Lord Chelmsford's
victory at Ulundi in the
Zulu War, July 1879.
Magnificent natural
soldiers, the Zulus
inflicted a serious
reverse on the British at
Isandhlwana, January
1879.

left
The Baluchi Regiment
on active service in
Abyssinia, 1868. They
formed part of a punitive
expedition of 32,000 men
under Sir Robert Napier.

above
The Crimean War was a
serious struggle that
showed up British
military unpreparedness
and foreshadowed
massive reforms. Here we
see the interior of the
Redan at Sebastopol,
after its capture.

right
The Boer War
administered another
major shock to the
British army. Boer
marksmen achieved many
surprising successes
over British regulars and
volunteers, none sharper
than their victory at
Colenso, the climax of
the 'Black Week' in 1899,
when the British
sustained three defeats in
seven days.

Of the two, Jomini was the more traditional. He strove to explain Napoleon's methods in terms of eighteenth-century traditions of precise operational analysis; he defined for the first time the nature of strategy, tactics and logistics, and postulated a number of principles of war – manoeuvrability, concentration of force, surprise and flexibility. A weakness lay in his assumption that the initiative, once gained, could always be maintained. Clausewitz stressed the unpredictability of war, the importance of chance and friction. He believed that the nature of war must be understood before the theory, and that the essential interrelation between armed conflict and political action was the key point. He also held that the strategic defensive, developing into an all-out retaliatory attack, was the stronger form of war, and appreciated the part that guerrilla warfare could play in defeating an invader. He also laid down a series of principles less rigid than Jomini's concepts, adding simplicity, by which he understood all-out attritional attack once the battle had been joined. Heavy casualties he considered as inevitable, and his famous although incomplete work *On War* described a form of total war as the ideal.

Jomini's teachings had a large following in North America and France. Clausewitz's doctrines were widely adopted in Prussia, and generations of soldiers paid tribute to his influence. These included von Moltke the Elder, mastermind of the Franco-Prussian War of 1870–71, General Meckel, the modernizer of the Japanese army, and Graf von Schlieffen, originator of the celebrated plan designed to encompass the defeat of France, which underlay, in a modified form, the great attack launched through Belgium on Paris in August 1914. Somewhat

belatedly, at the beginning of the century, the British army also studied Clausewitzian principles. In sum, Clausewitz was the truer prophet: he appreciated that war had changed radically in the Napoleonic period, whilst Jomini was far more traditional and conservative in his approach, deprecating the influence of psychological warfare. Clausewitz had recognized the new spirit of war.

In tactical terms there were scant developments in the art of war before 1861. The armies that fought in the Crimea might have come straight from a Napoleonic battlefield. However, considerable changes were taking place in weaponry as industrial inventiveness and production techniques improved. Where small arms development was concerned, Great Britain made a number of early contributions. The skilled gunsmith Joseph Manton developed an earlier idea of a Dr Forsyth and, by the 1820s, had perfected the copper percussion cap. This ended the long reliance on flint and steel for discharging firearms. The system was adopted by armies some ten years later, and by the innately conservative British army in 1842. Samuel Colt employed it in his development of the first practicable repeating revolver (1835), which also incorporated the novel feature of interchangeable parts.

The next developments related to the rifle. In 1847 Charles Minié developed a paper cartridge incorporating a hollow-based pointed and elongated bullet, which was easy to load down the rifling of a barrel, but which expanded on discharge to fit the bore very tightly, thus avoiding serious gas leaks. Already, in 1838, a breech-loading needle gun had been invented by Johann von Dreyse, and was soon adopted by the

Mukden, 1905, scene of a sharp Russian reverse at the hands of the Japanese during the Russo-Japanese War of 1904–05. The Japanese army, trained by German missions, and its navy, trained by the British, proved more than a match for the decaying power of Tsarist Russia.

Prussian army (1841) although its use spread slowly elsewhere. Next came the copper-cased, gas-tight cartridge and the rimmed cartridge, both French inventions, considerably improved by North American arms manufacturers. However, considerations of expense hindered their widespread adoption, and even in the early years of the American Civil War the muzzle-loading firearm was still much favoured. By the war's end, however, breech-loaders were on general issue in the North, including repeaters such as the Henry rifle and the famous Winchester cavalry carbine. By 1900, the Germans had the clip-loaded Mauser, and the British the Lee-Enfield.

By 1870 the French had equipped their infantry with the breech-loading 0·43-calibre *chassepot* rifle, which fired faster than the 0·66-calibre Prussian needle gun. They had also developed the *mitrailleuse*, a form of machine gun which had evolved on different lines from the earlier American Gatling gun (invented in 1862). The former had thirty barrels and was a bulky weapon, whereas the latter had only ten – or, in a later version, six. The French *mitrailleuse* was kept as a secret weapon, but was misused at too long a range in 1870, and was consequently put out of action by Prussian artillery fire. Next, in 1884, Hiram Maxim invented an automatic, water-cooled recoil-operated weapon, belt-loaded, and capable of firing 600 rounds a minute. This, together with the Hotchkiss gun (which used the gas of each explosion to recock the

piece), established the main principles for all later machine guns.

Artillery was also transformed in the course of the century. The muzzle-loading cannon gave place to breech-loaders, and the smooth-bore barrel to the rifled barrel. The army of Napoleon III employed the first breech-loading artillery at Solferino and Magenta. The American Civil War saw considerable use of iron-rifled cannon (mainly muzzle-loading), including the Brooke and Parrott guns. The smooth-bore 12-pounder Napoleon guns were still in common service producing massed fire from large batteries in the Napoleonic fashion. The next major advance in cannon design was in Germany, where the Essen-based firm of Krupp provided von Moltke with steel-cast, breech-loading cannon which proved far superior to the French artillery pieces in 1870. Within thirty years, the shock of artillery recoil was being compensated by hydraulic mechanisms, making faster rates of fire possible as it was no longer necessary to resite the piece between rounds. All shells had become conoidal in shape, and from 1884 smokeless powder had made shells and bullets both longer ranged and more accurate. The result was that infantry could now engage at 500 yards. Large howitzers were in use at the outbreak of the Russo-Japanese War, and the power of artillery appeared supreme. Firepower, it seemed, ruled the battlefield.

Inevitably, as the range and accuracy of both firearms and artillery increased, battlefield

casualties mounted alarmingly, until new tactical methods were developed. As always in warfare, tactics tended to lag behind technology. Thus the infantry formations used in the Crimea, and even in the first three years of the American Civil War, were still based on close-order linear and columnar drills reminiscent of Waterloo, although by the 1860s the rifled musket was in growing use. Indeed, its range and accuracy caused so much havoc amongst front-line artillery crews that field pieces had to be withdrawn from close-range positions. Battles such as Shiloh (6–7 April 1862), fought near the Tennessee River, saw heavy casualties on both sides, the Union forces losing 13,000 out of almost 63,000 engaged, the Confederates suffering 10,600 casualties out of 40,000 engaged.

Gradually the lesson sunk home that massed attacks were wasteful. New tactics were therefore introduced: infantry were trained to fight in loose screen formations, using cover, and it became appreciated that one great advantage of

THE BATTLE OF GETTYSBURG, 1-3 JULY 1863

The disposition of the forces on the third day of the battle will be found on the double-page spread overleaf, accompanied by a key. The captions below describe the crucial moments in the battle, which are to be found, in chronological order, on the page opposite and on the final page of the colour section. A full description of the battle will be found on pp 187–190.

1. On the morning of 1 July, the Union cavalry of General Buford, patrolling north-west of Gettysburg, contacts Confederate troops forming part of A P Hill's corps. A skirmish develops into a considerable action, as both sides send up reinforcements.

2. Ewell attacks the heavily outnumbered Union forces drawn up on Culp's Hill on the evening of 1 July. Ewell's failure to press home this critical advantage gives Union reinforcements time to reach the scene.

3. Longstreet's attack on Little Round Top on 2 July. He fails to carry this key position, occupied in the nick of time by the Union engineer General Warren, and is repulsed. Overnight, increasing numbers of Union troops reach Meade, the Union commander.

4. Pickett's charge at 2 pm on 3 July, Lee's last major assault, directed at the centre of the Union line. After a heavy preliminary bombardment, 15,000 Confederate troops sweep forward, to meet a hail of fire from Meade's carefully prepared position. Only 150 survivors reach the crest of the ridge; Lee, between two trees at bottom left of picture, accepts defeat.

5. At the same time, a few miles away at Spangler's Springs, 'Jeb' Stuart and the Confederate cavalry attempt to attack the rear of the Union army and fall into a trap laid for them by the Union cavalry under General Gregg. Attacked on three sides, the Confederates are overwhelmed.

Gettysburg is an example of a chance encounter escalating into a major battle. The tactics used by both sides were still basically Napoleonic. Lee failed to press home his advantage over the first two days, giving Meade the time to come up. Lee's two crucial mistakes were his sending Stuart on a raid, which deprived the Confederates of cavalry intelligence, and his failure to impose his will on his recalcitrant subordinates Ewell and Longstreet. After Gettysburg the Army of Northern Virginia was never again the superb offensive fighting machine it had been in its prime. Although the charge of Pickett's division is one of the most renowned in military history, it drove home the savage lesson that, in the face of the massed firepower of modern weaponry, attempts to apply Frederickan or Napoleonic tactical concepts were both futile and horribly wasteful of human lives.

1

2

3

The situation on the afternoon of 3 July

Terrain
1. Gettysburg
2. Seminary Ridge
3. Culp's Hill
4. Cemetery Ridge
5. The Peach Orchard
6. Little Round Top
7. Round Top

Confederates
8. Confederate II Corps, led by General Ewell
9. Confederate III Corps, led by General Hill
10. Confederate III Corps, led by General Longstreet
11. Pickett's Charge
12. Robert E Lee

Union
13. Union XIII Corps and part of I Corps
14. Union XI Corps
15. General Hancock's command, part of I Corps and all of II and III Corps
16. Union V Corps
17. Union VI Corps
18. General Meade, Union C-in-C

4   5

above
The Union's great siege
mortar, 'Dictator',
employed in the siege of
Petersburg during the
American Civil War. The
importance of artillery
of all types grew rapidly
during the second half of
the nineteenth century,
and by 1914 an obsession
with firepower had
become an overriding
factor.

left
The battle of Shiloh,
6–7 April 1862, was a
particularly gory
encounter in the
American Civil War.
General Rousseau's
troops are shown
recapturing a lost
battery.

the breech-loader was that soldiers could fire and reload lying down. It was realized that, when natural cover was not available, one answer lay in digging; in consequence field fortification was revived and developed. As smokeless powder became widely employed, the traditional fog of battle was greatly diminished, and colourful uniforms became increasingly unpopular as they presented too good a target. As a result, by the 1870s and 1880s armies were adopting drab or muted uniforms, and by the end of the century all British and American troops were in khaki and the Germans in field-grey. By 1914 the French was the only army that still did not have a field uniform. Their infantry went into the First World War wearing their beautiful gold-buttoned uniforms – the red kepi, the blue coat and the red trousers. Trench warfare, however, made uniforms of neutral colour essential and the French chose the horizon-blue of the *poilu*.

As the century progressed, the role of cavalry also underwent a change. Accurate rifle fire – and above all that of machine guns – spelt the end of the great cavalry charge with swords and lances, save for skirmishing and occasional colonial wars against ill-armed natives (as at Omdurman in the Sudan in 1898). Instead, cavalry became increasingly regarded as mounted infantry, using their mounts for mobility and range, before dismounting to employ their firearms once the scene of action had been reached. Thus the late nineteenth-century cavalryman had more in common with the Viking of the tenth century than with Prince Murat of the early nineteenth, although in mid-century there was still room for splendid mounted cavalry engagements such as the charge of the Heavy Brigade at Balaclava in 1855, which has undeservedly received far less attention than the suicidal charge of the Light Brigade under Lord Cardigan at the same battle. Another change affecting the tactical employment of cavalry was its increasing use as a weapon for interdictive raiding, one of many developments of the American Civil War, when far-ranging cavalry columns were sent deep behind enemy lines to attack depots and, above all, railway installations.

All these tactical trends were well established by the end of the century. Boer riflemen, fighting at long range from cover and trenches, hastened the processes of tactical reform and modernization in the British army. The losses of Colenso or Magersfontein could not be overlooked. The Boer War also saw cavalry used almost wholly in a strategical rather than a tactical role, at least in its mounted capacity, and showed the importance of first-class training. The Russo-Japanese struggle, with its heavy howitzers and long-range artillery, hastened the development of entrenched positions and the need for overhead cover and massive defences. A military revolution had almost been carried through. The age of the infantryman was giving way to that of the gunner.

The coming of the industrial age had as radical an effect on strategy as on weaponry and tactics. The age of steam led to a major revolution in naval warfare and also had a great impact on the prosecution of war on land. Railways, and the associated electric telegraph, transformed both the movement and the control of land forces. Troops could now be moved rapidly over large distances and arrive fresh at their destinations. At the same time, railways conferred certain limitations. Generals were often tied when selecting lines of advance to where railway lines ran – a fact that reduced strategical initiative until the network became comprehensive. Moreover, armies relying on railways for supplies presented their opponents with a tempting target for deep-penetration cavalry raiding, and therefore made them more conscious of the security of their lines of communication than ever before. Railways were first used for war on a large scale

in 1859, when both France and Austria moved troops into northern Italy, but they effectively came into their own in the American Civil War when it was partly the relative weakness of the South in terms of rail mileage and rolling stock that helped decide the ultimate issue, although paradoxically it was the Confederate use of the railroad to rush reinforcements to the front that enabled them to win the first major engagement of the war at Bull Run (21 July 1861). The Prussian army, inspired by von Moltke, also appreciated the full significance of railways, and it was Prussia's ability to mobilize 400,000 men on the frontier within twenty-one days of war's declaration in 1870, to France's 100,000 men, that underpinned Bismarck's triumph over Napoleon III. The limitations of railways were demonstrated in the Russo-Japanese War when the Trans-Siberian Railway proved incapable of sustaining the Tsar's army over 5,000 miles.

The development of the electric telegraph also had great implications at both grand strategic and strategical levels. In the American Civil War, the use of the railway telegraph system enabled governments to keep in very close touch with their armies in the field. This led to immense friction in the North, where President Lincoln interfered constantly with the conduct of day-to-day operations, to the fury of successive commanders. This highlighted the problem of relations between politicians and the military and emphasized the political control of the war effort in a democracy at war. At the strategical level, von Moltke demonstrated the significance of the new means of operational control during the Six Weeks War by running the entire war against Austria from his headquarters in Berlin. He only quitted them to follow the armies a mere four days before the decisive battle was fought at Sadowa (3 July 1866); in the meantime, using five

Franco-Prussian War, 1870–71. The French defence of the cemetery of St Privat, where the Prussians suffered heavy losses. A frontal attack by the Prussian Guard cost 8,000 casualties in a space of twenty minutes.

right
The modernized Prussian army was inspired and controlled by its incomparable General Staff. This group shows key figures in the Prussian unification of Germany, depicted on the battlefield of Königgrätz, 1866, where Austria was defeated at the end of a lightning campaign of seven weeks' duration. Third from the left is the great statesman, Otto von Bismarck, with, on his left, von Roon and von Moltke the Elder, the senior military men, and, on the extreme right of the picture, their master, King William of Prussia.

below
Omdurman, 2 September 1898. The rout of the Mahdi's forces avenged the murder of General Gordon at Khartoum, and demonstrated once again the effectiveness of well-directed firepower. Kitchener's success was the culmination of the age of 'little wars' fought by the Victorian army. Note the Maxim guns.

railways, he had controlled the deployment of 250,000 men along 275 miles of front. Thus dawned the age of remote control at the strategic level.

Great strides were also made in the realm of staff organizations, Prussia once again leading the way. Von Moltke's famous General Staff, subdivided into General (operational), Administrative and Quartermaster branches, largely evolved out of the need for a military railway office. The placing of trained staff officers at every major formation was made possible by instituting comprehensive training at special war or staff colleges. Von Moltke ran the wars of 1866 and 1870 by issuing broad directives for faithful implementation by his trusted subordinates serving at the front. After 1871, many nations hastened to copy the Prussian system. The conduct of war had become thoroughly professional, although it took the shock of the Boer War to induce Great Britain to create a General Staff in 1904. Further reforms of far-reaching importance were then rushed through by Lord Haldane, as the British army was belatedly

A world apart from the splendour of nineteenth-century European cavalry were the Boer commandos of the first years of the twentieth century. These tough farmers, with their deadly Mauser rifles and wiry ponies, combined mobility and accurate firepower. The British eventually responded by raising similar formations in South Africa, and mounted infantry became common.

brought up to date, to face the new century.

With industrial expansion came accelerated population growth, making possible larger armies, almost all of which were based upon conscription in varying forms. The American Civil War was the first major struggle to be fought by basically conscript armies, totalling several millions, on both sides. During the same period, economic and psychological warfare took on a new significance with the North's strangulation of the South's vital cotton trade, and General Sherman's deliberate harshness against the civilian population of the South during his march to the sea from Chickamauga to Savannah in 1864–65. The concept of unconditional surrender also underlined the growing totality of warfare. Equally significantly, military success was no longer seen to imply complete political victory. After the surrender of Napoleon III in 1870, the Prussians were forced to besiege Paris and quell popular resistance in the French provinces before imposing a dictated peace. Similarly, the British conquest of the Transvaal and Orange Free State in 1900 only served as the prelude to the bitter guerrilla phase of the struggle, which lasted into 1901. Here was a portent for the future: it was not only governments and armies that had to be cowed but also complete peoples, if victory was to have any meaning.

For the period between 1816 and 1914, four soldiers merit special mention. They all belong to the latter half of the period. The first two were the giants of the American Civil War, Robert E Lee and Ulysses S Grant. Lee is a romantic figure of great appeal and even greater abilities. In the first years of the war he served as the key adviser to the Confederate President, Jefferson Davis. The South's only real hope of success lay in securing European recognition and intervention, given the disparity of military, economic and population resources between North and South. This necessitated a strategic defensive fought by tactically offensive means–the defence of Confederate territory with the aid of strong offensives into the North. Lincoln's acumen,

and other circumstances, ultimately doomed this concept.

Lee's true greatness, however, lay in the field. His strategic expertise functioned best at the level of a single theatre of war, and his service commanding the Army of North Virginia from 1862 restricted his viewpoint. His skill at grand tactics on the battlefield was amazing, particularly when acting with 'Stonewall' Jackson as his subordinate, as his handling of the actions of Second Bull Run (1862) and Chancellorsville (1863) clearly demonstrated. Despite his inferior forces, he inflicted drubbing after drubbing on his Northern foes, until Gettysburg (see below).

Lee was not a 'modern' general. The epitome of the gentleman, he was the embodiment of Jomini's theories of warfare. For all his acumen, however, he never fully appreciated the significance of railways and did nothing to produce a first-class army staff. His skill at army administration and supply precluded an appreciation of the relationship between war and politics, and his abilities did not grow appreciably with the passage of years. Nevertheless, he was the inspiration of the Confederacy and its soldiers.

By contrast, Ulysses Grant was a commander who unquestionably grew in military stature as the war progressed. He was fully aware of the importance of politico-military cooperation. He was the first commander to appreciate the wisdom of Lincoln's preferred strategy, that of attacking the Confederacy at several points at once to make the most of the North's growing preponderance of men and material. He backed the strategy of splitting the Confederacy from north to south down the Mississippi (1862–63), and then from east to west (Sherman's march to the sea), whilst maintaining ceaseless pressure against Richmond from the north–the front that had absorbed almost all the attention of his predecessors (to the ruin of their reputations) in the first years of the war.

A man of immense character and moral strength, he relied on common sense. He once claimed, 'The art of war is simple enough. Find out where your enemy is. Get at him as soon as

General Robert E Lee (1807–70), the hero of the Confederacy and one of the most capable commanders of the nineteenth century.

General William Tecumseh Sherman (1820–91), who conducted the famous 'march to the sea' from Atlanta to Savannah in 1864, which split the land area of the Confederacy. A tough, brutal soldier, he coined the famous dictum, 'War is Hell', and deliberately harassed the Southern civilian population.

Field Marshal von Moltke (1800–91), mastermind of the Prussian General Staff and the ablest European soldier since Napoleon. He made the greatest use of railways and wireless telegraphy to achieve decisive victories over both Austria and France.

you can. Strike at him as hard as you can and as often as you can, and keep moving on.' These concepts were demonstrated in his famous Vicksburg campaign (1863). In this campaign he deliberately broke every rule. After the initial check to his plans, he was advised to return to Memphis to open a safe line of operations. Instead, he adopted a series of daring experiments, well aware of the political damage any great delay in the west could cause. At one stage he abandoned all lines of communication and fought a series of reversed-front actions, driving the enemy back into Vicksburg, which he then besieged and took after heroic resistance. He deliberately fostered good relations with Lincoln (unlike his predecessors), held press conferences and played along with the Government's whims. Cool, unexcitable and completely determined, he was a general cast in the modern mould.

Helmuth von Moltke was the greatest European general since Napoleon. His was an intellectual preeminence *par excellence*; he was a staff officer for more than sixty years, a student of war and a scholar of distinction, yet a soldier who never commanded a regiment. A convinced nationalist, he backed Bismarck to the hilt, and made possible the great successes of 1866 and 1870–71. Head of the Prussian General Staff from 1857, he advocated spending immense sums to develop the railway network on which he based his strategies. No dogmatist, he stressed the need for initiative at every level, and issued only the most essential directives, encouraging the use of independent judgement by subordinates to carry out their spirit if not the exact letter. Minimum interference from the top levels of the command system was his rule–and the fruit of his concepts were Sadowa, Gravelotte and Sedan.

Count Alfred von Schlieffen, German Chief of Staff from 1891 to 1905, was the most extreme example of the new generation of professional soldiers, possessing vast military knowledge and dedication but limited political awareness. His scheme for dealing with a war on two fronts, by smashing France first with a massive onslaught through Belgium before turning against Russia, was not flawless, as he himself realized before his death. It was carried out in a heavily modified form in 1914 by von Moltke the Younger, and led to failure. Nevertheless, its originator was perhaps the most noted strategist of the late nineteenth century.

At the beginning of the twentieth century, therefore, Europe was rapidly being turned into an armed camp, as each country modernized its forces along mainly German lines and chased alliances in the search for collective security. Arms races and international rivalries heightened the tension. Using the system of reservists organized into various classes, the great powers could mobilize between them some 14 million men within a few weeks. Europe teetered on the brink of catastrophe. The writings of a Polish banker, Ivan Bloch, prophesied the form of a future major war: a terrible struggle of attrition in which the defensive would have the advantage, resulting in the drawn-out stalemate of trench warfare, dominated by artillery, until one rival society or the other cracked under the strain. It was a grim prophecy, but it would come very near to the truth.

The Battle of Gettysburg, 1–3 July 1863

By the middle of May 1863, the Confederacy was growing weaker and the power of the North was at last being mobilized. Faced with Vicksburg in the last extremity on the western front, a receding hope of European intervention, and fruitless victories on the eastern front, Jefferson Davis decided on a last gamble. He ordered General Robert E Lee to launch an offensive into Union territory, in the hope of shaking Lincoln's resolve and earning an armistice.

On 3 June, Lee secretly left Fredericksburg and headed for Harrisburg. His move did not long go undetected by the Union General Hooker, who determined to place his 100,000 men between Lee and the capital, Washington. However, Hooker was replaced by General Meade on 28 June as a result of a dispute with the Federal Government.

On 23 June, Lee made the mistake of detaching J E B Stuart and much of the Confederate cavalry to make a raid. This lasted nine days, and for this vital period the main army was deprived of news and cover. Lee, therefore, had no idea how fast or exactly where Meade was moving until he learnt on the 29th that his communications with Virginia were threatened. He halted his northward march and concentrated at Cashtown.

That same day, a Union cavalry division on a reconnaissance under Buford reached Gettysburg, and camped near the town. Next day, a

General Ulysses S Grant (1822–85), the great Union Commander-in-Chief from 1863, who proved capable of both defeating the Confederacy and of cooperating to the full with President Abraham Lincoln.

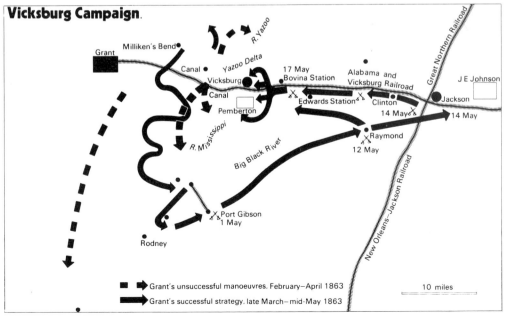

Vicksburg Campaign.

Grant's brilliant Vicksburg campaign, which achieved a strategic penetration of the Confederacy, cutting it in two and preventing the transfer of troops from the west to the east.

187

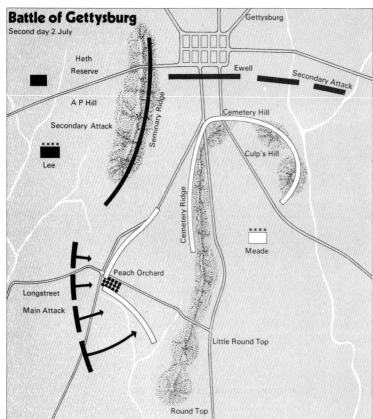

Battle of Gettysburg
Second day 2 July

Gettysburg

Heth
Reserve

Ewell

Secondary Attack

A P Hill

Cemetery Hill

Secondary Attack

Seminary Ridge

Culp's Hill

Lee

Cemetery Ridge

Meade

Peach Orchard

Longstreet

Main Attack

Little Round Top

Round Top

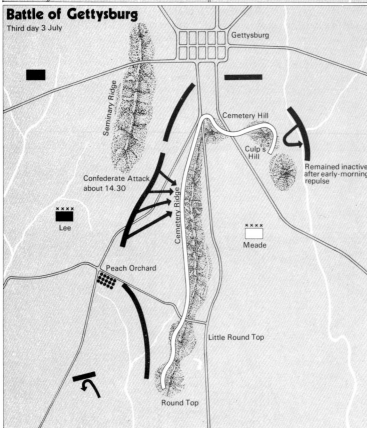

Battle of Gettysburg
Third day 3 July

Gettysburg

Seminary Ridge

Cemetery Hill

Culp's
Hill

Remained inactive
after early-morning
repulse

Confederate Attack
about 14.30

Cemetery Ridge

Lee

Meade

Peach Orchard

Little Round Top

Round Top

Confederate brigade on a foraging detail reported
Buford's presence to General A P Hill (commanding the nearest of Lee's three corps), who,
on his own authority, ordered all his men towards Gettysburg. On the morning of 1 July,
a tough fight broke out north-west of the town.
Buford held on manfully and alerted Meade,
who was eight miles away at Pipe Creek, and
soon the two small Federal corps were on their
way to his assistance. By mid-afternoon quite
a sizeable battle was raging, with the advantage
swinging in the Confederate favour. By evening,
the Union troops had been forced back with heavy
loss to Cemetery Ridge, south of Gettysburg. By
dusk, both Lee and Ewell's corps had joined Hill,
and the Confederates had thus built up a considerable numerical advantage. However, Ewell
disregarded a rather vague order from Lee to
attack Culp's Hill that evening, and a chance to
overwhelm the northern end of the Union line

left and bottom
Two views of Gettysburg
from Union artillery
positions.

was therefore lost.

Overnight saw the arrival of Meade with more troops. He decided to fight the next day and called up the rest of his army. By noon on the 2nd, Lee had been joined by Longstreet's Corps, bringing his strength to 83,000 men. Only Stuart's 5,000 cavalry were still distant. Throughout the 2nd, therefore, Lee retained the numerical advantage over the five Union corps in position, although the odds were steadily shortening. Lee then decided to launch a strong attack against Meade's left near Little Round Top, linked with a diversion by Ewell in the north. However, Longstreet delayed opening his attack until 4 pm, and this enabled General Sickles to extricate his exposed corps from the area of the Peach Orchard on the road to Emmitsburg, giving a sapper named Warren time to extemporize defences for Little Round Top. Both Confederate attacks finally foundered, although Ewell came

close to success in the north against Culp's Hill before night intervened.

By early on the 3rd, the remainder of Meade's army had appeared. The Union army's 88,200 men and over 100 guns gave the North the numerical superiority. Lee, conferring with the recently arrived Stuart, decided to make a major attack against the centre of the Union line, whilst his cavalry hit the rear simultaneously. Meade guessed that this was likely, and overnight he strengthened his centre, placing many guns in concealed positions. The morning passed with indecisive skirmishing, but shortly after 1 pm 138 Confederate guns opened fire, and at 2 pm some 15,000 Confederate troops (Lee's last fresh men) led by Generals Heth, Pender and Pickett, swept forward. As they advanced over open ground towards the ridge, Meade revealed his guns in a murderous cross-fire. Only 150 Confederates reached the summit of the ridge,

'the high-water mark of the Confederacy', and they were soon routed. Meanwhile, Gregg's Union cavalry defeated Stuart's cavalry near Spangler's Springs. By 5 pm the battle was over, and with it all hope of a Confederate victory in the war. Meade lost 23,049 casualties over the three days; Lee lost 23,063. The Union could afford these losses: the Confederacy could not. Davis' gamble had failed.

The Battle of Gravelotte-Mars-la-Tour, 18 August 1870

After a series of sharp frontier clashes with the Prussian forces, the French commanders found themselves everywhere at a disadvantage, and there was grave danger that their two field armies (one under MacMahon in the north near Sedan, the second under Bazaine in the general vicinity of Metz) would find themselves strategically divided. This was indeed the intention of the German general staff. Following the preliminary fighting at Mars-la-Tour on 16 August, Bazaine unwisely fell back eastwards, pivoting on his left flank, in order to take up a strong position enclosed on three sides by the rivers Orne and Moselle and the fortress of Metz. Von Moltke lost little time in following up the French, executing a daring swing to the northeast to bring his forces face to face with the new French position. By early on the 18th a reversed-front battle was about to begin, with each side facing its base.

Bazaine placed four of his corps in a line between Roncourt and the suburbs of Metz, and in anticipation of a Prussian attempt to turn his southern (or left) flank, he ordered the Reserve (the Guard Corps) to take up station behind his left wing. In all, the French had 150,000 men present.

Although the Prussians had selected a strong position, bottling the French into a restricted area, they had failed to reconnoitre fully on the 17th and therefore wrongly assumed that the French line only extended from Montigny to Rozerieulles. This could have been a fatal error. However, they deployed their 180,000 men as follows. XII Corps and the Prussian Guards were to envelop Bazaine's right flank (which they believed undefended) before rolling up his lines, whilst VIII and VII Corps attacked the opposite flank, aided by IX Corps. Two further corps, X Corps and III Corps, would serve as reserves behind the northern and central sectors, ready to exploit the anticipated collapse of the French right wing.

Soon after the battle opened, therefore, the Prussians discovered their error; instead of having an open area of countryside, denuded of French troops, on the northern sector, they found their advance hotly contested all the way from Roncourt to Rozerieulles. This inevitably upset the impetus of von Moltke's attack, and for much of the morning and afternoon little progress was made, as a series of rather poorly

Marshal Bazaine, the French commander decisively defeated at Gravelotte.

A scene at the battle of Gravelotte, 1870.

The French Montigny *mitrailleuse*, one ancestor of the machine gun. The French 'secret weapon' in 1870, it was misused in operations against the Prussians.

coordinated attacks were launched against Bazaine's line. For a time, indeed, defeat appeared to be staring the Prussians in the face. The German IX Corps and Guard Corps sustained crippling casualties when they marched forward in massed formation, the French *chassepot* muskets taking a heavy toll, whilst the attack against the French left was only saved from disaster by the opportune arrival of II Corps from Pont-à-Mousson. This timely reinforcement enabled the Prussians to withstand the French counterattack on this sector, mounted by the French Guards released from reserve by Bazaine –prematurely as it proved.

The decisive action took place at 7 pm, when part of the Prussian XII Corps, after making a long detour, succeeded in turning the extreme right flank of the French line. This manoeuvre induced the exposed French VI Corps to abandon its position and fall back southwards. This in turn forced the retirement of all of Bazaine's line. Overnight, Bazaine pulled all his men back from the front and shut them within the fortifications of Metz. During the day's fighting, the Germans had suffered an estimated 20,000 casualties, and the French some 13,000.

Although the Prussian techniques displayed at this battle were not particularly impressive (indeed it might be said that they snatched a minor tactical advantage at the eleventh hour) the strategic result was a major Prussian triumph. Bazaine, obsessed with the questionable need to employ all his resources to defend Metz (one corps would have sufficed), failed to achieve the desired concentration with MacMahon. He enabled von Moltke's strategy to succeed, and the twin disasters of Metz and Sedan sealed the fate of the French Second Empire.

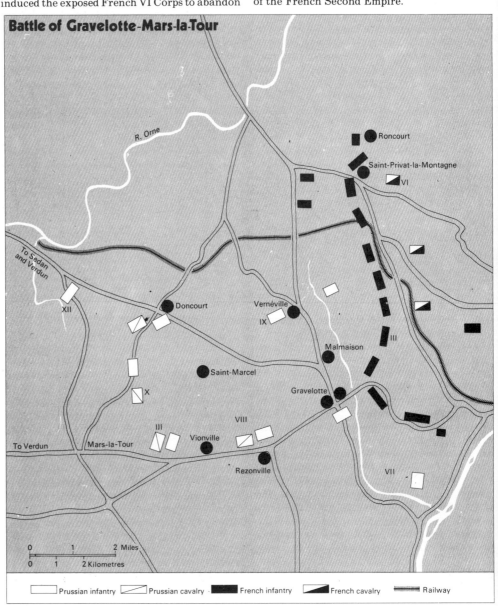

Battle of Gravelotte-Mars-la-Tour

R. Orne

Roncourt

Saint-Privat-la-Montagne

VI

To Sedan and Verdun

XII

Doncourt

Vernéville

IX

III

Malmaison

Saint-Marcel

Gravelotte

X

III

VIII

To Verdun

Mars-la-Tour

Vionville

Rezonville

VII

| 0 | 1 | 2 Miles |
| 0 | 1 | 2 Kilometres |

| | Prussian infantry | | Prussian cavalry | | French infantry | | French cavalry | | Railway |

THE FIRST WORLD WAR

In August 1914 there commenced a struggle the like of which mankind had never experienced before. By its close in November 1918 it is estimated that some 65 million men had been mobilized, and 29 million of these had become casualties (including 8 million dead). These grim totals take no account of civilian losses caused either directly or indirectly by the war, The cost in terms of money is incalculable, but a round sum well in excess of a billion pounds sterling would probably be a conservative estimate.

This was armageddon on a terrible new scale, involving, in the final count, twelve nations on the Allied side and four on that of the Central Powers. By its close, three mighty empires had fallen: Tsarist Russia, the German Second Reich and the Austro-Hungarian Empire. A period of economic dislocation gripped the world over the following decade and helped to contribute to the return of international tensions that would lead directly to another world cataclysm, just twenty years after the signing of the Peace of Versailles in 1919.

At the outset hardly anybody foresaw four years of war; most forecast a speedy conclusion, and 'Over by Christmas' was the popular slogan of the hour. The Germans were confident that the amended version of the Schlieffen Plan would see German troops in Paris within a month, and the consequent surrender of France. This would leave Germany free to redeploy its divisions to the east, ready to meet the legions of Russia, which the Austrian forces and residual German formations would meanwhile have kept occupied. Britain and France, on the other hand, felt sure that Plan XVII (which envisaged a mighty blow into Alsace-Lorraine whilst two French armies and the British Expeditionary Force guarded the Belgian flank) would keep the Germans occupied until the Russian 'steamroller' could roll in from the east. Both sides, however, made critical miscalculations. The Germans found that they could not muster enough men to make their great wheel through Belgium unassailable. Moreover, they found the railway network incapable of taking the traffic involved in even the abridged scheme. They also underestimated the fighting qualities of the British Expeditionary Force, the Old Contemptibles, who took their nickname from a derogatory remark made by Kaiser Wilhelm II. The French, on the other hand, overestimated the military strength of Russia, and seriously miscalculated the strength Germany could put into the field at the outbreak of war.

The result was stalemate on the Western Front by the end of 1914, and a rather more flexible situation in the east. Germany had sustained one considerable defeat at the Marne in September, and achieved two great victories at Tannenberg and the Masurian Lakes (August-September –see below), but nowhere was there the least prospect of a speedy end to the war. Indeed, its scope was spreading; Turkey declared war on the Allies on 29 October, and Italy entered the lists in March 1915. Now all the major participants, with the exception of the United States, were in the struggle, and a mighty war of attrition began, involving whole societies and economies. The nineteenth-century concept of the 'nation in arms' was soon transformed into that of the 'nation at war'. Britain continued to avoid recourse to conscription until 1916, but the mobilization of women to work in factories, on the land, and at many other tasks normally reserved for men, was one feature of the new dimension of war. The first tentative Zeppelin raids spelt the opening of the era of strategic bombing, in which civilian populations were effectively in the firing line. The growing U-boat campaign also began to have serious economic effects on the British Isles, traditionally vulnerable to blockade.

By Christmas 1914, therefore, far from being in Paris or Berlin respectively, the rival armies found themselves manning a series of trenches, sometimes only separated by a few dozen yards, stretching all the way from Switzerland to the English Channel. Lord Kitchener, British Minister of War, admitted his bafflement. 'I don't know what is to be done. This isn't war.' It was certainly not the kind of struggle that the generals and soldiers of 1914 had anticipated, although a close study of Vicksburg (1863), Mukden (1905) or even Magersfontein (1899) might have supplied a strong clue. With what was to prove ill-placed optimism, the Allies chose to ignore the stalemate and retained large bodies of cavalry behind the front, for the great breakthrough

that did not materialize until 1918. For three and a half years no offensive was to prove capable of moving the front line more than ten miles in either direction. The Germans were probably correct to adopt a basically defensive strategy, leaving it to the Allies to mount one costly offensive after another, such as the Somme (where the new British volunteer armies suffered 60,000 casualties on 1 July 1916) or the third battle of Ypres. Even when the Germans did launch a major attack at Verdun in 1916, it

was intended to trap the French into a grinding battle of attrition. By the time the eleven-month battle had burnt itself out in late December, the French had sustained over 500,000 casualties to the Germans' 430,000, most of them in a salient measuring barely fifteen miles.

The nature of trench warfare deserves a more detailed description, as it came to dominate the war not only on the Western Front but also in the Balkans and Middle East, amongst the Alps, and, to a slightly lesser degree, inside Poland and Russia. At first the trenches were mere ditches, but as time passed they became more elaborate, with belts of barbed wire, firing bays, dugouts of every size, and communication and support trenches. A description of part of the vaunted Hindenburg Line, near Cambrai, illustrates the complexity of field engineering by 1917. The position comprised three sets of double trenches. The front line consisted of advance posts, backed by a wide fire trench, supported in turn by a second trench some 200 yards to the rear. The main Hindenburg support line was dug a mile to the rear, again two trenches in depth, and finally, a further two miles back, was the nearly completed third line. In all, six belts of barbed wire, the densest being 100 yards thick, protected the main line alone, and the forward and rear positions were similarly provided for. Dozens of zigzag communication trenches linked the various lines, and to the rear were sited hundreds of guns zeroed to strafe no-man's-land with shrapnel and high explosive, or gas shells, the moment the alarm was raised. Further forward were sited strong machine-gun posts with interlocking zones of fire.

Living conditions in these trenches were often appalling. During the wet seasons the trenches became morasses; none who experienced it ever forgot the mud of Flanders, which could engulf without trace a man or animal straying from the

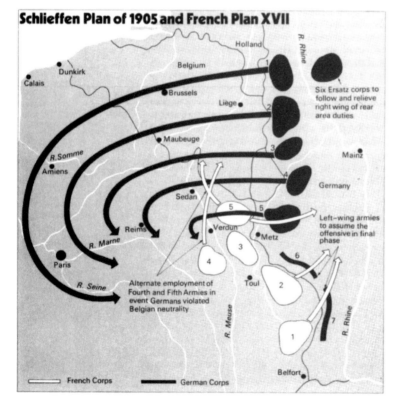

Schlieffen Plan of 1905 and French Plan XVII

Six Ersatz corps to
follow and relieve
right wing of rear
area duties

Left-wing armies
to assume the
offensive in final
phase

Alternate employment of
Fourth and Fifth Armies in
event Germans violated
Belgian neutrality

French Corps   German Corps

French quick-fire field guns, the famous '75s'. A battery going into action on the Aisne early in the war.

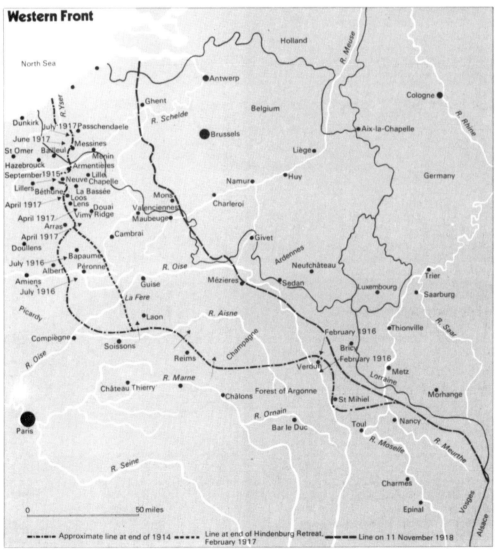

Western Front

North Sea

Holland

R. Meuse

Antwerp

Ghent

R. Schelde

Belgium

Cologne

R. Rhine

Dunkirk
July 1917 Passchendaele
June 1917
St Omer Bailleul
Hazebrouck Menin
September 1915 Armentières
Lillers Neuve Chapelle
Béthune La Bassée
April 1917 Loos Lens
April 1917 Vimy Ridge Douai
Arras
April 1917
Doullens
July 1916 Bapaume
Albert Péronne
Amiens
July 1916
Picardy
Compiègne
R. Oise Soissons

Messines

Brussels

Liège

Aix-la-Chapelle

Namur Huy

Germany

Mons
Valenciennes
Charleroi
Maubeuge
Cambrai
Givet

R. Oise

Ardennes
Neufchâteau

Guise
La Fere
Laon

R. Aisne

Mézières Sedan

Luxembourg

Trier

Saarburg

R. Saar

February 1916 Thionville
Bricy
February 1916
Verdun
Champagne

Reims

R. Marne
Château Thierry
Châlons Forest of Argonne
R. Ornain
Bar le Duc

Metz

Lorraine

St Mihiel

Morhange

Toul Nancy

Paris

R. Seine

R. Moselle *R. Meurthe*

Charmes

Epinal

Vosges

Alsace

0 _____ 50 miles

—·—·— Approximate line at end of 1914   ▪▪▪▪ Line at end of Hindenburg Retreat. ▬▬▬ Line on 11 November 1918
February 1917

Thirty-ninth Siege Battery, Royal Garrison Artillery, in action with their 8-inch howitzers near Mametz in 1916.

The battle of the Marne, September 1914. The German invasion was checked and each side, in attempting to outflank the other, began the 'Race to the Sea'. The lines reached the Channel near Dunkirk and quickly became stabilized.

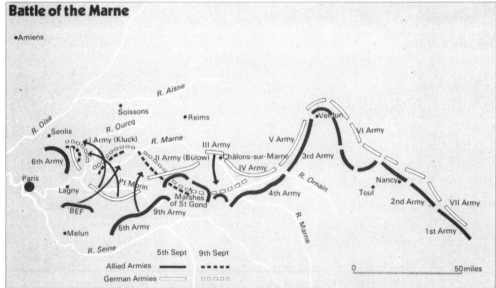

Battle of the Marne

Amiens

R. Aisne

R. Oise

Soissons

R. Ourcq

Senlis

Reims

I Army (Kluck)

R. Marne

Verdun

VI Army

6th Army

II Army (Bülow)

III Army

V Army

Châlons-sur-Marne

3rd Army

Paris

Lagny

Pt Morin

IV Army

Nancy

BEF

Marshes of St Gond

9th Army

R. Ornain

4th Army

Toul

2nd Army

VII Army

Melun

5th Army

R. Marne

1st Army

R. Seine

5th Sept   9th Sept

Allied Armies ▬▬▬   ▬ ▬ ▬

German Armies ▭▭▭   ▯▯▯

0   50 miles

Huge Turkish fortress gun in the Madjar-Kale battery near Chanak, part of the defences of the Dardanelles. The Turks proved doughty opponents at Gallipoli, in Mesopotamia, and in Palestine.

left
Isandhlwana, the scene of a desperate struggle in 1879 during the Zulu War. A British force of some 6,000 men was almost wiped out in a surprise attack by a force of 10,000 Zulus. The British were overwhelmed before they could use their firepower effectively. A year later, at Ulundi, concentrated rifle fire defeated the Zulus.

below
Bavarian troops, allied to Napoleon, fighting at the battle of Polotsk during the Russian campaign of 1812. A fine painting by W Kobell, showing the distinctive Bavarian uniforms and other equipment. *Schloss Nymphenburg, Munich.*

The charge of the Heavy Brigade under General Scarlett at the battle of Balaclava, 25 October 1854. Although less celebrated than the ill-fated charge of the Light Brigade at the same battle, this attack was far more successful, the Russian cavalry being routed as they strove to exploit the capture of some Turkish guns.
National Army Museum, London.

above
British troops man a
dilapidated fire post
during the German spring
offensive in April 1918,
as the enemy loom
through the rain soon
after sunrise.

right
French heavy tanks in
action near Soissons,
July 1918.

wooden duckboards. In the Middle East and Balkans, heat and thirst were the great slayers – as at Gallipoli, before Gaza or at Salonika – but the Middle Eastern winters could be bitterly cold as well. Disease was rampant: dysentery and trench foot in Flanders; malaria, cholera and heat exhaustion in the Levant. Deadly boredom was the inevitable lot of the soldier on the quieter sectors of the front. This was only alleviated by the German dawn barrage and the Allied reply at sunset, each side using the glare of the sun behind them to prevent the enemy from registering the positions of their batteries. Nights saw patrolling amongst the myriad shell holes and rotting corpses out in no-man's-land; wiring parties, burial details or resupply detachments would go cautiously about their business, keeping a wary eye open for star shells or rival patrols, whilst the latest batch of wounded would be sent 'down the line' to seek treatment in the rear areas.

Such was the daily routine of life in the trenches, with only the periodic rest periods out of the line to look forward to. From time to time a fresh attempt would be made to achieve a breakthrough. The vast preparations required were hard to conceal from enemy intelligence, particularly reconnaissance aircraft, and the tremendous artillery bombardments that preceded practically every offensive (that preceding the Somme lasted a week) also served notice on the enemy of what was afoot. These bombardments were supposed to cut the enemy's wire and shatter his morale prior to the attack, but very rarely did they achieve either objective. Once the gunfire lifted, wave upon wave of infantry rose out

of their trenches and poured over no-man's-land, to be met by enemy artillery fire, blasts from machine gun posts and rifle fire as the defenders rushed from their deep dugouts to man their weapons. Horrific casualties were the result, and success was measured in yards rather than miles, taking weeks to achieve.

Warfare had sunk to this level because the defensive had become demonstrably the stronger form of war. The combination of barbed wire, machine guns, fast-firing guns, trench mortars of all sizes, Mills bombs, stick grenades, and the magazine-fed, breech-loading rifle made frontal attacks prohibitively costly. However, the tactical theoreticians could envisage nothing

Trench warfare saw a partial return to the armoured suits of former ages. German infantry, armed with stick grenades, man a bomb bay in the Hindenburg line, 1918. Note the telephone wire running along the trench.

The first attempts to break the deadlock of trench war included poison gas. Mustard gas often blinded its victims, here seen awaiting evacuation to field hospitals.

Mud, duckboards and desolation – Château Wood, Ypres, October 1917. This was the all too typical face of trench war on the Western Front. Many men and animals drowned in the mud.

right
The passing of messages
presented great problems.
Radios were rare,
telephone lines were
almost invariably severed
by shell fire. Here, a
British signal post sends
out morse in
Mesopotamia.

opposite, top
British Mark V tanks,
manned by the Fifth
Australian Division,
move up in the assault on
the Hindenburg line. The
tanks carry cribs, which
were used as stepping
stones when crossing the
wide trenches of the
Hindenburg line.

but soldiers advancing in extended order, burdened with full equipment and extra ammunition.

Industrial mass production made available a profusion of sophisticated weaponry. The French 75-mm quick-firing field gun had its counterpart in the German 77-mm and the British 18-pounder. The British Lewis gun, and medium and heavy Vickers machine guns, met their technical match in the German Maxim, the French Hotchkiss and later the American Browning. The German trench mortars were rated as superior, and their medium and heavy artillery included 17-inch howitzers, numbers of Big Berthas and seven huge 9-inch railway guns with 117-foot barrels, which proved capable of bombarding

below
A messenger dog brings
up hot rations to a
German outpost on the
Western Front.

Paris from a range of 65 miles.

It had been hoped that the development of the internal combustion engine, allied to the complex network of railways, would make warfare on land both fluid and mobile, but the power of artillery, the size of armies and the hopelessly outdated tactics led to stalemate. Growing numbers of lorries could supplement horse transport in carrying supplies to the front, but they did not help troops fight, save, perhaps, at the Marne in 1914, when the Paris taxicabs were pressed into service to ferry Galliéni's garrison to the battle at a critical time. Once the trench lines had been established, there was no chance of outflanking manoeuvres at either the tactical or the strategic level.

Tactics existed for clearing trenches, but the crude rush, preceded by a creeping barrage of artillery fire, seemed the only method of large-scale attack. Communications posed a continuing problem. Wirelesses existed only at army and sometimes corps level. Telephone lines were invariably cut by shell fire; signal rockets were used by both sides and could lead to confusion. Finally pigeons and runners were used, the runners enjoying the shortest life expectancy of any soldier at the front. Poor direction from above and inadequate reporting of the current situation were the inevitable results, and it is hardly surprising that the great offensives petered out.

As time passed, however, certain developments seemed to promise a solution to the impasse of the trench war. In April 1915, at Ypres, the Germans introduced chlorine gas discharged from 5,000 large cylinders. This caused a panic amongst the Allies at the second battle of Ypres, but the Germans were not ready to exploit their advantage and the line held. The Allies developed forms of gasmask, and used poison gas in their turn, and the Germans soon realized the disadvantage of the prevailing westerly winds, which aided the Allies. Later, shells firing mustard and phosgene gas were used. They were far more effective than canister gas, as one part of gas could poison 4 million parts of air, blinding and burning those who came into contact with it. The main disadvantage was that the gas lingered for long periods. Gas warfare, however, was employed to the end of the war, but as both sides became used to the weapon its effectiveness decreased.

A more promising development was the British invention of the tank. Winston Churchill had ordered experiments with steamrollers, but the tank was really the brainchild of Colonel Swinton. It was designed to achieve three objectives: to afford protection for its crew from shrapnel and machine gun fire; to tear gaps in or flatten the barbed-wire entanglements defending the approaches to the enemy's positions, and, by the use of its continuous tracks supplemented by fascines, to enable the vehicle to pass over shell holes and trenches whilst its gunners shot up the defenders and aided the supporting

infantry to reach their objectives. The first British tanks, nicknamed 'Mother', 'Big Willie' and 'Little Willie', were cumbersome machines, weighing twenty-eight tons or more, and capable of only three to four miles per hour. They were extremely noisy and prone to many mechanical problems. Not the least of these were breakdowns in steering: the early models relied on moving a vulnerable two-wheeled gun carriage, towed behind the tank, and it was some time before track steering was developed. Another difficulty related to communication with the tank crews once they were battened down. The tank crews had also to be equipped with face visors and special clothing to ward off the white-hot metal flakes from the inside of the tank, which were caused by bullet hits on the outer casing.

Nevertheless, the tank did offer a solution to the deadlock on the Western Front. Unfortunately many conservative Allied generals had limited faith in its potential effect, and it was first used only in penny packets at Flers during the battle of the Somme in 1916. Early next year, tanks proved incapable of dealing with the mud at the third battle of Ypres. It was only in November 1917 that tanks were employed in sufficient strength and under the right conditions at Cambrai (see below). The effect on enemy morale was shattering, but, as with the first gas attacks, the surprise element was not exploited properly. In any case, by Cambrai the Allies were too exhausted to mount another major offensive that year. The Mark IV tank was, however, a great improvement on earlier versions, and its hour

came at Amiens in August 1918 when 430 were used in the first attacks. Ludendorff declared 8 August to be the 'black day of the German army,' and the long war was at last moving towards its close. The French developed the heavy Saint Chamand (armed with a 65-mm gun) and smaller but well designed tanks, such as the six-and-a-half-ton Renault. From March 1918 the Germans half-heartedly produced a few *Sturm-panzerwagen*. A new phase in the development of the art of war had begun.

Of almost equal significance was a change in infantry tactics by the Germans. Appreciating that frontal attacks in extended lines were horribly wasteful of human life, they developed

below
The advent of the internal combustion engine revolutionized warfare. The lorry was first on the scene. Here, frostbitten British soldiers are evacuated at Suvla Bay, November 1915, during the ill-fated Gallipoli campaign.

Hutier tactics. Storm-troopers were trained to infiltrate the enemy lines in small parties, and to head for the rear areas, deliberately bypassing strongpoints. First used at Riga on the Eastern Front in 1917, these concepts also played a part in the German recovery at Cambrai, and were of major importance in the great spring offensives of 1918, which almost shattered the Allied lines. Another German invention was the flame-thrower, a devastating close-range weapon for trench warfare.

Warfare had assumed a new dimension with the advent of air power. Balloons had periodically been used for spotting from as early as the 1790s, but aerial warfare as such only dates from 1914. The development of the internal combustion engine was of central importance for aircraft. Both lighter-than-air (the German Zeppelins) and heavier-than-air machines were developed. They began to exercise a profound influence on the conduct of war. At first, two-seater aircraft were regarded as an ancillary part of the army, and were used largely for artillery spotting and intelligence surveys. Then improvements in machine guns, particularly the French development of synchronized firing through the propeller, encouraged the development of single-seater fighters, which could contend for air supremacy over sectors of the front in defence of their vulnerable spotter aircraft. Thus Sopwith Pups and Camels fought for mastery against German Fokkers. Next, small bombs were dropped on ground targets, at first by hand, later from racks. Gradually the concept of close air tactical support of land operations was evolved. The famous German 'flying circuses' were amongst the first large formations to be organized to battle for air superiority over the front. German aircraft also aided their ground troops to good effect in December 1917 and from March to July in 1918. The Allies were not slow in adopting similar measures, and their final offensives in 1918 made considerable use of close air support. In Palestine, General Allenby's army made telling use of strafing and bombing, after the victory at Megiddo in September 1918, to close the passes behind the retreating Turkish armies. Six months

General von Hutier's Infiltration Tactics

Moving or 'creeping' barrage

Strongpoint

Strongpoint

Reserve

Picked storm–troop units

Reserve

Sequence

1 Short, intensive artillery bombardment
2 Assault force moved into position at last moment by night
3 Infantry advance covered by a creeping artillery barrage, accompanied by light guns
4 Storm troop units infiltrate through 'soft' sector, leaving reserves to engage and mop up the strongpoints

earlier, the independent Royal Air Force had been founded in Great Britain. Fighter aces such as Baron von Richthofen, Hermann Goering and Lieutenant Luke became popular heroes.

Strategic bombing also made its first appearance from 1914 onwards with the Zeppelin raids on London and other centres of industry and population. This was later supplemented by Gotha bombers raids. By 1918 the Allies were planning to bomb Berlin, but the Armistice prevented any operations. These activities, striking directly at both civilian morale and war industries, involved to a greater degree than ever before populations living far from the war fronts. Countermeasures included searchlights, tracer bullets and anti-aircraft guns. Aerial warfare was another dimension, and by the war's end Allied factories were producing over 20,000 aircraft a year.

War at sea saw equally significant developments. In so far as the convoy war had a direct bearing on the ability to maintain the war on land, this is relevant to this volume. The war saw the switch of emphasis from the major fleet action, gun against gun (as at Jutland in 1916), to the more insidious struggle against the submarine and torpedo, which at one point in 1917 had caused such losses to British and Allied shipping that the possibility of Great Britain being reduced to starvation level indubitably existed. The convoy system together with improved submarine detection and hunting methods were employed in the very nick of time. But unrestricted German submarine warfare was a material cause of the entry of the United States into the war in 1917.

War had taken on a new and more terrible form in terms of both scale and human misery. To find the men to fight, and the munitions, weapons, machines and food to back them, governments had to adopt extraordinary measures including food rationing. By 1917, all major belligerents in Europe had adopted universal conscription and the direction of civilian labour. Women were playing a larger role than ever before, in the women's services, on the land and in factories. Submarine and air operations

Two important German commanders: Field-Marshal Paul von Hindenburg (1847–1934), left, and his Chief of Staff and *éminence grise*, General Ludendorff. Between them they won a crushing victory at Tannenberg on the Eastern Front in 1914, but they proved somewhat less successful on the Western Front from 1917, although the spring offensives of 1918 came close to success.

meant that whole populations were in a state of siege. Even democratic governments had to become increasingly authoritarian for the duration and rule by decree or Order in Council. To produce the shells required for the Western Front, Lloyd George, as Minister of Munitions and later Prime Minister, assumed vast powers. Friction bedevilled civil-military relations at the top; Premier Asquith was often at odds with Lords Kitchener and Fisher; Lloyd George strongly disliked Sir Douglas Haig. In the British cabinet, 'Westerners' clashed with 'Easterners' over how to conduct the war. Ultimately the democracies produced in Woodrow Wilson, Clemenceau and Lloyd George three strong statesmen capable of imposing their wills on the complexities of the war effort. Centralized authority became more effective, an advantage enjoyed by the Central Powers from the outset. However, Tsarist Russia cracked beneath the economic and social strains in 1917.

Friction between allies was another phenomenon repeated on a new scale. The Germans were unhappy with the Austrian war effort; both criticized the Turks. The French tried to dictate to Great Britain; the Americans insisted on imposing their terms on both powers in return for their entry into the fighting on the Western Front. This was vital to ultimate Allied victory, as was proved in 1918. The dangers implicit in the successes of the German spring offensives of that year, as German armies transferred from the victorious Eastern Front swept into action in the west, at last persuaded the Allies of their need for a single supreme commander, and Marshal Foch shouldered the responsibility. The

weary French and British armies welcomed the fresh energy of the new troops pouring over the Atlantic, and the tide was checked and then turned. At last the guns fell silent in Europe, the Middle East and those parts of Africa that had become involved in the gargantuan struggle.

In terms of leadership, the First World War produced no commanders of the front rank. Most of them were competent mediocrities, whose occasional blunders or short-sightedness were often mitigated by the General Staff system which the elder von Moltke had first perfected, and which such statesmen as Haldane or the American Eli Root had copied and adapted. This is not to say that there were no important military figures. The Germans had able chiefs of staff in, successively, von Moltke the Younger (a mere shadow of his famous uncle, however), Falkenhayn and Ludendorff. Paul von Hindenburg, victor of Tannenberg in 1914 (see below), was a formidable soldier, as was the Austrian Conrad von Hoetzendorf, who scored telling victories on both the Eastern and Italian Fronts, including Caporetto in 1917. Good fighting generals of the Central Powers included von Mackensen, conqueror of Rumania, Liman von Sanders (mastermind of the defence of the Gallipoli Peninsula against the Allies in 1915–16, and subsequently the ill-fated commander of Turkish armies in Palestine), Mustapha Kemal, the ablest of his Turkish subordinates, and Lettow von Vorbeck, whose intrepid defence of German East Africa against overwhelming odds earned him the unique distinction of being accorded the 'honours of war' when he was forced to capitulate. Many of these leaders had the seeds of greatness, but none was quite worthy of being included amongst the great captains of history.

The same was true of the Western Allies. The French produced a fine supreme commander in Ferdinand Foch, however questionable his mania for massed attacks. 'Papa' Joffre was no mean commander-in-chief, although the battle of Verdun ruined his reputation and career. Amongst the younger generals, Pétain and Weygand were outstanding. The Russian Archduke Nicolas made reasonable use of Russia's poorly organized resources until disastrously superseded by Tsar Nicolas II, whilst by 1916 Alexei Brusilov had emerged as the most able of the Russian commanders. He was in command of the great offensive in 1916 which did much to relieve pressure on the British at the Somme and the French at Verdun. The most notable American general to emerge was John Pershing, organizer of the American Expeditionary Force in 1917, and eventual victor of the great battles of St Mihiel and the Argonne in September and October 1918.

What of Great Britain and her empire? Four senior soldiers merit honourable mention, although many lower commanders also acquitted themselves worthily. Field-Marshal Lord Kitchener was an effective, if controversial, Minister of War until his untimely death *en route* to

Russia in 1916. Sir John French took the British Expeditionary Force to France and helped to win the vital battle of the Marne in 1914. But he lacked dynamism and failed to win the confidence of his political masters. In 1915 he was replaced by Field-Marshal Sir Douglas Haig. This general's abilities have also been the centre of controversy. Although an unimaginative soldier, and very inarticulate, he was a 'stayer' who would accept responsibility for the failures of his subordinates as offensive followed offensive with little to show but appalling casualty lists. He also stood up to the mercurial Lloyd George, and possessed an unshakeable belief in ultimate Allied victory. He saw the potential of the tank when many another doubted its effectiveness, and encouraged its developers. He proved adept at cooperation with both the French and Americans, but was not keen on establishing a supreme command. As even his critic Lloyd George admitted, 'Who could we send in his place?' At a slightly lower level stand generals such as Byng, near-victor of Cambrai, and the brilliant Australian commander, Monash. The South African General Smuts, sometime sworn foe of the British, also served with some distinction in East Africa. One commander, Sir Edmund Allenby, once he was transferred from the deadlocked Western Front to Palestine in 1917, proved his great ability at the third battle of Gaza and Megiddo. In the same theatre of war, Lawrence of Arabia refined the techniques of guerrilla warfare. However, the fact that it is necessary to cite so many names proves the overall mediocrity of the generalship displayed. As Winston Churchill perceptively remarked, 'the Great War owned no master; no-one was equal to its vast and novel issues'. The result was the slaughter of almost an entire generation of European manhood and an unsatisfactory peace – a breeding ground for future conflict.

The Battle of Tannenberg, 26–31 August 1914

As the situation became increasingly critical for the British, Belgian and French armies on the Western Front, and as the German armies swept through Belgium towards Paris, the French Government urged Tsar Nicolas II to launch an offensive against East Prussia without delay in the hope of easing pressure in the west. The Russians agreed, although their mobilization was still incomplete. They were soon to rue the decision, for one of the most comprehensive military disasters of modern history was to overtake them.

The Russians advanced into East Prussia in two masses under the overall control of General Jilinsky. The First Army, commanded by General Rennenkampf, moved in from the east towards Stallupönen and Gumbinnen, and the Second, under General Samsonov, moved up from the south to the east of Soldau. Facing them was the widely dispersed German Eighth Army under

General von Prittwitz. At first the Russian numbers told, and despite a repulse at Stallupönen on 17 August and a drawn battle at Gumbinnen three days later, their slow, steamroller advance made ground on both sectors. In fact the two Russian armies were drawing apart, for Samsonov's army soon lost most of its impetus owing to a combination of poor Polish roads, inadequate transportation and shortage of rations.

Nevertheless, von Prittwitz was becoming increasingly alarmed. He urged von Moltke to send reinforcements from the west and announced his decision to retreat behind the Vistula. Von Moltke duly detached two corps from von Kluge's army in the west, but replaced von Prittwitz with General Paul von Hindenburg (with Ludendorff as his chief of staff) on 20 August.

The new command decided to concentrate against Samsonov and merely to shadow Rennenkampf's advance. When they reached the front on the 23rd they found that an intelligent staff officer, Lieutenant-Colonel Hoffmann, had already anticipated these orders; this precise situation had been the subject of a General Staff war game in 1912. Therefore, after halting Rennenkampf's advance at Stallupönen, the Germans rapidly transferred their Eighth Army (minus a single cavalry division, left to observe the First Army) to the south-west to confront the fumbling Samsonov, using the railways and roads to make the most of their advantage of interior lines. Some of Samsonov's advisers sensed the peril, but he ignored their warnings and moved forward into the developing trap. His five corps became hopelessly dispersed, and their

Three significant Allied leaders on the Western Front; 'Papa' Joffre, left, General Sir Douglas Haig, centre, and General Ferdinand Foch, right. Only in 1918, faced by the threat of a massive German breakthrough, did the Allies appoint Foch to supreme command over all their forces.

above
Tannenberg, August 1914. Russian infantry fording a stream. Ill equipped and badly led, the peasant soldiers of Tsarist Russia were outclassed by the more efficient German war machine. By 1917 their morale had reached breaking-point, and they joined the ranks of the revolutionaries in hundreds of thousands. Even the dash and courage of the famous Russian Cossacks, *opposite page,* availed the Tsar's generals nothing at Tannenberg.

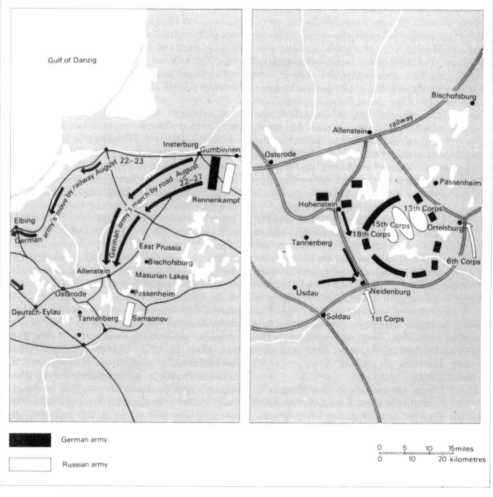

Battle of Tannenberg

Gulf of Danzig

Insterburg
Gumbinnen
German army's move by railway August 22–23
German army's march by road August 22–27
Rennenkampf
Elbing
German
East Prussia
Allenstein
Bischofsburg
Masurian Lakes
Osterode
Passenheim
Deutsch-Eylau
Tannenberg
Samsonov

Bischofsburg
Allenstein
railway
Osterode
Passenheim
Hohenstein
13th Corps
5th Corps
18th Corps
Ortelsburg
Tannenberg
6th Corps
Usdau
Neidenburg
Soldau
1st Corps

■ German army

☐ Russian army

0   5   10   15 miles
0   10   20 kilometres

exact locations were revealed to the Germans by the uncoded Russian telegraph signals.

As a result, Ludendorff was presented with the opportunity of carrying out a classical double envelopment. His nerve almost failed him when the Russians scored a few minor tactical successes on the 24th but the commander of the German I Corps, von François, ignored the Chief of Staff's contradictory orders and pressed ahead to envelop the Russian left and rear after a long railway journey from Insterburg to Deutsch Eylau via Königsberg and Marienburg, Jilinsky's orders on the 27th for Rennenkampf to support the Second Army were ignored. By that time, the German corps were closing in on all sides of Samsonov, who had begun a tentative withdrawal through Tannenberg. Von François' bold sweep through Soldau severed the last avenues of escape on the 29th. Two Russian corps were obliterated and the remainder reduced to half their original strength. By the 31st, the Russians had lost 125,000 men and 500 guns to the Germans' 15,000 casualties. Samsonov shot himself.

This German success shook the Allies' faith in Russian military capability and raised the German morale to a pitch which even the defeat at the Marne in the west (two weeks later) could not reduce. Hoffmann and von François were perhaps the true heroes, but Hindenburg and Ludendorff reaped the honours, and in any case had borne the responsibility. Without delay the Germans now turned on Rennenkampf, and between 9 and 14 September shattered his army at the Masurian Lakes, inflicting another 125,000 casualties and taking 150 guns. Thus the concepts of Hannibal at Cannae and Napoleon's strategy of the central position were put to devastating twentieth-century use. But Russian incompetence and unpreparedness lay at the root of their defeat.

The Battle of Cambrai,
20 November–7 December 1917

The persistent state of deadlock on the Western Front from late 1914 resulted in enormous casualties for negligible gains. Compared to the great offensives that both preceded and followed it, Cambrai was little more than a raid carried out in strength. Nevertheless it is a landmark in warfare in that it saw the first large-scale employment of tanks. It also showed that surprise could achieve far greater results, at much cheaper cost, than massive frontal attacks following days of artillery preparation of the type represented by the battles of the Somme or the third battle of Ypres.

The attack was prepared in the greatest secrecy. General Byng, commanding the British Third Army (nineteen divisions strong) ruled out the use of a conventional preliminary barrage, and the squadrons of tanks were carefully concealed in woodland until the last minute. The site of the battle had the advantage of being well-drained, chalk-based land on a quiet sector of the front. The plan was based on a scheme of Colonel Fuller, and envisaged a quick breakthrough by the infantry-supported tanks of Brigadier-General Ellis, creating a 'cavalry gap' towards the important rail and road centre of Cambrai, which could then be exploited. Unfortunately, some generals regarded the project with suspicion, or as merely an experiment, especially as the season of the year was so advanced, and neglected to make adequate arrangements.

Early on 20 November the battle opened. Almost 1,000 guns sent a sudden hail of fire towards the lines occupied by elements of General

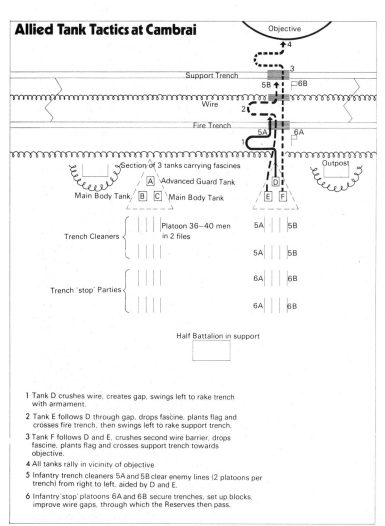

Allied Tank Tactics at Cambrai

Objective

Support Trench

5B   6B

Wire

Fire Trench

5A   6A

Outpost

Section of 3 tanks carrying fascines
A Advanced Guard Tank
Main Body Tank B C Main Body Tank
D
E F

Trench Cleaners { | | | | Platoon 36–40 men in 2 files   5A | | 5B

| | | | 5A | | 5B

Trench 'stop' Parties { | | | | 6A | | 6B

| | | | 6A | | 6B

Half Battalion in support

1 Tank D crushes wire, creates gap, swings left to rake trench with armament.

2 Tank E follows D through gap, drops fascine, plants flag and crosses fire trench, then swings left to rake support trench.

3 Tank F follows D and E, crushes second wire barrier, drops fascine, plants flag and crosses support trench towards objective.

4 All tanks rally in vicinity of objective

5 Infantry trench cleaners 5A and 5B clear enemy lines (2 platoons per trench) from right to left, aided by D and E.

6 Infantry 'stop' platoons 6A and 6B secure trenches, set up blocks, improve wire gaps, through which the Reserves then pass.

right
Cambrai, 9 October 1918. The important railway centre never fell into British hands during the celebrated Cambrai offensive of November 1917, but next year it was occupied after the collapse of the morale of the German army on the Western Front. Note the field combat order of the British troops, and the entrenching tools strapped below the waist belt. Some officers still carried canes and map cases and wore polished riding boots.

von der Marwitz's Second Army. At the same moment, 324 fighting tanks, supported by 98 supply and other specialist tanks, followed by infantry, surged forward into no-man's-land. Five British divisions were in the line, with four cavalry divisions waiting to the rear; German strength totalled barely four divisions at the outset. The attack extended over a ten-mile front.

Surprise was complete. Many Germans turned to flee, and within a few hours a six-mile gap had been torn through the vaunted Hindenburg Line. The tanks operated in sections of three, each followed by infantry companies advancing in file. The tanks crushed the wire barricades, dropped their fascines into the trenches and supported the infantry with fire. For a time it appeared that the British had achieved the long-sought breakthrough, and the cavalry began to move forward. Sadly, the initial advantage did not prove capable of full exploitation. When the 51st Highland Division advanced, the infantry were kept too far back from the tanks, and as a result the strongpoint of Flesquières held out, the German guns accounting for 39 British tanks on the sector. This setback

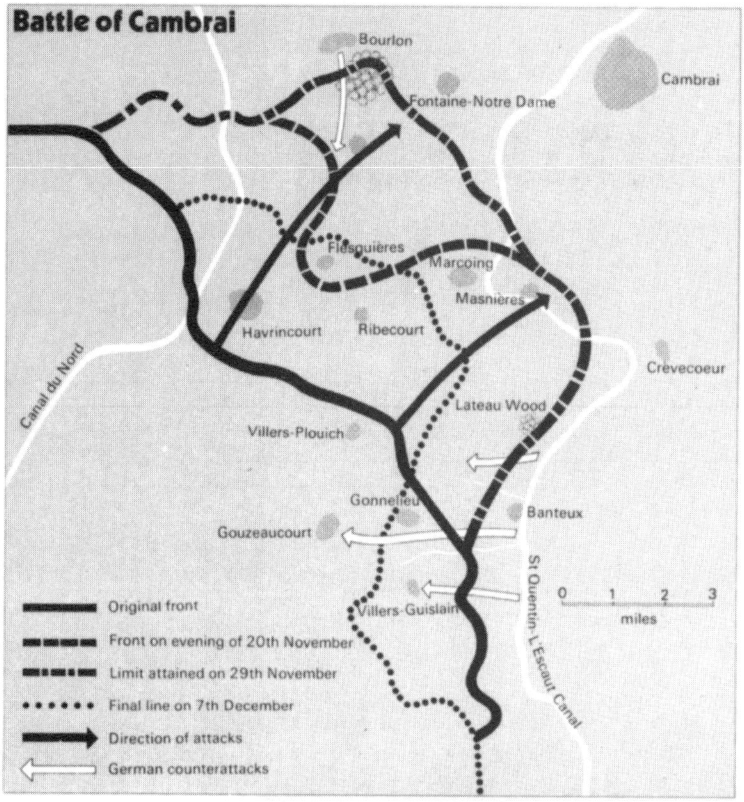
Battle of Cambrai
Bourlon
Cambrai
Fontaine-Notre Dame
Flesquières
Marcoing
Masnières
Havrincourt
Ribecourt
Crevecoeur
Canal du Nord
Lateau Wood
Villers-Plouich
Gonnelieu
Banteux
Gouzeaucourt
St Quentin-L'Escaut Canal
Villers-Guislain
0 1 2 3
miles
Original front
Front on evening of 20th November
Limit attained on 29th November
Final line on 7th December
Direction of attacks
German counterattacks

badly disrupted the advance in the centre, and robbed the British of their ultimate objective, Bourlon and its dominating ridge. Progress on other sectors, however, was excellent.

Unfortunately, the Germans received a windfall in the arrival of the fresh 107th Division by rail from the Eastern Front. These troops helped to rally morale and contain the extent of the break-in. As hour followed hour, more German reinforcements reached the front. Although they abandoned Flesquières late on the night of the 20th, they were strong enough to withstand the seven-day British offensive against Bourlon Wood. On the 27th, Haig ordered Byng to close down the offensive.

The brief stalemate that ensued was rudely shattered when, early on 30 November, the Germans (now twenty divisions strong) launched a sudden counteroffensive, concentrating against the southern sector of the battlefield, and also pressing south from Bourlon. Employing infiltration tactics, and supported by low-flying aircraft, the Germans made considerable headway. By 6 December their impetus was running out, but they had recovered two-thirds of their lost ground. The British Third Army had lost some 44,000 men; the Germans admitted 41,000 casualties. The battle thus ended indecisively, but a new era of warfare, that of the tank, had effectively dawned.

right
The battlefield at night: tracer flares and signal rockets weave intricate patterns across the sky. Note the wire entanglements dominating no-man's-land.

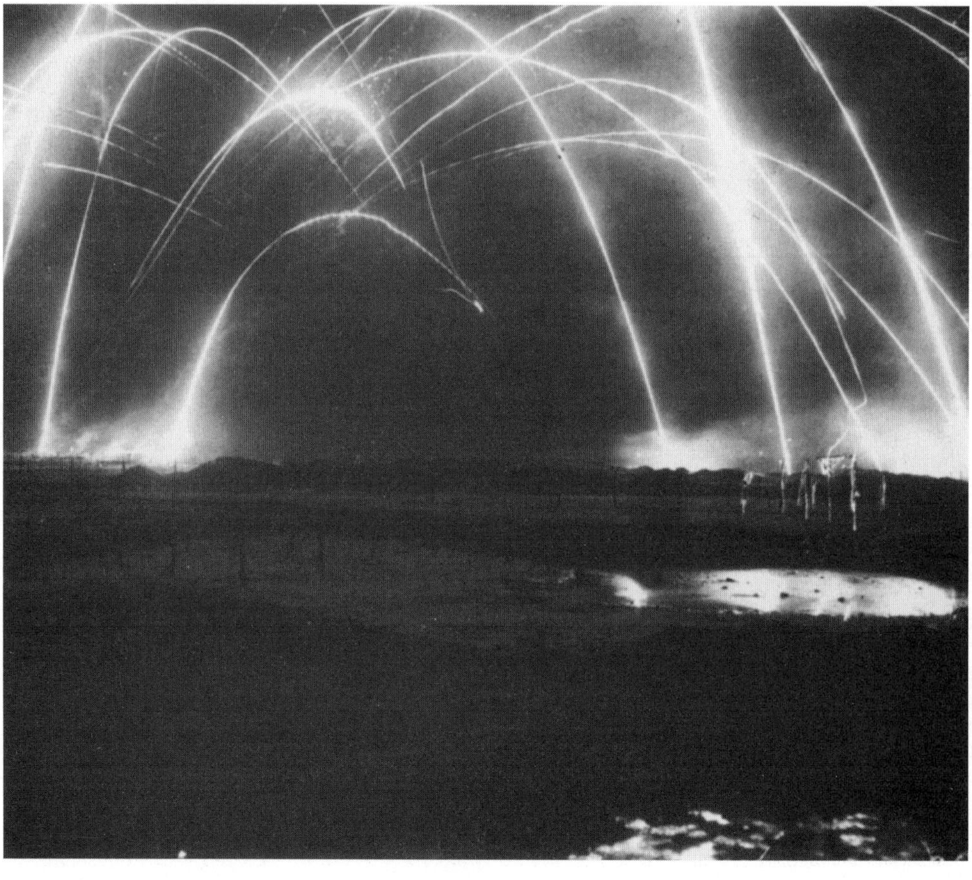

THE SECOND WORLD WAR

Hopes that mankind had seen the end of large-scale conflict died hard, but the brave attempt to solve the world's problems through the League of Nations, and numerous efforts to limit armaments through negotiation, proved to be in vain. The refusal of the United States to join the former, and the blatantly selfish interest of many of the parties in the latter, were not good omens for the future. Economic dislocation leading to worldwide recession, and a festering sense of injury and growing desire for revenge on the part of the defeated (in part due to the harsh terms of the Treaty of Versailles) were equally unpropitious auguries, and very soon for the percipient, including Winston Churchill, there was evidence of a new slide towards a major war.

As in the years before 1914, there was a crop of premonitory symptoms in the shape of local wars. The 1920s saw crises in Eastern Europe and the Balkans; a bitter civil war tore the Soviet Union; Communist agitation was widespread throughout Europe. Then, in 1931, Japanese hunger for what Hitler would later call *Lebensraum*, or living-space, led to the invasion of Manchuria and the start of a fourteen-year struggle with China. In 1935 came Fascist Italy's attack on Abyssinia—caused by outdated imperialistic ambitions which belonged more to the nineteenth than to the twentieth century. The year 1936 saw two more fatal steps. First Adolf Hitler's brazen reoccupation of the Rhineland, a deliberate gamble which revealed the reluctance of the Western powers to honour their declarations. Then the outbreak of civil war in Spain, which became for three years the testing ground for new German and Italian weaponry and techniques. Emboldened by his early success, Hitler (who had taken Germany out of the League as early as 1933) demonstrated his scorn for international opinion by successively annexing Austria, and seizing large areas of Czechoslovakia in 1938, before completing the process by occupying Bohemia in January of the following year. Britain and France stood by, apparently impotent. Confident that his *coup* in securing a non-aggression pact with the USSR (August 1939) would utterly dumbfound any attempts at an effective Western riposte, in early September Hitler sent his armies marching into Poland. To his surprise, he found himself at war with England and France from 3 September. The dominions and colonies rallied to Britain's call, as they had done in 1914, and once again a major war had begun. For the moment it focused on Europe, but it was soon to spread to almost every quarter of the globe.

Such military interest as had existed between the two world wars had been devoted to the consideration of two fields of activity: the development of air power and the role of the tank. In the case of the former, the theories of the Italian Douhet had wide influence. Convinced that 'the bomber will always get through', Douhet prophesied that future wars would be decided by the strategic bombing not only of industrial areas but also of centres of population. Advances in aircraft technology—more powerful engines and the advent of the metal-skinned monoplane—and such ghastly experiments as the destruction of Guernica in Spain by aerial bombardment caused many to believe him right. Meanwhile, in the democracies, such lone voices as Mitchell in the United States and Trenchard in Great Britain argued for the building of effective air forces as a safeguard against future aggression. Little heed was paid them. Fortunately, such international competitions as the Schneider Trophy enabled designers to develop the prototypes of the Spitfire and the Hurricane, but as war approached it was Germany who possessed the only effective air force. Germany had been secretly rearming since the late 1920s and blatantly doing so since 1935. As a result she was able to enter the struggle with over 3,000 first-line aircraft. Nevertheless, the Germans still thought of air power as essentially an adjunct of war on land.

Since 1918, a number of military thinkers had been considering the implications of the tank. Although the Germans were to make the most effective use of the ideas that emerged, the originators were two Englishmen and a Frenchman: Colonel (later Major-General) J F C Fuller, Captain Basil Liddell Hart and Colonel Charles de Gaulle. Liddell Hart was the most influential. In many newspaper articles and several books he argued in favour of a new approach to military strategy, combining highly

'Scramble!' The pilots of a Hurricane fighter squadron rush to their aircraft as an alarm reports the approach of enemy aircraft, 1940.

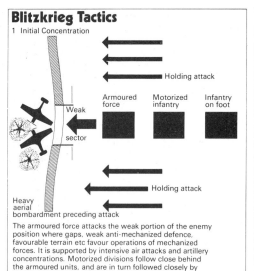

Blitzkrieg Tactics

1 Initial Concentration

Holding attack

Weak sector

Armoured force

Motorized infantry

Infantry on foot

Heavy aerial bombardment preceding attack

The armoured force attacks the weak portion of the enemy position where gaps, weak anti-mechanized defence, favourable terrain etc favour operations of mechanized forces. It is supported by intensive air attacks and artillery concentrations. Motorized divisions follow close behind the armoured units, and are in turn followed closely by infantry divisions on foot.

Blitzkrieg Tactics

2 Breakthrough

Holding attacks

Armoured units

Motorized infantry

Armoured units

Motorized infantry

Infantry on foot

Armoured units

Motorized infantry

Armoured units

Holding attacks

The breakthrough is achieved. Armoured and motorized units widen the gap and advance to seize the objective, supported by aviation and artillery. Infantry on foot follow close behind to relieve the armoured and motorized units.

mechanical all-arm formations (tanks, mobile guns, carrier-borne infantry and support services) with closely associated air support. Fuller, on the other hand, believed in a massive all-tank force supported by infantry and machine guns borne in lorries, and questioned Liddell Hart's conviction that an even higher degree of cross-country mobility was required for all the elements of a strike force. Liddell Hart foresaw the use of such forces in 'an expanding torrent', beginning with violent air attacks as a prelude to achieving a penetration through the enemy's defences on a narrow front; then, bypassing centres of strong defence, the armoured spearhead would exploit

The vaunted Maginot Line, with its huge reinforced concrete steel casemates, underground railways and retractable gun turrets, was an expression of French national faith in fixed defensive positions. It was, in fact, an enormous military white elephant.

towards the enemy's open rear on an ever-expanding front, spreading confusion and terror behind the lines.

The disagreements between the rival proponents of armoured warfare provided the excuse for years of inaction by the British army, in which the process of mechanizing the cavalry was still being strongly challenged by influential senior cavalry officers. In Europe, however, these ideas had a more immediate influence. De Gaulle was an early disciple, but his recommendations were ignored by a government which placed all its faith in the vast defensive works of the Maginot Line, being constructed at huge expense along the eastern frontiers of France. In effect, the Maginot Line was the supreme rationalization of the trench systems of the First World War, transformed into steel and concrete. It would prove the ultimate expression of passive defence –the surrender of all initiative to the foe. Similarly, many generals on both sides of the Channel believed that in any future war the tank would repeat its First World War role as a slow-moving, massively armoured weapon for infantry support. Seldom have the dangers of victory–in encouraging false economy and a belief that the military arts had reached their final development–been more graphically demonstrated. The Allied defeats of 1940 and 1941 were in large measure the fruits of victory in 1918.

In the Soviet Union, and above all in Germany, the new ideas did not go unheeded. Although Stalin's great purges of the Russian officer corps in the 1930s did much to delay the implementation of the new ideas, in Hitler's Germany, smarting to avenge defeat and willing to try new ideas, the concepts gradually took hold in influential quarters. Men like Hans Guderian were fervent disciples of Liddell Hart, as was Ernst Udet, the developer of dive-bomber tactics in close support of advancing armour. They were firmly backed by Hitler. By 1939, Hitler had at his disposal ten Panzer divisions. Britain had barely a single armoured division and France only three. The result would be a series of stupendous German successes in the first two years of the war, including the conquest of Poland and France (see below) and the first months of the invasion of the Soviet Union.

The German Panzer was the twentieth-century development of the Mongol *touman*, Saxe's *légion* and Napoleon's *corps d'armée*. It conferred the same advantages, namely a fast-moving, balanced striking force, virtually self-contained, which was capable of dealing a weighty blow. Its organization varied, but the 1941 version comprised a tank regiment of 150 to 200 tanks, a regiment of artillery (24 150-mm medium guns, 30 105-mm guns, 30 88-mm dual-purpose guns and a light flak battalion), a brigade of four battalions of Panzer grenadiers, a motorcycle and sidecar battalion, signals, reconnaissance, army air corps and supply detachments–a total of 14,000 men and some 4,200 vehicles. In addition there were the closely associated squadrons of Stuka dive bombers (Junkers Ju 87s), which served as heavy artillery. This was the weapon of *Blitzkrieg* that overwhelmed France, won crushing victories at Kiev and Kharkov in Russia and, on a smaller scale, won victory in the Western Desert at such battles as Gazala-Tobruk in 1942.

Fortunately, some Allied generals also adopted the new methods. Generals Wavell and O'Connor employed their armour in a similar way, and with telling effect, against the Italians in 1940–41 in North Africa. In due course the British and American armoured divisions organized their brigades along self-sufficient lines, whilst the

Russian 'tank armies' proved capable of resounding victories such as Kursk (1943). But apart from the American George Patton, the great armoured leaders of the Second World War were Germans: Manstein, Kleist, Guderian and Rommel.

Although the democracies initially lagged behind the totalitarian powers in the development of new weapons made possible by advances in technology, the process of rearmament developed apace from the mid 1930s onwards. Tanks could now move at up to 30 miles per hour, with ranges of 200 miles or more. The German *Pzkw* tanks, Marks I to IV, were eventually replaced by the

A determined German storm trooper puts a bunker in the Maginot Line out of action.

Following the fall of France, Rommel was sent to North Africa, where he made the most of the open terrain to exploit the characteristics of fast-moving armoured warfare. His greatest success was at Gazala-Tobruk in May–June 1942. Here, a *Pzkw* Mk III moves up over the desert.

above
The ten German Panzer divisions of 1940, with their mobility, flexibility and daunting striking power, almost won the land war for Germany. This photograph, taken by General Rommel from his command vehicle, shows part of his Seventh Panzer Division advancing through France. The tanks are medium *Pzkw* Mk IIs; note the small command cars.

right
One of the most successful artillery weapons of the Second World War was the German 88-mm. Originally an anti-aircraft weapon, it proved equally effective as an anti-tank and general-purpose field gun.

dreaded Tigers and Panthers. The obsolete British medium and light cavalry tanks of 1939 gave way to the infantry-support Matilda, the cruiser Crusader, and ultimately the Churchill. American factories provided numbers of Stuarts, Pattons and Grants before developing the powerful Sherman which, with its range and 75-mm main armament, was the key tank from Alamein (see below) to Berlin. The Russians produced the

TU 14 and the Joseph Stalin. Of the major contestants, the French, Japanese and Italians lagged behind in this respect. The overall effect of the tank was to ensure that almost all campaigns of the land war were based on manoeuvre.

Artillery was also altering. The British 25-pounder gun-howitzer and the German 88-mm were amongst the most important weapons. The latter was originally designed as an anti-aircraft

gun, but it proved equally effective against armour or as a field gun, and was a considerable thorn in the side of the Allies. Medium and heavy artillery played an important role on the Eastern Front, where the Germans deployed railway guns capable of penetrating concrete from twenty-five miles, and the Russians possessed effective 280-, 305- and 406-mm howitzers. However, most major developments related to smaller weapons. The German *Panzerfaust* was matched by the US bazooka as a close-range anti-tank weapon. The British 6-pounder anti-tank gun, firing armour-piercing shells, replaced the less effective 2-pounder of the first years of the war. Anti-tank minefields were widely employed by all combatants from the outset. Field mortars and flame-throwers remained much the same as in 1918, apart from technical improvements and the development of special tanks to carry enlarged versions, for example the 'flying dustbin' and 'crocodile' tanks of Hobart's 49th Armoured Division of specialized armour in 1944. A new weapon, however, was the Russian multi-barrelled rocket-launcher, the *Katiusha,* and its German and American counterparts, the *Nebelwerfer* and the US 4·5- and 7·2-inch rockets. In the case of small arms, the German Spandau machine gun and machine pistol, not to forget their light, accurate, selective-fire weapons, the MP 43 and MP 44, all earned a reputation. The British Bren gun (of Czechoslovak origin) supplemented the ·303 clip-loaded Lee-Enfield rifle, and was soon joined by the Sten gun. The American semi-automatic Garand and M-2 infantry carbine were superior weapons as was the Russian

Master of tank warfare, Erwin Rommel with part of the staff of the Desert Afrika Korps. His charisma extended to his enemies, and Eighth Army HQ had to forbid direct mention of his name in orders and messages. Hitler made him a field-marshal after Tobruk in 1942; two years later, however, he was forced to take poison, after implication in the attempted assassination of Hitler in July 1944.

fully automatic *Dektyarov.* Certain weapons of the First World War remained in use: the Vickers heavy and medium machine guns, the Lewis gun (until superseded) and the Mills bomb and the German stick grenade. The trend was towards automatic and semi-automatic weaponry.

Although mechanization of the British and American armies was almost complete, it is sometimes overlooked that the German armies,

Strategic and tactical bombing were of critical importance in the Second World War. Here, an American Air Command Baltimore bomber attacks Japanese supply depots in Burma, 1944.

An Italian gun crew in action on the North African coast, 1942.

for all their vaunted Panzer spearheads, re-mained reliant to a surprisingly marked degree on horse-drawn transport for as many as seventy-five per cent of their infantry divisions. Similarly, the Russians retained the services of large num-bers of mounted Cossacks.

Air power, however, now came fully into its own. Air forces were developed to an unpre-cedented degree and aircraft design was rapidly improved. The bomber was the strategic weapon for crushing enemy war industries and breaking the morale of the home populations–or so the experts foretold. How effective it proved in the former role is still hotly debated. The Allied strategic bombing offensive of 1944–45, involving huge raids by 1,000 or more bombers, employing either RAF carpet bombing by night or USAAF precision bombing by day, did immense damage to German industrial centres, but thanks to the decentralization masterminded by Albert Speer, German war production of tanks and aircraft actually increased over the period. More telling were the Allied blows aimed at key targets such as the Schweinfurt ball-bearing plants, the Mohne and Eder dams and the Ploesti oil refin-eries in Rumania. As for the attempts to wreck civilian morale by terror bombing, these proved largely counterproductive, despite the appre-hension the prospect had caused during the 1930s. The German blitz against Rotterdam in 1940

horrified the world, but the *Luftwaffe*'s offensive against London and other British centres rallied rather than destroyed morale, and the same was true of the later Allied blows against German cities, although such horrors as the Hamburg fire-storm of 1944 or the destruction of Dresden in 1945 were largely planned as deliberate blows against the German people. In the case of Japan, although USAAF raids had by 1945 destroyed forty per cent of the land area of the sixty-six major cities, ninety-seven per cent of her industrial war effort continued.

Aircraft grew in size and effectiveness; the twin-engined Whitleys, Wellingtons, Dornier Do 17s and Heinkel He 111s of 1939–40, with their half-ton bombloads and 1,250-mile range, gave way to the Lancasters and Stirlings of Bomber Command,. with their ten-ton bomb-loads, and above all to the American Flying Fortresses, Super Fortresses and Liberators, with their 3,000-mile range and five-ton bomb-loads. Bomb design also developed from the incendiaries and 100- and 200-pounders of 1939 to the German parachute-borne landmines, and thence to the British ten-ton blockbusters, de-signed to crack the strongly protected German submarine pens.

To protect the bombers and carry out the functions of tactical air support, fighter aircraft changed out of all recognition. The biplane soon

disappeared, as the single-wing fighter, capable of speeds in excess of 300 miles per hour and ranges of about 250 miles, became the norm. The British answer to the Me 109 and the nightfighting Me 110 were the Spitfire, Hurricane and Beaufighter. The American Mustang was the answer to the later Focke-Wulf 190, and both the Typhoon and the Lightning were superior to the Japanese Zero. Fighters were adapted to carry bombs and rockets to support landings from the sea and land attacks–including the Hurricane and the Typhoon–and naval battles in the Pacific Ocean hinged on the issue of air power, as the great aircraft carriers replaced the battleships as the key vessels of fleets at war. Reconnaissance aircraft, such as the fast and high-flying Mosquito or the slower German Condor, photographed enemy installations or shadowed convoys. More cumbersome flying-boats, including the Sunderland and the Catalina, watched for U-boats to the limits of their range. Aircraft delivered paratroops in divisional strength to attack Crete in 1941, to secure the flanks of the D-Day landings, and to attempt the seizure of the Rhine crossings in Holland in 1944. In Burma, the second Chindit operation began with a large-scale fly-in of glider-borne troops, and the stalwart defence of the isolated position of Imphal earlier the same year was facilitated by the fly-in of the Fifth Indian Division at the height of the

The epic struggle for Stalingrad, which lasted from September 1942 to February 1943, saw much hand-to-hand fighting amongst the ruins of the city on the River Volga. Here, lightly equipped Russians advance cautiously over the rubble.

crisis. Air supply became increasingly important. It had its failures, as at Stalingrad, where Goering's promise of 500 tons of supplies per day was never once met, or at Arnhem, where a combination of bad weather and poorly defined drop zones disrupted the operation. But it also had its triumphs, particularly in Burma, where many a beleaguered 'box' position was sustained by parachuted or free-fall supplies. The maids of all work in these operations were the three-engined German Junkers Ju 52 and the ubiquitous American Dakota, or DC3. Few transport aircraft, however, could carry much more than three tons in a single sortie, and the further the distance to and from the objective the lighter the load, for extra fuel had to receive top priority.

Thus the aeroplane came to fulfil a vital role in support of both armies and fleets. If its significance in an independent strategic role was less than had been anticipated, the role of air power in support of land operations was of critical importance. As Rommel learnt in North Africa and again in Normandy, it was virtually impossible to move large armoured formations by day under conditions of enemy air superiority.

The Allied tactical air forces played a vital part in ensuring the success of Operation Overlord in June 1944. Before the operation they paralysed the enemy's rail and road communications and radar installations. During and after the invasion, fighter-bombers on the 'cab rank' system gave invaluable close support to the land forces. When poor weather grounded the aircraft, dire results could ensue – as the German Ardennes offensive of late 1944 demonstrated to the Allies during its early phases.

Another important feature of the Second World War was the key role of the scientist. The new tanks and aircraft demanded ceaseless improvement and modification, and the contribution of the scientist was vital in this process. Such men as Winston Churchill's chief scientific adviser, Lord Cherwell, or J R Oppenheimer, head of the Manhattan Project working towards

the production of the first atomic bomb in the New Mexico Desert, had an important contribution to make. So had Wernher von Braun, Hitler's leading expert on the production of flying bombs (the V-1) and early rockets (the V-2). The scientific arms race was as critical as any aspect of the struggle. It is only possible here to mention a few of the key developments which embraced every field of warfare. On the medical side, the improvements in antibiotics and blood-transfusion techniques saved countless lives both on and off the field of battle. Electronics saw immense developments, including radar (originally developed by Robert Watson-Watt). Radio communication improved beyond all recognition, transforming the problems of control. Many new weapons were developed, including the 'hedgehog' rocket system for destroying U-boats, which with improved sonar equipment were easier to detect. Better bomb sights and new types of bomb and explosive, including RDX, the blockbuster and the bouncing bomb, not to forget proximity and delayed-action fuses, contributed to the air war. The scientific race for the atomic bomb, probably the most critical of all, was won by the Allies because of the German shortage of heavy water and the emigration of many Jewish scientists from Germany to the democracies before the war. The Germans developed the first supersonic strategic rockets, but the V-2 came too late to sway the fortunes of war in late 1944. Whittle's original jet engine was only applied to military aircraft in the last year of the war; the German Me 262 was too short-ranged to be fully effective, whilst the British Meteor did not fly operationally until 1945.

To sustain the huge armies, navies and air forces and to keep them equipped and supplied called for an unparalleled degree of organization. Because of their initial advantages, including rearmament throughout the 1930s, the Germans did not resort to full-scale rationing or the wholesale direction of female labour until well into the war. Great Britain, on the other hand, had to

A V-2 rocket leaves its firing table. The first operational V-2 was fired on Paris on 6 September 1944; by the end of the war about 4,000 of these missiles had been launched from mobile bases against Allied targets. Although the V-2 was not a decisive weapon, it was nevertheless a monumental engineering achievement.

The 'Big Three', Stalin, Roosevelt and Churchill, confer at Teheran.

maquis, the Yugoslav partisans and other underground organizations, and the BBC ran Radio Free Europe. In the Far East, special forces kept in touch with such bodies as the Malayan People's Anti-Japanese Army, and kept the flame of defiance alight. Many techniques of guerrilla and popular warfare were developed and taught during these years by the British Special Air Service and the American OSS.

All these were features of warfare between 1939 and 1945. The problems of coalition warfare had to be resolved in the context of a truly global war. The Big Four, Churchill, Roosevelt, Chiang Kai-shek and Stalin, faced many problems of rival ideology and clashing strategic priorities, and these tensions and disagreements were transmitted to their military subordinates. Nevertheless, the Alliance survived and came through to ultimate victory. In the end, cooperation and coordination triumphed, despite major disagreements concerning the 'Hitler first' decision (much vocal American opinion backed Admiral King's rival belief that the Pacific theatre should absorb the bulk of American attentions), and over the relative importance of the Mediterranean theatre as against north-west Europe once the decision to invade had been given priority. Nevertheless, such operational and administrative masterpieces as the invasion of Sicily on 9/10 July 1943 (involving seven assault divisions, 3,000 ships and two brigades of paratroops, besides some 3,700 aircraft), or that of Normandy on 6 June 1944 (involving three divisions of paratroops, five divisions of seaborne assault troops, 4,600 vessels and warships and over 9,500 aircraft) were successfully planned

resort to strong measures from the outset. Conscription came in 1939, and direction of labour was total. Rationing of food and resources was rigidly controlled. Press and radio censorship was tight, as the propaganda war swung into action, and some other civil rights had to be suspended for the duration. When it was necessary, the National Government was prepared to rule by decree or Order in Council. The United States, with its immense resources of both men and material, did not need to adopt all these measures, and held a presidential election in 1944. Britain held a General Election in 1945.

Another important Allied role was the support of resistance movements in Occupied Europe prior to and during the liberation. British agents and equipment were parachuted to the French

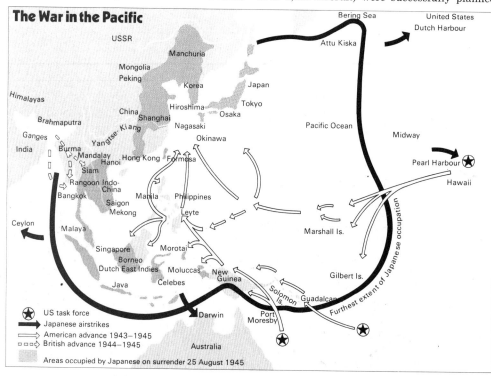

The War in the Pacific

- ⭐ US task force
- ▶ Japanese airstrikes
- ⇨ American advance 1943–1945
- ⊡⊡⊡⇨ British advance 1944–1945
- ▒ Areas occupied by Japanese on surrender 25 August 1945

and carried through. They required the most unselfish cooperation and tact between the British and Americans, and between their respective land, sea and air commanders. Such immense enterprises would never have been possible had not the Battle of the Atlantic against the U-boat 'wolf packs' been won in 1942–43. Shipping losses were immense, but ultimately Allied hunter-killer groups, improved detection and more destructive depth charges, together with better convoy techniques, radar, air searches and increasingly effective bombing of the U-boat pens in French ports, enabled the menace to be contained and then beaten.

The Royal Navy and mercantile marine also kept open – at terrible cost – the sea-lanes to Malta, the Middle East and the Far East, and (via the North Cape) to Soviet Russia, ensuring the transfer of troops, equipment and munitions of war to the land fronts. The aid supplied to Russia in 1941–42 was of critical importance in helping the Soviet forces to absorb their initial losses in military material, and thus made a vital contribution to victory over Germany.

In strategic terms, two world fronts were of critical importance to the outcome of the war. The first was the Eastern Front. Although it was understandable for the British and Americans to stress the importance of the North African, Italian and north-western European campaigns, the war against Germany was won and lost in Russia and Eastern Europe. The Soviets alone are estimated to have lost 21 million military killed and wounded, besides a further 15 million civilian dead. The Germans lost over two-thirds of their 10 million military casualties on the

Eastern Front. All other operations and theatres pale into relative insignificance besides these figures. This is not to discount the importance of other war fronts in distracting enemy forces from the critical theatre of war. Britain's part in sustaining the whole war effort alone in the dark days of 1940 and 1941, before the Soviet Union or the United States became involved in the struggle, was clearly of the greatest significance.

The second crucial theatre was the Pacific. The Japanese Imperial Army was still capable of massive resistance in August 1945, but their country had already been decisively defeated at sea and in the air. The loss of their aircraft carriers at such battles as Midway (1942) and Leyte Gulf (1944) destroyed their maritime empire and the South-East Asia Co-Prosperity

above
The Italian campaign saw some large-scale landing operations from the sea. Besides Sicily, the Allies mounted major seaborne attacks at Salerno, shown here, and Anzio. A landing-ship-tank (LST) disgorges men and material, September 1943.

below
The war in the Far East saw much bitter fighting in Burma by Slim's Fourteenth Army. Here, British troops manoeuvre during the double defensive battle of Kohima-Imphal, 1944.

Sphere. This enabled the American submarine offensive to take a stranglehold on the Japanese economy by starving its industries of raw materials and reducing civilian rations to 1,680 calories a day. Nine-tenths of the Japanese mercantile marine (originally totalling more than 10 million tons of shipping) was destroyed. Over half of it was sunk by American submarines, carrier- or land-based aircraft only accounting for twenty per cent, as priority was given to Japanese cities for the Strategic Air Forces. The bitter struggles for the Japanese-occupied islands, with their determined garrisons who fought to the death, and the reconquests of New Guinea, Borneo, the Philippines and Burma, were some indication of what would have been involved in a direct conquest of the Japanese home islands. The decision to drop the atomic bomb was taken as a result of this estimate. The American decision to use these weapons against Hiroshima and Nagasaki on 6 and 9 August 1945 is still a cause of heated debate, but President Truman's steadfast belief that this action shortened the war dramatically and saved huge casualties was probably justified.

Five years of war had caused immense destruction and dislocation, and the world needed peace to try and bind up the wounds. It is estimated that 100 million people were mobilized, that 15 million military and up to 34 million civilians lost their lives, and that at least 30 million combatants were gravely wounded. In terms of financial cost a figure of $1,650 billion has been suggested, but such figures are suspect, as the economic effects of such a war are barely calculable. However, it would seem that the

top
The chiefs confer. The American General Patton, with pearl-handled revolver, in an amicable exchange with his superiors, General Omar Bradley, and General Bernard Montgomery, Normandy 1944. Unfortunately their relationship was not always so unclouded.

above
General Hans Guderian inspecting tank crews on the Eastern Front, September 1941.

right
The Americans undertook the reconquest of many Pacific islands from the Japanese. They faced bitter opposition from their fanatical opponents, who rarely allowed themselves to be taken alive. Here, American marines take cover on Rendova island in the central Solomons.

Second World War proved five times as costly as the First in terms of economic and financial considerations, and proved three times as destructive in terms of total deaths.

The postwar period has been far from peaceful, as the wars in Korea, Indo-China, the Middle East and Vietnam have shown. However, in terms of scale these have all been limited confrontations. The progressive retreat from empire faced by the British, French and Dutch has also been far from bloodless, and the forces of subversion have been much in evidence in many countries. But fear of the effects of all-out nuclear war has radically redrawn the concepts of strategy, and reduced the likelihood of a return to total conventional war on a global scale.

What of leadership displayed in this long struggle? Many notable commanders emerged, and (on the basis that this book is a study of *land* warfare) it is impossible to compile a list of notable generals which omits the British Montgomery, Wavell and Slim, the Americans Eisenhower, Bradley and Patton, or the Frenchmen de Gaulle and Leclerc. The Germans produced fine soldiers in Manstein, von Rundstedt, Model, Guderian and Rommel, one of the few romantic figures to be found in this conflict. Japanese

leaders of note included Yamashita, and the Russians produced a number of talented if somewhat stolid generals, including Timoshenko.

However, three commanders probably merit inclusion in the company of the great of former ages. One of these, being in fact a sailor, can only be accorded a mention. The Japanese Admiral Yamamoto was the mastermind behind the air attack on Pearl Harbor and the synchronized attacks on several parts of South-East Asia by sea, land and air forces. A realistic assessor of the true Japanese war situation, he would only guarantee his political masters a single year of victory. The second place must go to the American general, Douglas MacArthur. However tactless and naïve his political convictions, and however justly he may be criticized for the conduct of his retreat in 1942 to Bataan and Corregidor, he nevertheless remains one of the outstanding figures of the war. His reputation was made secure by his brilliant reconquest of New Guinea, Borneo and the Philippines. Whatever the circumstances of his dismissal by President Truman in 1950, at the height of the Korean War, he must also be credited with inspiring the beginning of Japanese rehabilitation and recovery after 1945. The third figure of gigantic

The price of war in terms of material destruction. Cassino, in central Italy, after conventional air and artillery bombardment.

stature was Marshal of the Soviet Union Grigori Zhukov. For much of the Russo-German struggle he was Deputy Supreme Commander-in-Chief, second only to Stalin in military affairs. Zhukov made a positive and personal contribution to final victory during the mammoth campaigns for Moscow, Leningrad, Stalingrad, Kursk, the Dnieper and ultimately the conquest of Germany itself. He was no courtier, but stood up to Stalin, and twice assumed personal command of an army group at critical times. These men were the military giants of the Second World War.

The Battle of France, 10 May–22 June 1940

Early on 10 May the Germans launched heavy air and land attacks against Holland and Belgium. Paratroops seized the outskirts of Rotterdam, and by the 12th the Belgian fortress of Eben Emael had fallen to special shock formations. Meanwhile, Von Bock's Army Group B surged into the Low Countries, and the Allies crossed into Belgium to meet the threat, they hoped, along the River Dyle, as laid down in Plan D. Thus the 'phoney war' in the West was rudely shattered by German *Blitzkrieg*.

However, the Germans had not yet revealed their main attack. Following the Manstein plan, the main assault was to be launched through the supposedly impassable Ardennes region after a feint attack in the north. Accordingly, on 13 May, seven of the ten German Panzer divisions, forming the spearhead of von Rundstedt's Army Group A, headed over difficult terrain for the River Meuse. Surprise was complete. The indifferent French Ninth Army disintegrated, Sedan fell, and on the 15th the Germans were over the Meuse, punching a fifty-mile gap in the Allied front. Supreme Commander Gamelin found his armies split in two; he had no strategic reserve to plug the gap, and transfers of part of the French Seventh Army from the north (where Holland had already capitulated) proved too little and too late.

Worse was to follow. Daringly, General Guderian disobeyed the cautious orders of his superior, von Kleist, and with von Rundstedt's approval headed west and north to exploit the breakthrough to the uttermost. In growing alarm the Allies pulled back from Belgium, striving to re-establish the front. But the tide of the German armoured advance was too fast for them. Within two days, parts of their armour (one division commanded by Rommel) had reached the Channel coast near Abbeville. This was a war of movement with a vengeance, with German Stuka dive bombers replacing the ponderous heavy artillery. The vast and incomplete Maginot Line to the south, in which the French had placed so much faith, was completely bypassed by the enemy and its flank turned.

The Allies, now commanded by General Weygand, Gamelin's successor, attempted to launch counterattacks against the flanks of the German corridor, but despondency was spreading.

above
US General of the Army, Douglas MacArthur, Commander of Allied Forces in the South-west Pacific region, lands at Humboldt Bay, Dutch New Guinea on 22 April 1944.

right
Marshal of the Soviet Union Grigori Zhukov, second only to Stalin in Russian military councils, seen during the advance through central Poland, 1944.

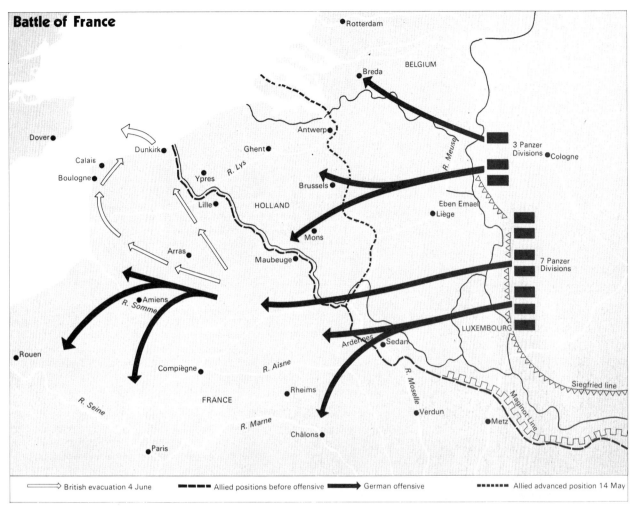

Battle of France

Rotterdam

BELGIUM

Breda

Antwerp

Dover

Calais

Boulogne

Dunkirk

Ghent

R. Lys

Ypres

Lille

HOLLAND

Brussels

R. Meuse

3 Panzer
Divisions

Cologne

Eben Emael

Liège

Arras

Maubeuge

Mons

7 Panzer
Divisions

R. Somme

Amiens

Rouen

Compiègne

R. Aisne

FRANCE

Rheims

R. Seine

R. Marne

Châlons

Paris

Ardennes

Sedan

LUXEMBOURG

R. Moselle

Verdun

Metz

Maginot Line

Siegfried line

| ⇨ British evacuation 4 June | ▰▰▰ Allied positions before offensive | ➤ German offensive | ▪▪▪▪ Allied advanced position 14 May |

left
The battle of France
disastrously lost, the
British evacuated some
330,000 troops (including
French and Belgians)
through the small
Channel port of Dunkirk,
28 May–4 June 1940. In
the background ships
burn, while a hospital
ship takes wounded from
the mole. Many other
troops were taken off the
open beaches in small
boats.

Hiroshima, where the
first atomic bomb was
dropped on Japan in
August 1945.

A long-range desert patrol group.

From the south, only the attacks led by Major-General de Gaulle's armoured division made the least impression, whilst from the north a single British armoured brigade–Frank Force–made a telling attack near Arras on the 21st. Their effect, however, was only temporary. The Germans went on to the defensive along the Somme, and swooped north for the kill.

By 26 May it was clear that the Belgian army– holding the coastal flank–was on the verge of surrender. General Lord Gort, commanding the ten divisions of the British Expeditionary Force, requested and obtained from Churchill permission to take his forces out of French command and to head for the port of Dunkirk. French recriminations were strident, but Gort's timing was exemplary, and he completed the Dunkirk perimeter in the very nick of time before the Belgian collapse exposed his flank. The Germans, in the meantime, had for some still undisclosed reason called a two-day halt in their advance– probably to carry out maintenance on their much-travelled tanks–and Goering promised that the Luftwaffe could complete the destruction of the British, French and Belgians in the Dunkirk pocket. This pause enabled Gort to complete his perimeter, and to begin Operation Dynamo, the evacuation by sea.

The miracle of Dunkirk was an astounding feat. Despite the relentless pressure of the *Luftwaffe*, and the resumed attacks by the German ground forces from the 28th, no less than 330,000 Allied troops (one-third of them French and Belgians) were taken from the moles of Dunkirk and from the neighbouring beaches. On 5 June the remaining 40,000 of the French rearguard surrendered. However, as Churchill remarked, 'Wars are not won by evacuations.'

The Germans now turned south, swept on Paris from the Somme, and occupied the French capital on 13 June. Soon after, Pétain's new government sued for terms from the Axis (Italy had entered the war on 10 June), and on 21 June an armistice was signed at Compiègne. The whole world, and not least the Germans, were astounded by the brilliance of this brief and decisive campaign.

The Battle of El Alamein, 23 October–5 November 1942

At much the same time as the great battle of Stalingrad was raging in Russia, another important struggle was taking place in North Africa, almost at the gates of Cairo and Suez. Two months earlier, the battle of Alam Halfa had exhausted the last of the German and Italian energy. Thus there was no longer much danger that the Suez Canal and, beyond it, the oilfields of the Middle East, would pass into Axis hands, or that Rommel would thereafter blast a course northwards through Asia Minor to open a new front against the southern flank of the Soviet Union. But it still remained for the Eighth Army to defeat their opponents and reconquer the northern littoral of Africa.

Since Erwin Rommel had arrived in North Africa in February 1941, the struggle for control of the Western Desert had swung to and fro. However, the combination of scanty local resources, over-extended lines of communication and an invariable loss of impetus as the advance continued had time and again led to stalemate–the precursor of another offensive in the opposite direction. Neither side had sufficient strength to win a decisive victory: Rommel was starved of tanks and petrol by the requirements of the Eastern Front; Wavell and Auchinleck had vast responsibilities from Persia to Abyssinia and an inadequacy of men and equipment to fulfil them all.

From 15 August, however, new commanders reached the front: General Alexander to the top

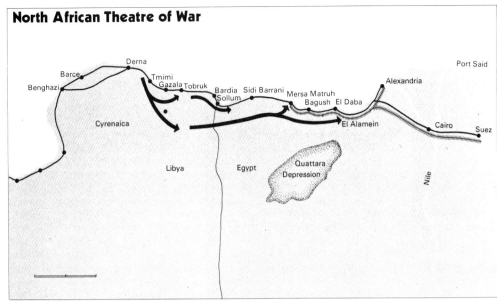

North African Theatre of War

The second battle of El Alamein, October 1942, in which Montgomery and the British Eighth Army finally defeated Rommel and the Axis forces in the Western Desert. Motorized troops under heavy fire as they pass through a gap in the German minefields at the height of the long battle.

235

post, and General Bernard Montgomery to take over the Eighth Army. Confidence returned to the troops, especially after the repulse of Rommel at Alam Halfa, and soon large reinforcements were reaching the theatre. They included new divisions from the Commonwealth and new Sherman tanks from the USA, together with many more British 6-pounder anti-tank guns. Montgomery refused to be rushed into a premature offensive by Churchill's eagerness, but by mid-October everything was ready. Three British armoured and nine infantry divisions were in place along the Alamein front, where each end was securely anchored by the Mediterranean and the Qattara Depression respectively. Facing them were four Axis armoured divisions, two German and two Italian, and eight infantry divisions, seven of them Italian. Thus the British fielded 130,000 men and 1,200 tanks against Axis forces comprising 96,000 men and 400 armoured vehicles. The Desert Air Force also enjoyed a decisive superiority over the *Luftwaffe*. Rommel's army, moreover, was tired and battered, and its dynamic commander away ill in Germany.

At 21.40 hours on 23 October, 1,000 British guns opened fire. Twenty minutes later the first troops advanced. Surprise was achieved in respect of both timing and direction of attack, Montgomery having created the illusion of wanting to attack in the south, not in the north. However, despite surprise and superior men and material, the Eighth Army failed to punch the pair of corridors towards Miteiriya Ridge, and by the 25th its advance had been halted. The enemy minefields had proved more extensive, and the Italians' defence tougher than anticipated. Moreover, Rommel had flown back to take over the battle from the third day. Montgomery realized that he must regain the initial impetus of the attack. He reorganized his forces, launched a feint attack with his Australian division along the coast road, and then launched Operation Supercharge against the weak Italian Trento Division in the centre on 2 November. This time the breach was made, and the superior British tanks poured through to do battle against Rommel's fewer and petrol-starved armour. Within two days the issue was decided; Rommel had only thirty-five tanks still operational, and despite Hitler's orders to fight to the last, he began to retreat towards Tripoli, an inevitable step, as from 8 November Allied armies were invading north-west Africa in Operation Torch. Caught between two fires, Rommel had to look to his base.

Montgomery had inflicted 30,000 casualties and destroyed 350 tanks and 1,000 guns for a loss of 13,500 men and 450 tanks. The Desert War had passed its final turning point, and within six months Africa would be clear of the Axis forces. Montgomery's success was based upon preparation, pertinacity and strategic timing. Rommel's final thrust had been thwarted.

El Alamein

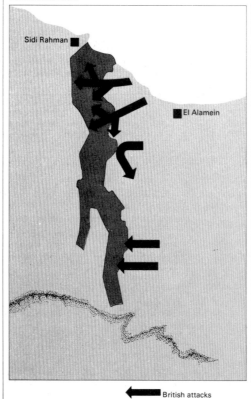

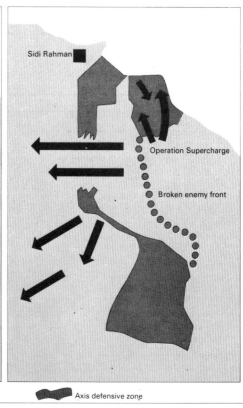

Sidi Rahman

El Alamein

Sidi Rahman

Operation Supercharge

Broken enemy front

British attacks

Axis defensive zone

Select reading list

General works

J Boudet. *The Ancient Art of Warfare*, 2 Vols (English Edition), 1969
D G Chandler. *A Traveller's Guide to the Battle-fields of Europe*, 2 Vols, 1965
J Colin. *The Transformation of War*, (English Edition), 1912
H Delbruck. *Geschichte der Kriegskunst*, 4 Vols, 1900–20
R E and T N Dupuy. *Encyclopaedia of Military History*, 1970
D Eggenberger. *A Dictionary of Battles*, 1967
C Falls. *The Art of War from the Age of Napoleon to the Present Day*, 1961
J F C Fuller. *The Decisive Battles of the Western World*, 3 Vols, 1954–56
J F C Fuller. *The Conduct of War, 1789–1961*, 1961
B H Liddell Hart. *Strategy, the Indirect Approach*, 1954
F Lot. *L'Art Militaire et les Armées au Moyen Age*, 2 Vols, 1946
B L Montgomery. *A History of Warfare*, 1968
C W C Oman. *The Art of War in the Sixteenth Century*, 1937
Preston, Wise and Werner. *Men in Arms*, 1956
Spaulding, Nickerson and Wright. *Warfare*, 1925
E Wanty. *L'Art de la Guerre*, 3 Vols, 1967
J A Weller. *Weapons and Tactics*, 1966
A number of these volumes contain useful bibliographies.

Recommended works:
a personal selection

Classical Warfare

T A Dodge. *Hannibal*, 1891
J F C Fuller. *The Generalship of Alexander the Great*, 1958
J F C Fuller. *Julius Caesar*, 1965
H M D Parker. *The Roman Legions*, 1928

Y Yadin. *The Art of War in Biblical Lands*, 1963
Asian Warfare: The Chinese, Indians and Mongols
V R R Dikshitar. *War in Ancient India*, 1948
H Lamb. *The March of the Barbarians*, 1941
H Lamb. *Genghis Khan, Emperor of All Men*, 1927
A Waley. *The Secret History of the Mongols*, 1964
Sun Tsu. *The Art of War*, 1963
The West: The Rise and Fall of Feudalism
A H Burne. *The Agincourt War*, 1956
P M Kendall. *The Yorkist Age*, 1962
H Lamb. *Charlemagne*, 1954
E Perroy. *The Hundred Years War*, 1951
The Eastern Mediterranean: Byzantium, The Arabs and The Crusaders
J B Glubb. *The Great Arab Conquests*, 1963
H Lamb. *The Crusaders*, 1930
R C Smail. *Crusading Warfare*, 1956
D M Vaughan. *Europe and the Turk, 1350–1700*, 1954
The Emergence of Modern Warfare
T A Dodge. *Gustavus Adolphus*, 1890
C Firth, *Cromwell's Army*, 1902
M Roberts. *The Military Revolution, 1560–1660*, 1956
J W Thompson. *The Wars of Religion in France*, 1957
C V Wedgewood. *The Thirty Years War*, 1938
The Eighteenth Century: The Age of Limited Warfare
D G Chandler. *Marlborough as Military Commander*, 1973
W S Churchill. *Marlborough, His Life and Times*, 2 Vols, 1946
G A Craig. *The Politics of the Prussian Army, 1640–1945*, 1955
G Ritter. *Frederick the Great*, 1968
J M White. *Marshal of France . . . Maurice de Saxe*, 1962

S Wilkinson. *The French Army before Napoleon*, 1915
French Revolutionary and Napoleonic Warfare
A Brett-James. *Wellington at War, 1794–1815*, 1961
D G Chandler. *The Campaigns of Napoleon*, 1966
R W S Phipps. *The Armies of the First Republic and Consulate*, 5 Vols, 1923–
Y von Wartenburg. *Napoleon as a General*, 2 Vols, 1897
J Wellar. *Wellington in the Peninsula*, 1962
S Wilkinson. *The Coming of General Bonaparte*, 1921
The Nineteenth Century
B Bond. *Victorian Military Campaigns*, 1967
B Catton. *Centennial History of the Civil War*, 3 Vols, 1963–65
M E Howard. *The Franco-Prussian War*, 1961
R Hargreaves. *Red Sun Rising: the Siege of Port Arthur*, 1962
R Kruger. *Goodbye Dolly Gray: the Story of the Boer War*, 1959
The First World War
C Barnett. *The Sword-Bearers*, 1963
B H Liddell Hart. *The War in Outline, 1914–18*, 1965
A J P Taylor. *The First World War*, 1963
J Terraine. *The Western Front*, 1964
A Wavell. *Allenby–a Study in Greatness*, 1940
The Second World War
W S Churchill. *The Second World War*, 6 Vols, 1948–53
F W von Mellinthin. *Panzer Battles*, 1955
B L Montgomery. *El Alamein to the River Sangro*, 1946
W Slim. *Defeat into Victory*, 1956
C Wilmot. *The Struggle for Europe*, 1952
P Young. *World War, 1939–45*, 1966

Acknowledgments

The illustration on page 77 is reproduced by courtesy of the Archbishop of Canterbury and the Trustees of the Lambeth Palace Library, the lower illustration on page 132 and that on page 134 by courtesy of his grace the Duke of Marlborough, and the upper illustration on page 93 by courtesy of the Master and Fellows of Corpus Christi College, Cambridge. The photographs on pages 22, 50 (bottom), 70 (bottom) and 133 (top) are crown copyright and are reproduced with the permission of the Controller of Her Majesty's Stationery Office.

Photographs Graphische Sammlung Albertina, Vienna 118–19; Antikvarisk-Topografiska Arkivet, National museum, Stockholm 55; Archives Photographiques, Paris 130 bottom; B Arthaud Editeur, Grenoble 24 top; Associated Press, 228 top, 228 centre; Bayerische Staatsgemäldesammlungen, Munich 106, 115; Bayerische Verwaltung der Staatlichen Schlösser, Gärten und Seen, Munich 154; Biblioteca Apostolica Vaticana 86 bottom; Bibliothèque Nationale, Paris 80; Bodleian Library, Oxford 72; E Boudot-Lamotte, Paris 45 top, 65; British Museum, London 30, 32, 59, 73 centre, 102, 110 top, 111 top, 162 top, 168, 169; E J Bulloz, Paris 36 bottom left, 182–3; Camera Press, London 20; J. Allan Cash, London 39; Chicago Historical Society, Chicago, Illinois 181 top; Corpus Christi College, Cambridge 93 top; Department of Archaeology, Government of Pakistan, Karachi 45 bottom; Department of the Environment 22, 50 bottom, 70 bottom, 133 top; Deutsche Fotothek, Dresden 173; Edinburgh University Library 53 top, 53 bottom; W Forman, London 43; A Frequin,

The Hague 79 right; Photographie Giraudon, Paris 64 top, 75 bottom, 76, 90, 91, 95, 105, 117 bottom, 123 top, 140, 161 top; Hamlyn Group-Hawkley Studio Associates 137 top, 197 top, 198–9, 200 top; Hamlyn Group–Philip O Stearns 97, 98–9, 100, 157, 158–9, 160, 170, 178–9, 180; Hamlyn Group Picture Library 57, 58, 60 bottom, 71 top, 88, 109, 112–13; Heereschichtiches Museum, Vienna 163 top; Michel Hétier, Paris 61 bottom; Hirmer Verlag, Munich 23, 24–5, 25 top, 26, 27, 29 bottom, 33, 34 top, 34 bottom, 82, 83 top, 83 bottom, 84, 85; Historisches Museum der Stadt, Vienna 126 bottom; Hunting Aerosurveys Limited, London 92; Imperial War Museum, London 10–11, 171 bottom, 172 top, 196 top, 201 bottom, 202–3, 204 top, 204 bottom, 205 top, 205 bottom, 206, 207 top, 207 bottom, 209, 212–13, 214, 216–17, 219 bottom, 220 top, 220 bottom, 221 top, 221 bottom, 222, 223, 224, 227 top, 227 bottom, 228 bottom, 229, 230 top, 230 bottom, 231, 234, 235; Institut Géographique National, Paris 71 bottom; A F Kersting, London 93 bottom, 107 bottom; Kunsthistorisches Museum, Vienna 126 bottom, 131 bottom right; Kunstsammlungen der Veste Coburg 87; Kupferstichkabinett, Staatliche Museen Preussischer Kulturbesitz, Berlin 114 top; Editions Robert Laffont, Paris 197 bottom, 200 bottom; Lambeth Palace Library, London 77; Librairie Larousse, Paris 48, 62 top, 152, 174 bottom; L E A London 171 top; Mansell Collection, London 47, 49, 54, 74, 86 top, 89, 94, 108 top, 124–5, 131 top right, 136 top, 144–5, 151 top, 153, 162–3, 166, 188–9 top, 188–9 bottom; Mansell-Alinari 36 bottom right, 40–1, 107 top; Mansell-Anderson 31; Bildarchiv Foto Marburg 38, 44 top, 62 bottom, 67; Mas, Barcelona 104, 116 top; Metropolitan Museum of Art, New York 35;

Musées de la Ville de Strasbourg 138–9; Museum of Fine Arts, Boston, Massachusetts 50–1; National Army Museum, London 137 bottom, 165, 184 bottom; National Gallery, London 75 top, 150 bottom; National Maritime Museum, Greenwich 130 top right; National Portrait Gallery, London 131 bottom left, 164 bottom; Österreichische Nationalbibliothek, Vienna 46, 56, 101, 194 right; Pierpont Morgan Library, New York 73 bottom; Paul Popper Limited, London 19, 28, 29 top, 37, 44 bottom, 64 bottom, 122 centre, 122 bottom, 131 top left, 174 top, 186 top, 196 bottom, 208, 210, 218, 219 top, 223 top, 225, 226, 232–3; Radio Times Hulton Picture Library, London 70 top, 175 bottom, 181 bottom, 186 centre, 186 bottom, 187; Réunion des Musées Nationaux, Paris 136 bottom, 142–3; Roger-Viollet, Paris 36 top, 161 bottom, 195; ScaJa, Antella, Florence 60 top, 78–9, 117 top, 120; Schweizerisches Landesmuseum, Zurich 66 top, 66 bottom, 108 bottom, 111 bottom; Staatsbibliothek Preussischer Kulturbesitz, Berlin 110 bottom, 114 bottom, 121, 141 top, 141 bottom, 142 bottom left, 146, 150 top, 151 bottom, 172 bottom, 184 top, 185, 190 bottom, 211; Statens Museum for Kunst, Copenhagen 116 bottom; Süddeutscher Verlag, Munich 194 left, 210 top; Svenska Porträttarkivet, Nationalmuseum, Stockholm 122 top, 130 top left, 133 bottom; Swiss National Tourist Office, London 61 top; Trinity College, Cambridge 63 top, 73 top; Ullstein Bilderdienst, Berlin 148, 190–1; Victoria and Albert Museum, London 52, 68–9, 132 bottom, 134, 135, 155, 164 top; Weidenfeld and Nicolson Limited, London 191 bottom; Winchester Gun Museum, New Haven, Connecticut 175 top; Yan, Toulouse 63 bottom, 129 top.

Short glossary of military terms used in the book

Army large number of formations and troops, commanded by a senior general.

Arquebus predecessor of musket, fired by lighted match, barrel supported by a rest.

Bailey courtyard of a medieval castle.

Ballista ancient military engine-of-war for hurling rocks, fire arrows, etc.

Barbican exterior set of defences protecting a city or castle gateway.

Bataillon carré Napoleonic strategic formation of corps (qv), often diamond-shaped.

Battalion infantry formation comprising varying numbers of companies.

Blitzkrieg trans. 'lightning war': German strategy based on speed and manoeuvrability.

Bombard early form of medieval cannon made of iron firing stone cannonballs.

Breech-loader musket or rifle reloaded at the breech, not at the muzzle.

Bridgehead a limited area of enemy territory occupied by an army; e.g. over a river.

Brigade a group of three or more battalions (qv) commanded by a brigadier-general or (today) a brigadier.

Burgh a fortified town or city, especially ninth and tenth centuries AD.

Cab-rank system form of continuous tactical air support by fighter-bombers in Second World War, a squadron always being overhead and 'on call' to assist ground formations with guns, bombs or rocket fire.

Caracole sixteenth- and seventeenth-century cavalry manoeuvre, designed to make use of horse pistols.

Cataphract Byzantine or Sassanid Persian heavily armed horse archer.

Centurion Roman NCO commanding theoretically 100 (but usually 80) legionaries.

Circumvallation trenches protecting a besieging force from outside interference.

Cohort Roman formation of approximately 650 legionaries.

Colunella a Spanish sixteenth-century column, commanded by a colonel.

Company basic unit of infantry, 100–150 strong, commanded by a major or captain.

Condottiere leader of troop of mercenary soldiers, especially in fifteenth-century Italy.

Concentration a collection of military formations or a close pattern of firepower.

Contravallation trenches protecting a besieging force from attacks by the besieged.

Corps major formation comprising several divisions (qv) of all arms, 20,000–100,000 men, often commanded by a lieutenant-general; also a specialist force of troops.

Corps d'armée as above; introduced in Napoleonic period; commanded by a marshal.

Crow instrument of Ancient warfare designed to tear down city walls with giant hooks.

Curtain wall area of fortifications linking towers or bastions.

Decurion Roman junior NCO commanding eight to ten legionaries, or a tent party.

Deep penetration strategic movement driving deep into the enemy's rear areas.

Division formation of several brigades (c. 16,000 men) under a major-general.

Enceinte a total area of continuous fortifications forming a defended perimeter.

Enfilade fire brought to bear on a line of men from end to end, or from a flank.

Envelopment manoeuvres designed to trap an enemy force, or sever its line of retreat.

Exterior lines troops holding a concave line or extended position; hard to reinforce.

Falconet light sixteenth-century cannon, often used on galleys, galleons and city walls.

Fascine bundle of branches used in constructing trenches and other field works.

Fifth column agents or disaffected part of population working secretly for an army.

Flak anti-aircraft guns of many calibres and types producing concentrated fire.

Flank area of ground beyond the wing of an army or force, often exposed to enemy attack.

Flintlock seventeenth-century musket fired by action of flint, held in a lock, striking steel.

Front a war area of considerable size and importance.

Fyrd Anglo-Saxon regional force formed by mobilizing all able-bodied peasants.

Gabion hollow cylinder of wickerwork filled with earth; used in fortifications.

General staff the officers of varying ranks responsible for the running of administration, supply and quartermastering operations in the field.

Glacis area of sloping ground, cleared of all cover, leading up to fortifications.

Glaive broadsword or sword of medieval period.

Guerrilla lit. 'little war'; member of secret irregular military force using subtle or evasive tactics.

Halberd pole or staff weapon with a spear and axehead combined.

Hauberk suit of medieval chain or ring mail.

Hoplite heavily armed foot soldier of Ancient Greece, carrying twenty-one-foot spear.

Hornwork forked defence work often placed in a fortress's ditch to protect a curtain.

Howitzer high-trajectory artillery piece used for dropping shells behind cover, etc.

Huscarle bodyguard of Anglo-Saxon and Danish monarchs; lit. 'house-carl' or 'man'.

Hypaspist lightly armed soldier of Ancient Macedonia, armed with sling or javelins.

Interior lines a force drawn up on a short front, which facilitates transfers or sector reinforcement.

Keep main building of medieval castle; chief defence centre.

Legion Roman force of about 5,000 infantry, with cavalry support and engines-of-war.

Levée-en-masse first attempt at creation of a mass army; used in France in 1793.

Logistics the science of supplying, equipping and moving armed forces.

Machicolation defences along a medieval castle wall-top; gaps through which boiling oil can be poured down.

Mangonel ancient and medieval artillery for hurling stones.

Maniple Roman formation of c. 300 men, forming a web of tactical units in the legion.

Maquis underground movement of irregular troops waging guerrilla warfare; originally in the Corsican maquis or scrubland.

Masse de rupture reserve troops, often élite, held back for the final, critical attack.

Matchlock early form of musket, firing by a burning slow-match; heavy and slow-firing.

Muzzle-loader all cannon or muskets prior to introduction of breech-loaders (qv).

Needle-gun Prussian rifle, c. 1870, using a metal cartridge fired by a striking-pin.

Numerus 400-strong formation of a Byzantine army or thema (qv); equivalent of a battalion (qv).

Oblique order a formation that brings troops progressively into action, thus building up a mounting pressure against one enemy sector; eighteenth century.

Ordre mixte French tactical formation combining troops in line and column, fire and shock action.

Orlok commander of a Mongol Horde or army; twelfth to fourteenth centuries.

Panzer German word for tank; or armoured formation of mixed capability, 1939–45.

Peltasts lightly armed Greek mercenary troops of the Ancient World; slingers and javelin throwers, sometimes bowmen.

Percussion cap explosive device fired by a sharp blow; used to detonate shells, etc.

Phalanx dense Ancient Greek infantry formation, mainly armed with the pike.

Picket a patrol or guard of mounted troops; also a pointed iron stake.

Platoon minor tactical and administrative formation; commanded by a subaltern or sergeant.

Poilu lit. 'hairy' or 'unshaven'; nickname for French soldier; twentieth century.

Pot helm medieval helmet of simple design that rested on the shoulders.

Pre-emptive strike a strategic blow launched to anticipate an enemy attack and thus prevent it.

Psiloi lightly armed Ancient Greek soldier, usually young.

Quaestor senior Roman official, civil or military, often a treasurer or paymaster.

Ravelin outwork with two faces used to protect bastions and curtain walls.

Redan large earthwork, usually with two faces forming an angle.

Reverse slope the rearward side of a hill, giving protection from sight and fire.

Reversed front a battle in which each side faces towards its own base area.

Regiment important formation comprising one or more battalions (qv).

Saker 6-pounder artillery field gun.

Salient an area of occupied ground jutting out into enemy-held territory.

Salvo a number of guns fired together.

Samurai Japanese heroic warrior imbued with a fierce military code of honour.

Sap a trench driven towards an objective, often with overhead cover.

Saphead the furthermost point reached by a sap (qv).

Satrap senior Persian government official; a governor of a province or satrapie.

Screen formation troops in loose or skirmishing order rather than in close lines.

Scorched-earth ruthless strategy to deny an enemy resources by destroying one's own country and crops.

Scutage a medieval money tax paid instead of personal military service.

Siege train the heavy guns and materials needed to undertake a siege.

Shock-troops special élite forces trained to lead attacks.

Surcoat a cloth garment worn over armour, often embellished with heraldic devices.

Strategos a Byzantine general commanding an army.

Telamon instrument of Ancient siege warfare, used to lift troops over city walls.

Tercio seventeenth-century formation comprising c. 5,000 men; lit. 'a third' of an army.

Testudo Roman formation of troops with interlocked shields on their backs, used for undermining walls.

Thegn Anglo-Saxon minor nobility; equivalent to the feudal knight.

Thema Byzantine army, often all-mounted, used to garrison a theme or district.

Tirailleur French light infantryman; period of the Revolutionary and Napoleonic Wars.

Touman Mongol formation of c. 10,000 mounted warriors; the command of an orlok (qv).

Trebuchet large medieval siege engine for hurling rocks etc.

Train formation including gunner and engineer units; also supply organizations.

Triarii senior Roman legionaries, usually aged forty to forty-five, placed in the third line.

Tribune Roman officer, often serving on the staff.

Trunnion metal protuberance at point of balance on a cannon barrel, used for mounting this on a carriage.

Turma squadron of Roman cavalry, approximately 150 horsemen.

Velites young Roman legionaries, often used as a forward screen.

Voltigeur French light infantryman belonging to the light company of a battalion.

Wheel-lock seventeenth-century musket incorporating features of both match and flintlocks.

Index

239